P9-BTY-025

DISCARDED

FINDING YOUR ONLINE VOICE

STORIES TOLD BY EXPERIENCED
ONLINE EDUCATORS

FINDING YOUR ONLINE VOICE

STORIES TOLD BY EXPERIENCED ONLINE EDUCATORS

Edited by

J. Michael Spector
Florida State University

LAWRENCE ERLBAUM ASSOCIATES, PUBLISHERS

2007   Mahwah, New Jersey   London

Copyright © 2007 by Lawrence Erlbaum Associates, Inc.
All rights reserved. No part of this book may be reproduced in
any form, by photostat, microform, retrieval system, or any
other means, without prior written permission of the publisher.

Lawrence Erlbaum Associates, Inc., Publishers
10 Industrial Avenue
Mahwah, New Jersey 07430
www.erlbaum.com

Cover design by Tomai Maridou

Library of Congress Cataloging-in-Publication Data

Finding your online voice : stories told by experienced online
educators / edited by J. Michael Spector.
    p. cm.
  Includes bibliographical references and index.
ISBN 978-0-8058-6219-5 — 0-8058-6219-6 (cloth)
ISBN 978-0-8058-6228-7 — 0-8058-6228-5 (pbk.)
ISBN 1-4106-1606-1 (e book)
1. Computer-assisted instruction. 2. Distance education. I. Spector,
  J. Michael.

LB1028.5F49 2007
374'.26—dc22   2006027752
                                        CIP

Books published by Lawrence Erlbaum Associates are printed on
acid-free paper, and their bindings are chosen for strength and
durability.

Printed in the United States of America
10 9 8 7 6 5 4 3 2 1

We dedicate this volume to the memory of
Peter B. Mosenthal
who died suddenly and unexpectedly in the summer of 2004.
Peter was a distinguished Professor in the
School of Education at Syracuse University,
co-editor of the Handbook of Reading Research,
and former President of the National Reading Conference.
It was Peter who had the idea that led to this book.
Peter's enthusiasm, dedication, and wisdom remind us all
that we can be more than we have been.

On behalf of all who have contributed to this volume,

—J. Michael Spector

Contents

Foreword

Donald P. Ely
Syracuse University

When professionals gather at a conference and are chatting informally with colleagues in the hallway, conversations often turn to pedagogical procedures that are used in teaching. When the topic is distance education, the dialogue often turns to technology. Later, instructional strategies are discussed and finally, the various methods of evaluation are exchanged. Professionals are usually curious about the way colleagues plan and deliver instruction at a distance. As new tools become available, the older procedures change, often mimicking the traditional instructor—learner dyad. One of these changes is the use of online communication as the major approach to teaching and learning at a distance. Where does an instructor learn about the procedures and interactions in this new approach?

The serious instructor who is about to begin teaching an online course will usually seek out colleagues who have had some experience with the new pedagogy. For some, there will be reservations about teaching individuals whom they cannot directly see or hear. Some instructors may feel that they should be able to teach in this new way but do not have sufficient experience to do so. How is a neophyte distance educator going to find the path to successful teaching when the primary vehicle is one computer connected to another computer? From this initial concern, there usually are follow-up questions about "how to do this or that" in this new environment. This book is a welcome addition to the distance education territory. It offers solid advice about teaching and learning at a distance. The wealth of wisdom about online learning is a bonus. A theme that permeates each chapter is a focus on the individual learner who is connected to the instructor using a computer connection.

DISTANCE LEARNING: EARLY EFFORTS

The isolated student *was* not unknown in the past. The Chautauqua education movement in the late 19th century was organized for students in remote locations using postal communication. In the mid-20th century, the International Correspondence School served students in many parts of the world from its headquarters in Scranton, Pennsylvania and Sunrise Semester in the early 1960s offered early morning television courses throughout the United States. Radio courses from the University of Iowa and the Articulated Instructional Media (AIM) from the University of Wisconsin were designed for learners at a distance. These distance learning programs focused on the individual learner even though there were hundreds and even thousands in many of the classes.

As I began to think about these early efforts that permitted students to learn wherever they might be, I recalled a paper that I delivered more than 30 years ago: *The Most Important Number is One* (Ely, 1970). The subtitle was "The Potential of Individualized Instruction in Higher Education."

From an earlier time, when educators were asked to provide *the greatest good for the greatest number*, the new theme became *the best for each*. For decades, educators have discussed individual learning in remote settings but the results were minimal. The means of communication were occasional dialog or written correspondence. The goal of learning independently at a distance was usually an attempt to provide learning that was equal to the face-to-face classroom exchange. It was based on a dream envisioned by many progressive educators since the early 20th century. Then, the internet entered the education scene. New and creative approaches were possible. At last *"the most important number is one"* became a possibility. When the potential of teaching and learning online became a way to reach the long-held dream of independent learning at a distance, new vistas were developed that brought teacher and learner into direct contact.

Distance learning is the term from which online learning emerged. Distance learning enjoys a checkered history over the past 100 years or so. Five generations of distance education have been described by Moore and Kearsley; (1) correspondence, (2) broadcast radio and television, (3) open universities, (4) teleconferencing, and (5) internet/web (Moore & Kearsley, 2005). Although this book does not explicitly review the history of the movement, it is important to acknowledge that much of the current and future distance learning will be delivered using the fifth generation tools with computer and internet-based virtual classes (Moore & Kearsley, 2005). Where does the neophyte online instructor go to prepare for the new assignment? Will trial and error take over? What has worked (or not worked) in other environments? *Finding Your Online Voice* will help both new and veteran distance educators profit from the experience of designers and instructors who have "been there" and "done that."

WHERE TO BEGIN?

This book is an encyclopedia of comprehensive, substantive information about distance education and online learning. Most of the content is based not only on field experience but also on sound research. The rationales and specific details in each chapter spell out recommendations for design and delivery of online learning. It is a distance instructor's guide through the maze of online teaching/learning process. The first chapter spells out expectations for the entire volume. It describes in brief detail the content of the book and its potential application for readers. It is loaded with concepts and references that are amplified later in the volume. It also contains specifications for online instructor competencies. Look at the competencies and evaluate the extent to which you have achieved each one. This private assessment should give you a sense of what you need to know and how online education differs from traditional teaching and learning. Remember ... *the most important number is one.*

From this point on, the emphasis is on the student's role in the learning process online. Begin to read here where the learner is the client. Collis and Moonen focus on distance students and how they embrace the learning process. The authors advocate the use of student contributions as motivating factors in online practice. Providing opportunities for distance learners to communicate with each other via a *digital workbench* creates an environment where ideas can be initiated and discussed without fear of retribution. In this setting, the role of the instructor shifts from linear lectures to self-study and group work. The ideas and suggestions of this chapter are based on more than 10 years of reflective practice. Examples are given; lessons learned are spelled out, and alternative approaches to learning online are recommended. Candid observations about the "good," "bad," and "ugly" of the online process offer sage advice. Collis and Moonen demonstrate that *the most important number is one,* and variations on this theme recur in nearly every chapter in this volume.

Further into the book, Jan Visser reflects on his many international experiences. The pluses and minuses of online learning are viewed and assessed by a UNESCO professional who has observed the "good and the bad" of distance learning practice. The examples are worthy of contemplation, especially those about online learning experiences in developing nations. Online learning is blended with face-to-face learning in some of the examples. This type of flexibility is a plus for online learning. As always, in this context ... *the most important number is one.*

One of the issues facing online instructors is the matter of discourse between student and teacher as well as among the students themselves. New instructors to the distance process often try to mimic the face-to-face classroom. Soon after such efforts are begun, it becomes clear that online learning is not a classroom full of students; this point is especially emphasized by Lya Visser, Deb LaPointe, Barbara Grabowski, and Vanessa Dennen, and it is also clearly evident in the other chapters as well. The resources, the exercises, and the discussions are designed so that *the most important number is one.* True, there is a virtual class but it is dispersed in time and place.

How does a teacher deal with students who are in many places and at different times? An overview of how the various authors view teaching and learning processes is provided in nearly every chapter. The successes and failures of earlier studies are discussed in chapter 1. Suggestions for overcoming some of the failures are discussed from experiences in the field and from online evaluations. Read chapter 1, and indeed all of the 11 chapters, with these thoughts: "If I were teaching a course online, what would I do to insure maximum levels of learning? What are the alternatives? Are there other activities that could be combined with the online effort?"

This book represents a blending of theory and research with examples of best practices and personal evidence collected by experienced online instructors. These are stories from the trenches that are meaningful and that provide help to practitioners who are seeking scholarly substance in this new world of teaching. Each chapter stands on its own merit. The notion of learning environments permeates chapters 2 through 10. These environments offer the substance in this section. They can be read selectively according to individual interests and needs. These rich examples help to identify specific key ideas about online learning. Problems are spelled out. Research and theory are imbedded in the description of personal evidence collected by experienced online instructors.

THE "NUTS" AND "BOLTS" OF ONLINE LEARNING

These 11 chapters delve into the important details of online learning. We see an emphasis on teaching in higher education. Alternative instructional designs developed by instructors prepare online learners to consider how to understand and process substantive information on their own. This section of the book touches not only the "how to" techniques but also introduces contemporary research and states the competencies required by professionals who design, develop, and evaluate online learning.

Collectively, these chapters offer a comprehensive encyclopedia of online learning that stems from a worldwide perspective. Detailed explanations of "what works" in online settings seem to cross political borders. These scenarios offer a rich source of worldwide online pedagogy. And the theme, *the most important number is one*, permeates the examples throughout the book. The publication of this volume marks a maturity of the online process and presents ideas beyond a mere catalog of "how to do it." Remember that we are "talking" to the lone student in a remote location who is seeking new knowledge. With an image of one person communicating with another, new possibilities for teaching and learning emerge in the online world.

Is online distance learning the wave of the future? Perhaps is not *the* way but one of the ways that learning can be extended to more people. Some people will have, maybe for the first time, an opportunity to gain new knowledge and skills that would not be otherwise available. Professional instructors will have to acquire new teaching skills for this 21st century opportunity. This book will be an important reference, especially for educators who have to acquire new approaches and skills for teaching in the digital world. The best advice for the online instructor is to remember that *"The most important number is one."*

REFERENCES

Ely, D. P. (1970). *The most important number is one*. Syracuse, NY: Syracuse University School of Education.
Moore, M. G., & Kearsley, G. (2005). *Distance education: A systems view* (2nd ed.). Belmont, CA: Wadsworth.

Preface

This volume resulted from a dissertation conducted by Radha Ganesan at Syracuse University (Ganesan, 2005). That research was a qualitative study of the perceptions and practices of highly experienced online teachers. She recruited six distinguished online educators in North America, Europe, and Australia. As the work evolved, Peter Mosenthal, one of her committee members who died unexpectedly and tragically just after her defense, remarked that the data that she was collecting was so rich in content and insightful with regard to online teaching, that the work should reach a much wider audience than that normally reached by a dissertation study. As her committee chair, I agreed to help her find a publisher. Our first choice was Lawrence Erlbaum Associates (LEA), and Lane Akers, Editorial Vice President at LEA, liked our proposal so the book effort began in 2003. We met to discuss strategy at the 2003 and 2004 meetings of the Association for Educational Communications and Technology, where Radha and several of the authors also made presentations related to the work that led up to this volume. Radha successfully defended her dissertation in July 2004. Due to personal circumstances, Radha had to withdraw from the book effort; we decided that Peter's idea and Radha's investigations were worth presenting as originally planned, and the project moved forward.

When the book effort began in 2003, we asked all six of Radha's subjects to contribute a chapter and all initially agreed. In addition, we asked six additional experienced educators to contribute chapters to ensure broad and deep coverage of online teaching. The focus was on how highly experienced teachers conceptualized and organized online courses including:

- Teaching orientations and philosophies.
- Perspectives on and approaches to learning and instruction.
- Orientation to and uses of technology.
- Models and methods of technology-based teaching.
- Reflections and self-assessments.

This volume contains invited contributions from expert teachers who specialize in online learning. The book includes best practices and guidelines for effective online teaching and a set of instructor skills and competencies specific to online learning environments. This book addresses how the significant but ill-defined area of online education can benefit significantly from the wisdom and perspective of expert practitioners—those with extensive online teaching experience and published research about those experiences.

The book consists of 11 chapters. The first chapter presents a research-oriented historical context for online teaching and learning. In chapter 1, readers find a description of historical approaches to teaching, some research findings pertaining to online teaching, and an elaboration of the notion of teaching competency especially as it pertains to online teaching.

Chapters 2 through 10 represent stories from the trenches, so to speak. Experienced online teachers present their views on general perspectives and approaches and lessons learned from their various experiences. These chapters all include stories that illustrate and emphasize particular aspects of online teaching, as do the first and last chapters of the book, although the focus of the first and last chapters is to frame the problems related to finding one's online teaching voice and to synthesize what these experienced online teachers have discovered through their various experiences. These stories from the field are supported with research and empirical evidence, all of which is intended to help online teachers become more effective—that is to say, to find their online voices. These key chapters range over many different issues and concerns, including the design of online activities, online collaboration, online interactions, authenticity in online settings, assessments in online settings, and much more. The concluding chapter by Dennen provides a synthesis, encapsulates key points, and hopefully provokes ongoing reflection and dialogue among online teachers. Enjoy.

—*J. Michael Spector*

REFERENCES

Ganesan, R. (2005). *Perceptions and practices of expert teachers in Technology-based distance and distributed learning environments*. Unpublished doctoral dissertation, Syracuse University, Syracuse, New York.

The Authors

Zane L. Berge
Associate Professor, University of Maryland, Baltimore County
Department of Education, 1000 Hilltop Circle, Baltimore, MD 21250 USA
Email: berge@umbc.edu

Bethany Bovard
Regional Educational Technology Assistance (RETA) Program
New Mexico State University, Las Cruces, New Mexico USA
Email: bbovard@nmsu.edu

Betty Collis
Shell Professor of Networked Learning, University of Twente
Postbus 217, 7500 AE Enschede, The Netherlands
Email: betty.collis@utwente.nl

Vanessa P. Dennen
Assistant Professor, Instructional Systems, Florida State University
305 Stone Building, Tallahassee, FL 32306 USA
Email: vdennen@fsu.edu

Donald P. Ely
Professor Emeritus, Syracuse University
704 Hamilton Parkway, DeWitt, NY 13214-2338 USA
Email: dely@ericir.syr.edu

Barbara L. Grabowski
Professor, Instructional Systems, The Pennsylvania State University
314 Keller Building, University Park PA 16802 USA
Email: bgrabowski@psu.edu

Chandra Gunawardena
The Open University of Sri Lanka
Nawala, Nugegoda, Sri Lanka
Email: ggunawardena@hotmail.com

Shironica Karaunanayaka
The Open University of Sri Lanka
Nawala, Nugegoda, Sri Lanka
Email: spkar@ou.ac.lk

Dayalata Lekamge
The Open University of Sri Lanka
Nawala, Nugegoda, Sri Lanka
Email: gdlek@ou.ac.lk

Deborah K. LaPointe
Assistant Professor, Organization Learning and Instructional Technologies
College of Education, MSC 09 5100, University of New Mexico
Albuquerque, NM 87131-0001 USA
Email: debla@tvi.edu

Mohan Menon
Commonwealth of Learning
Vancouver, Canada
Email: mmenon@col.org

Jef Moonen
Professor Emeritus, University of Twente
Postbus 217, 7500 AE Enschede, The Netherlands
Email: Jef.Moonen@Utwente.nl

Somaiya Naidu
Associate Professor, Educational Technology
The University of Melbourne, VIC, Australia, 3010
Email: s.naidu@unimelb.edu.au

Wilhelmina Savenye
Associate Professor, Educational Technology
P.O. Box 870611, Arizona State University
Tempe, Arizona 85287-0611 USA
Email: savenye@asu.edu

Roderick C. Sims
Knowledgecraft
PO Box 109, Woodburn NSW 2472, Australia
Email: rodsims@knowledgecraft.com.au

J. Michael Spector
Professor and Associate Director
Learning Systems Institute, Florida State University
C 4622 University Center, Tallahassee, FL 32308 USA
Email: mspector@lsi.fsu.edu

Jan Visser
Learning Development Institute
5, rue du Figuier, 13630 Eyragues, France
Email: jvissser@learndev.org

Lya Visser
Learning Development Institute
5, rue du Figuier, 13630 Eyragues, France
Email: lvisser@learndev.org

Chapter 1

Competencies for Online Teachers

J. Michael Spector
Florida State University

What is it to be a teacher? What is the nature of teaching? Some may say that teachers provide information and explain the nature of apparently complex things. Others may say that teachers bring understanding and impart knowledge and wisdom. Still others may say that teachers promote and support learning. Surely we can identify teachers and describe what they do. We should also be able to develop ways to measure the quality of teaching and to provide guidelines to help improve teaching. Surely.

The purpose of this volume is to explore such questions within the context of online teaching. This book is intended to be a practical guide for those who are or might become involved with online teaching—that is, teaching with the support of a web-based learning environment, especially one in which asynchronous discussions, synchronous chat sessions, and email exchanges are used to support learning. We focus on these forms of communicating in web-based learning environments because they differ in significant ways from face-to-face communications that take place in traditional classrooms and other face-to-face situations, and because they are so common in current online learning environments. Such forms of communication in online environments place particular demands on both students and teachers and are often the cause of less than desirable outcomes. Stated generally, this might be called the problem of finding one's voice as an online teacher or online student. In this volume, the focus is on helping online teachers find effective ways to communicate in online learning environments. Similar issues arise for students and also deserve elaboration. Indeed, the International Board of Standards for Training, Performance, and Instruction (IBSTPI; see http://www.ibstpi.org) has research projects aimed at standards and competencies for online teachers as well as for online learners. We begin with this question: what is it to be a teacher?

BECOMING A TEACHER

One could explore the nature of teaching by examining what teachers do. One could then identify teaching activities and practices that do or should contribute significantly to learning and those that appear to contribute very little to learning. Then, one could focus on ways that specific activities might be structured and conducted so as to optimize outcomes for particular learning and instructional situations. This scheme is widely recognized as rational and has informed instructional design research for more than a generation (see, for example, Reigeluth, 1983). Parts of this scheme have informed and still shape various teacher preparation programs. It is perhaps worthwhile to revisit what teachers do as a precursor for setting the stage for online teaching practice and associated problems.

What is it that teachers do? Teachers talk. Teachers present information. They demonstrate how to solve problems. They help students solve similar problems. They provide guidance to students when needed. They encourage students who are struggling. They discourage students who are disruptive or otherwise disturbing others. Teachers ask questions, suggest places to look for answers, direct activities, talk to other teachers, examine student work, provide feedback to students on their work, assign grades, fill out forms, talk to administrators and parents, and so on.

Teachers do many different things. Teaching is certainly not like driving a bus or serving food in a cafeteria. Nor is teaching like being an accountant or being a dentist, although some have compared some teaching situations with pulling teeth. The notion we are pursuing here is to think about all the things that teachers do and then focus on those things that might be done better. The difficulty is that teachers do so many different things. It is difficult to capture the essence of teaching in a few words. Indeed, one might begin to suspect that teaching is not a simple or single thing at all—teaching is, in a way, an illegitimate concept in that it refers to many fundamentally different kinds of things, none of which in and of itself represents the essence of teaching.

Driving a bus always involves a particular sort of vehicle that is clearly distinguishable from motorcycles and pick-up trucks. Serving food in a cafeteria always involves food. Being an accountant typically involves debits and credits and balance sheets. Being a dentist typically involves ... okay, we can forego the unpleasant memories in this case. What does teaching nearly always involve? Students and content. Being a teacher implies involvement with students aimed at understanding or mastering a subject or skill. This is not at all surprising.

Perhaps not. However, when the list of activities is revisited, one can then focus on those involving students as central to teaching. Although a teacher may need to speak with an administrator or fill out a form requesting a book to be ordered, such activities are not central to being a teacher. Instructional interactions with students are central to teaching. Although this point is quite obvious, many teachers when asked to identify where their time is spent will list many things that do not involve instructional interaction with students. Some of these other activities may be trivial or entirely unnecessary; some are probably unavoidable. Nonetheless, the intent hereafter is to focus on teacher interactions with students aimed at supporting understanding and mastery of some particular body of knowledge or set of skills.

TEACHING COMPETENCIES

My father described a teacher as the ear that listens, the eye that reflects, the voice that comforts, the hand that guides, the face that does not turn away (Spector, in press). There are of course other models of teaching. Klein and colleagues (2004) identified several traditional perspectives on teaching, including:

- The didactic tradition, associated with the Sophists who would expound on a topic in front of an attentive audience, often for a fee;
- The apprenticeship tradition, associated with craftsmen who would train their workers on the job and earn a living together;
- The Socratic tradition, associated with Socrates who had an informal but probing questioning style and who refused to accept any fees for his so-called teaching.

In modern times, these three traditions have all found a place in various contexts and the methods associated with these traditions are still practiced to some extent by many educators. Some teachers often blend various methods together in the course of an instructional program. Such blending is arguably very much in line with the instructor competencies developed by the International Board of Standards for Training, Performance, and Instruction (see Klein et al., 2004). These competencies are depicted in Table 1.1. The Board conducted an extensive review of the literature, numerous focus group discussions, a large-scale international survey, and many internal discussions and reviews to establish 17 competencies in five domains; (a) professional foundations, (b) planning and preparation, (c) instructional methods and strategies, (d) assessment and evaluation, and (e) management. Not all teachers do all of these things, but the variety of things identi-

TABLE 1.1
Instructor Competencies (see www.ibstpi.org)

Professional Foundations
    Communicate effectively.
    Update and improve one's professional knowledge and skills.
    Comply with established ethical and legal standards.
    Establish and maintain professional credibility.

Planning and Preparation
    Plan instructional methods and materials.
    Prepare for instruction.

Instructional Methods and Strategies
    Stimulate and sustain learner motivation and engagement.
    Demonstrate effective presentation skills.
    Demonstrate effective facilitation skills.
    Demonstrate effective questioning skills.
    Provide clarification and feedback.
    Promote retention of knowledge and skills.
    Promote transfer of knowledge and skills.

Assessment and Evaluation
    Assess learning and performance.
    Evaluate instructional effectiveness.

Management
    Manage an environment that fosters learning and performance.
    Manage the instructional process through the appropriate use of technology.

fied by ibstpi as critical to the role of an instructor are reflective of the earlier discussion of the many different kinds of things that teachers do.

It is noteworthy that the first competence for a teacher is to be able to communicate effectively. The ibstpi survey indicated that this particular competence was regarded as the most critical competency (Klein et al., 2004). Teachers must be able to communicate effectively. This competency establishes an important part of the context for online teaching and problems with online teaching. How can teachers develop competence in communicating effectively in online environments? How can teachers find their voice in online settings? How have effective online teachers managed to achieve competence in this area? The remainder of this chapter and this volume are aimed squarely at these questions. First, however, we need to consider a bit more about the context and the nature of teaching competencies.

What is competence? Competence is commonly conceptualized in terms of being adequately qualified to perform a reasonably well-defined task (Spector et al., 2006). According to ibstpi, a competency is a related set of knowledge, skills and attitudes that enable one to perform the activities associated with a task, job or occupation according to expectations or standards (Klein et al., 2004). The 17 competency statements in Table 1.1 have associated performance statements that indicate how one would recognize that a person had that particular competency. For example, with regard to the comforting voice competency (#9–demonstrate effective facilitation skills), the associated performance statements are (Klein et al., 2004, p. 40; © 2003 ibstpi):

a. Draw upon the knowledge and experience of all participants.
b. Give directions that are clearly understood by all learners.
c. Keep learning activities focused.
d. Encourage and support collaboration.
e. Bring learning activities to closure.
f. Monitor, assess, and adapt to the dynamics of the situation.

With regard to the Socratic competency (#10–demonstrate effective questioning skills), the associated performance indicators are (Klein et al., 2004, p. 41; © 2003 ibstpi):

a. Ask clear and relevant questions.
b. Follow up on questions from learners.
c. Use a variety of question types and levels.
d. Direct and redirect questions that promote learning.
e. Use questions to generate and guide discussions.
f. Build on responses to previous questions in subsequent learning activities.

The point is that a competency statement is somewhat broad and indicative of having achieved a certain level of mastery with regard to fairly challenging or complex tasks such as facilitating discussions or using questions to promote learning. In order to make a judgment that someone has in fact achieved that level of mastery, some more or less standard indicators are required. The ibstpi performance statements are not intended to dictate how one should perform a task; rather, they serve as markers to indicate where one might look to see if someone was competent with regard to a particular task or skill (Klein et al., 2004).

Let us assume that we are now in a position to determine that a teacher has gained the appropriate competency. A critical question is then: How does one go about gaining or developing competence in teaching? Indeed, this is a central question for many teacher preparation programs, although how many of these programs are successful in this regard is difficult to determine. We might revisit the three traditional approaches to teaching for clues. In a didactic approach, those with experience and insight with regard to effective teaching would tell novices how to become effective teachers. Indeed, there is much such telling in many teacher preparation programs. Telling alone, however, is not likely to be adequate to the task of developing skill in such a complex task area as teaching (Merrill, 2002).

In an apprenticeship approach, novice teachers would be placed under the supervision of experienced teachers and gain competence by teaching—learning by doing on the job, so to speak, in situ. Most teacher preparation programs also include some aspects of learning by doing, through practice teaching in mock classrooms and especially through required internships and supervised teaching in actual classrooms.

In the Socratic approach, experienced teachers would ask novices probing questions aimed at getting them to challenge their unstated assumptions about teaching and to explore the value of teaching, among other things. It should be obvious that the Socratic approach can be integrated with both the didactic and the apprenticeship approach. Such a blending of all three of these approaches can be found in many teacher preparation programs.

Whether or not particular blends lead to desired outcomes and are conducive to developing teaching competence has not been very well researched. Part of the difficulty in this regard is that teaching involves many complex and somewhat ill-structured activities; as a consequence, establishing reliable and relevant performance measures for teaching competence is difficult. Moreover, comparing one teaching situation with another or one teacher with another is particularly challenging because there are so many variables that might convolute meaningful comparisons and analyses (Falk, 2001).

Nevertheless, there are research projects aimed at investigating teaching competence and performance, such as Project 2061 sponsored by the Interagency Education Research Initiative (DeBoer et al., 2004). Serious research on teaching in the United States has developed especially with regard to mathematics and science education, where significant deficiencies in American education have been identified (AAAS, 1993). Indeed, improving learning and instruction, especially in the areas of mathematics and science, has become an issue of national policy in the United States and in many other countries (see, for example, National Research Council, 2002). Many efforts to improve learning and instruction have attempted to integrate and leverage technology, particularly Internet-based technologies. Outcomes are difficult to assess, with some apparent successes but also with many failures (Feldman, Konold, & Coulter, 2000). Few studies take into account relevant policy considerations, federal and state mandates, and other limitations and constraints. In short, few research studies are aimed at educational systems as systems. More typically, research focuses on an isolated part of an educational system and ignores interactions with other parts of the system not being investigated.

The general line of thought in research and development on learning and instruction is fairly straightforward. It is sometimes possible to identify serious deficiencies in student or worker performance. When a deficiency is identified, it becomes a target for systematic improvement. Two kinds of improvement are generally developed, both hopefully (but all too rarely) based on research. First, improved instructional methods are developed; these may and often do include new technologies and new approaches (possibly new blends of traditional approaches). As already noted, research establishing that a new method is more effective than a different method is a significant research challenge, and only a few good empirical studies along these lines exist (Richey, Klein, & Nelson, 2004). Second, improvements in teacher preparation are developed; these may also include new technologies and approaches. Research in this area is still more challenging due to the time required to determine that teaching competence developed in ways that resulted in improved learning and instruction.

In sum, findings from empirical research targeting improved learning and teaching are limited and only partially inform how best to improve teaching and learning. This means that watching master teachers engage students in learning, listening to the voices of experienced teachers, and trying out various skills and techniques are reasonable supplements to existing research. This book focuses specifically on the voices of experienced teachers with regard to online teaching—voices from the *cyber-trenches*, so to speak.

Listening to these voices is neither necessary nor sufficient for the development of competency. However, hearing what experienced educators say about their teaching can help an individual develop a focus and strategy for self-improvement. Following a regimen for self-improvement is certainly one way to develop competence. Some researchers call this pathway to expertise deliberate practice (Ericsson, Krampe, & Tesch-Römer, 1993).

A precursor to deliberate practice is the notion of the reflective practitioner (Schön, 1983), which contrasts knowledge developed in action and practice with knowledge imparted in school and classroom settings. Schön emphasized the dynamic aspects of teaching and in effect argued for integrating aspects of reflective reasoning in problem-based learning in school contexts. Given this alternative pathway to competency development through reflective reasoning and deliberate practice, the voices in this volume can be heard as intended to give cause for reflection as a precursor to developing competency as a teacher.

It is in fact possible to create this kind of reflective blend for preparing classroom teachers, and many programs do so either intentionally or unintentionally. Preservice teachers watch experienced teachers ply their trade. They may be encouraged to reflect on why that teacher took that action in that situation. Additionally, preservice teachers get to try out their own knowledge and skills in the action of the classroom. Many times they are asked to reflect on why particular things occurred the way they did and what alternatives might have been considered. Although teacher preparation programs that involve some traditional schooling are not likely to be eliminated anytime soon in favor of learning entirely on the job by doing—by teaching, in this case—it is quite reasonable to see that these programs are involving more experiential and reflective activities than before. Our general argument is that listening to voices such as those expressed herein can promote a useful kind of reflection and thereby facilitate the development of competence, although teaching competence is admittedly difficult to assess.

ONLINE TEACHING

Having set the stage with this discussion of teaching and competence, we are prepared to address issues that pertain specifically to online teaching. First, we have to indicate what we mean by online teaching. We have interpreted online teaching very broadly to include both synchronous and asynchronous modes of communications—especially email, threaded discussions, chat sessions, and text messaging. None of these experienced voices were very much engaged in real-time audio- or video-based systems. Clearly the mode of communication affects how one might appropriately adjust one's voice. For example, in an audio-based environment, one ought to speak in such a manner that participants are likely to understand and follow—this might mean speaking more slowly and less colloquially than one might in casual conversation and it certainly requires keeping in mind the location of the microphone so as to avoid muffled or missing words on the receiving end.

Competencies for online teaching have been discussed for several years (see Goodyear et al., 2001; Spector & de la Teja, 2001). Moreover, a number of popular books on topics such as facilitating discussions and implementing effective online environments can be found, many of which are generally helpful (cf. Collison, Elbaum, Haavind, & Tinker, 2000; Kearsley, 1999; Ko & Rossen, 2001; Sales, 2002; Simonson, Smaldino, Albright, & Zvacek, 2003). However, what is missing in these practical, how-to guides is the richness of specific teaching experiences as told by master educators. Some of those voices can be found at a general and more academic level elsewhere (see, for example, Hativa & Goodyear, 2002). What we are aiming to provide in this volume are those voices articulated in very specific and personal terms in a way that might be useful to educational practitioners.

The forms of online teaching that are involved in subsequent chapters are primarily those found in colleges and universities around the world. As already mentioned, in such environments (BlackBoard, Moodle, Sakai, TeleTop, WebCT, etc.) the place where the teacher is most often heard is on the discussion board, in an email or text message, or in a chat session. Consequently, it is the difficulty of adjusting one's voice appropriately for such settings that is the focus in this volume. There is no need to discuss those challenges here as they are best heard firsthand and in a personal and practical manner in subsequent chapters. A brief review of research on online teaching is provided next, followed by a few closing remarks intended to promote reflective practice.

RESEARCH ON ONLINE TEACHING

Ganesan's (2005) review of the pertinent research literature focused on a number of dimensions, including (a) attitudes, (b) interactivity, (c) pedagogy, (d) perceptions, (e) policies, (f) systems, and (g) time. In each case, there are multiple subcategories to consider, such as those associated with students, teachers, designers, and administrators. Because this is a practitioner-oriented volume rather than a research volume, only a few highlights and representative findings of research pertinent to online teaching in these seven dimensions is mentioned here. Hopefully this brief review of some of the relevant research will serve the purpose of promoting reflective practice.

Attitudes

Teacher resistance to online teaching is often mentioned but rarely examined from a research perspective. A resistant or reluctant attitude to online teaching will certainly influence one's development of competence. However, teachers do believe communication is critical to effectiveness (Klein et al., 2004) and a study by Jones and colleagues (2002) indicated that receptiveness to online teaching and subsequent skill development was generally correlated with self-assessed competence with digital technologies, a general attitude about teaching with technology, and the availability of technology and technology support.

As it happens, faculty attitudes with regard to online teaching are partly shaped by policies pertaining to tenure and promotion, partly by anticipated time demands, and partly by pedagogical inclinations (Spector, 2005; Spector, Doughty, & Yonai, 2003). Determining faculty attitudes with regard to online teaching (i.e., especially such things as (a) attitudes and expectations about related time pressures, (b) tenure and promotion opportunities, and (c) teacher vs. learner centeredness—whether or not the teacher is or ought to be the focal point for learning) is certainly relevant to selecting likely faculty for online teaching and judging how much of an obstacle to competency development these attitudes represent. Negative attitudes in these areas are well founded in many cases (Spector, 2005; Spector et al., 2003). Changing attitudes is always a challenge. Perhaps listening to the cautiously enthusiastic voices in subsequent chapters will help in some cases.

Interactivity

Research has generally demonstrated that online courses involve specific and relatively high levels of interactivity, especially on the part of instructors in online discussions (Hiltz & Turoff, 2002; Hislop & Ellis, 2004). Stacey and Rice (2002) examined online learning in terms of communities of inquiry—that is to say, in terms of cognitive presence, social presence, and teacher presence. Consistent with findings in traditional settings, students who are engaged typically learn more or more quickly, and the teacher can help or hinder student engagement by promoting or failing to promote meaningful interactions. Consistent with Schön's (1983) notion of the reflective practitioner, however, there are no simple, straightforward, algorithmic rules for promoting meaningful interaction. Variations due to individual learner characteristics and local learning situations require highly flexible teachers; this appears to be true for online teachers just as it is true for traditional teachers.

Pedagogy

In general, there has been a shift in pedagogy away from didactic approaches and toward more apprenticelike approaches, with particular emphasis on activities and environments that are learner centered, problem oriented, inquiry based, socially situated, and technology facilitated (see, for example, Jonassen, 2000; Spector, 2002; Spector & Anderson, 2000). The Internet has become a powerful and widely accessible source for resources to support learning and instruction (Rosenberg, 2001; Steeples & Jones, 2002).

Technology changes. Technology changes what people actually do and are able to do. This, of course, applies to those who teach with technology. Although research on learning has generally demonstrated that active learner engagement with content in meaningful contexts is effective, technology has been evolving in ways that make possible a variety of such engaging and meaningful activities (Goodyear, 2001; Jonassen, 2000). It should not be a surprise that teaching with technology is much more challenging than teaching in a traditional classroom with minimal teaching and learning tools. Research with regard to online teaching suggests that the role of the teacher changes significantly from face-to-face settings (Peterson & Bond, 2004). New instructional approaches and technologies create a particular challenge for teachers to find a helpful and meaningful voice in support of learning and their students.

Perceptions

Given this sea of change in learning and instruction, it is not at all surprising to find that teachers often view technology in general and online teaching specifically with some suspicion and caution (Kanuka, Collett, & Caswell, 2002). Jones and colleagues (2002) found that teacher attitudes with regard to online teaching were often correlated with their self-assessed levels of general technology competence. There is surprisingly little research on faculty perceptions with regard to various aspects of online teaching, just as there is very little research with regard to general teacher attitudes about online teaching (Ganesan, 2005). Some practical advice can be found in various articles and guidebooks (see, for example, Ko & Rossen, 2001; McKinnon, 2002; Sales, 2002). When one examines those and other guides, there is very little concern with teacher attitudes and perceptions about online teaching. Ganesan (2005) reported that the subjects in her dissertation study were generally enthusiastic about online teaching (an attitude) because it afforded new kinds of teaching opportunities and learning affordances (a perception). Her subjects reported spending more time teaching online but they also reported that the outcomes were generally more satisfactory, due in large part to much more meaningful discussions. One can conclude that those experienced online teachers had found their voices. Those new to online teaching are still at the *stuttering* stage,[1] perhaps. What is clear is that perceptions and attitudes do influence what one is willing to undertake. There are many wrong-headed perceptions about online teaching (e.g., it is easier or less time consuming than face-to-face teaching). There are also many nonproductive attitudes about teaching online (e.g., students will not learn anything and simply appear to be active and complete minimal requirements). My sense in this regard is that more research on teacher attitudes and perceptions would be useful in contributing to more realistic beliefs about the possibilities for meaningful online discourse.

---

[1]In this context, 'stuttering' refers to the hesitancy of online expression caused by feeling uncertain in a new or unfamiliar environment. This is not a reference to a speech disorder nor is it intended to demean those who involuntarily stutter when speaking.

Policies

Policy issues are addressed in a few research studies (see, for example, Chizmar & Williams, 1998; Spector et al., 2003). These studies tend to report unintended institutional barriers to progress with regard to online teaching and learning. These unintended barriers take many forms, including inadequate technical support, unreliable or out-of-date equipment and infrastructure, lack of faculty incentives, and an intellectually hostile environment to teach online (e.g., no recognition of excellence for online teaching and disadvantages with regard to tenure and promotion for those who teach online).

Such institutional barriers and various policies of tacit resistance to online teaching are not generally conducive to improving the quality of online teaching and may impede some from undertaking the challenge of online teaching. The marketplace may drive organizations to take online teaching much more seriously and to develop appropriate incentives and institutional support. Regardless, those who choose to teach online often do so in spite of discouraging policies and institutional barriers. It is their voices that can and should be heard—hopefully this volume makes a small contribution in that regard.

Systems

Online learning and instruction, like other types of learning and instruction, occur within the context of an educational or performance system (Moore & Kearsley, 2005). An educational system is comprised of an organizational structure that encompasses administrators and support staff, teachers with various areas of expertise, learners with various characteristics and prior knowledge, learning and teaching spaces, and so on. Policies and procedures, whether explicit or tacit, should be considered part of an educational system. The various curricula, courses, and instructional materials are part of the system. What is unique or unusual to online learning systems is that these various system components and aspects are more highly distributed than in a traditional system; many of these system components are located at different places and interactions among the various system components often occur with delays due to that physical separation. The challenges of separation in time and space between teachers and students are relatively well addressed in the literature. What have been less well addressed are the effects of separation on other aspects of an educational system. Interacting system components and delayed effects are particularly difficult aspects of complexity to understand (Dörner, 1996). With regard to a teacher–student interaction, a teacher naturally wants to help a student who has misunderstood a particular point or who has a problem; the delay

introduced in an online environment makes identifying such a need and offering help more of a challenge. With regard to administrator–teacher interactions, particularly as they pertain to policies, the inability to have an
immediate face-to-face exchange about the reasons for or difficulties with
regard to a particular policy may create unnecessary tension between teachers and administrators. Many more such challenges that are unique to online educational systems can be identified and only add to the difficulty of
finding one's voice as an online teacher.

Time

Several studies have explored the time demands placed on online teachers
(Collis & Gervedink Nijhuis, 2000; Hislop & Ellis, 2004; Spector, 2005;
Spector et al., 2003). The consistent finding reported in these studies is that
online teaching generally requires more time than face-to-face teaching. In
some cases, the extra time is associated with administrative online course
management tasks and various technology issues that would not arise in a
traditional classroom. In other cases, the extra time is associated with online discussions that can occupy much more of a teacher's time than would a
normal lecture period. As already noted, experienced online instructors accept this particular time burden willingly because it is associated with improved learning. One may find one's voice in moderating and contributing
to online discussions, but it may take some time.

CONCLUSION: FINDING YOUR VOICE

To conclude these initial remarks about finding one's online voice, I
would like to share a few personal experiences. I have selected three
brief online teaching examples as they illustrate things that may be
somewhat counterintuitive or surprising. It is my hope that these examples and the remainder of the book will generate reflection about online
teaching and perhaps help a few to overcome their online stuttering, to
which I readily ad-ad-admit.

The first example has to do with how online discussions were designed
and implemented in a graduate course in instructional design that typically
had about 20 students enrolled. The way the course was organized was that
each week there was a primary presentation about a selected topic, associated individual and small group student assignments, occasional individual
and group presentations, and a weekly discussion thread. As the instructor,
I was responsible for the course design and implementation in WebCT. For
no particular reason, I left discussions open after the scheduled week for
discussion. I was active in the discussions during the week they were scheduled but then went on to the next week's discussion. In this particular

course, there was an early module about ethics as it pertains to instructional designers. This module had been neither a much discussed nor a well-received topic in the face-to-face version of this course, which I had taught several times prior to the online offering. Near the end of the semester and about 2 months after the ethics discussion thread, I happened to go back and look at that discussion, along with all the others. What I discovered, much to my surprise, was that this discussion was still active. It had more postings than any other thread and it had evolved into a high-level debate about the ethical responsibilities of instructional designers. On the last day of class, I noted this fact on the discussion board and the general response was that the topic had caused them to rethink their initial lackadaisical attitude with regard to ethical obligations. I had done very little to generate this debate other than post the initial trigger question and ask a few probing questions the week the thread was active. My conclusion was that simple design choices (in this case, the choice to leave the thread open, which could only be considered a choice by default) can significantly influence the nature and quality of learning and instruction. My naiveté in this regard might be considered a kind of stuttering. In this case, my online stuttering did not inhibit student engagement with the content—perhaps it even facilitated that engagement.

The second example also addresses the issue of design more than the issue of voice. At one of my former institutions, I encountered much resistance to online teaching, especially at the doctoral level. Many of my colleagues have encountered similar resistance. The resistance might be captured in this assertion: "One cannot possibly teach a doctoral seminar online." There is also an active debate within the instructional design and technology community with regard to the design of online learning environments. One of the mantras often repeated in this community is this: "An online learning environment must be designed to be entirely different from a traditional face-to-face environment." I was reluctant to accept either of these positions without qualifications, partly because I generally regard such strong statements with suspicion. So I set out to design and implement an online doctoral seminar on the topic of issues pertaining to instructional design research, which I had previously taught as a face-to-face seminar with about eight or 10 students. I designed the course to be an online replica of the face-to-face course I had taught the previous year. I used the same readings, required the same assignments, and had the same discussion questions as before. The outcome was a dramatic improvement in the quality of the discussions. The papers delivered by students were of a similar quality to those I was used to getting, and participation was also at a relatively high level, as one would expect in a doctoral seminar. The primary difference was that the discussions were significantly richer—students posted often and their postings were substantial. Threads were followed to many levels and new threads were often introduced by students seeking to explore a different line of thought. As it happened, I had left the chat feature of WebCT turned on and made the chat room available to students, but I never intended to use it nor did I ever tell them how to organize their own sessions. In spite of this negligence on my part, these students decided to meet on their own in the chat room and discuss specific topics outside the context of the scheduled discussions. Perhaps my face-to-face students had done something analogous and met in a coffee shop to discuss topics and exchange ideas; I do not know. What I do know is that this particular design choice—leaving the chat room accessible—had dramatic and positive consequences for that group of students. My silent online voice was not such a deterrent as it might have been in this case.

The third and final example concerns a blended learning environment. In this case, the course was intended to be a face-to-face course with support materials made available through BlackBoard. This was a doctoral seminar with nine students. We met every week for 3 hours to discuss readings selected from the *Handbook of Research on Educational Communications and Technology* (Jonassen, 2003). I posted the course syllabus, many readings, links to other resources and more on the course Website. Each week, I asked two students to present a summary of the readings. The course evolved much differently than I had planned. I had planned to lecture for 2 hours and give the students one hour for their presentations. This only happened the first week. The students basically took over both the face-to-face course and the online discussions. Their presentations in the classroom were very elaborate and typically took 2 hours or more. So, I shifted what I wanted to say to the discussion board—more stuttering on my part. The discussion board then developed into a much richer sharing and exchange than I had expected, especially given the effort the students were putting into the face-to-face meetings. The first week, there were 47 messages posted—23 of these were from me. By the 5th week, the number of messages had risen to 159—41 of these were from me. While my contributions almost doubled, student contributions increased almost seven-fold. This pattern was sustained for the remainder of the semester. The postings were generally thoughtful and substantial, which was my experience in the other two cases.

What have I learned from these and my other online experiences? I think I have learned that one ought to remain open to change and be willing to consider alternative explanations and approaches. I may have learned what I sometimes tell my students about the need to be clear about the differences between science and advocacy—to realize that one may know less than one is normally inclined to believe. The remaining paragraphs, save the last, are taken from a message I posted to that third group of students discussed earlier.

What constitutes a scientific statement and a scientific attitude? How is this different from or similar to advocacy? A scientific claim is one in which evidence can be gathered to show that the claim is very likely true or false

(Popper, 1963). Scientific statements are subject to evidentiary confirmation or refutation—the latter requirement probably being the more critical. The notion of evidence involves associated concepts of public scrutiny—examination by those who are convinced as well as by those who are doubtful. Evidence in this sense refers to publicly observable data—things or events that others could in principle observe independently or replicate. A scientific attitude, then, is one that is open to both confirmation and refutation (Popper, 1963). This corresponds with the classical notion of skepticism found in Pyrrho and Sextus Empiricus. A skeptic is one who is engaged in a search for an answer—as the Greek root word suggests. A skeptic is a seeker—one who admits to not knowing but wanting to understand. A scientific attitude is precisely the attitude of not knowing how to explain an event or phenomenon or group of events or phenomena along with the willingness to explore alternative explanations in an attempt to understand. The scientific attitude is characterized by a willingness to be wrong. It is the openness to refutation and the associated commitment to engage in disciplined exploration of alternative explanations that distinguishes science from advocacy. It is not that one is better than the other. They are simply quite different enterprises. When one further examines the things that advocates do and compares those activities with things that scientists do, the differences become even sharper. The language of an advocate is designed to persuade; in that sense, effective advocates are good rhetoricians. The language of a scientist is designed to explain; in this sense, effective scientists find likely causes and effects or refute alleged causes or effects. Confusing these different attitudes and activities can undermine the growth of knowledge, as should be evident with regard to educational research. Although instructional scientists have identified much that can be done to improve learning and instruction based on empirical inquiry, very little of that research has made its way into practice. In closing, it is my hope that educational researchers will learn to couple their scientific voices with informed advocacy and make positive contributions to the practice of teaching, whether it be in online environments, in classrooms, in coffee shops, or in hallways, homes, shopping malls or wherever one finds the opportunity to facilitate and support learning.

REFERENCES

AAAS (American Association for the Advancement of Science). (1993). *Benchmarks for science literacy*. New York: Oxford University Press.
Chizmar, J. F., & Williams, D. B. (1998). Internet delivery of instruction: Issues of best teaching practice, administrative, hurdles, and old-fashioned politics. *Campus-wide Information Systems, 15*(5), 164–173.
Collis, B., & Gervedink Nijhuis, G. (2000). The instructor as manager: Time and task. *Internet and Higher Education, 3*(2000), 75–97.

Collison, G., Elbaum, B., Haavind, S., & Tinker, R. (2000). *Facilitating online learning: Effective strategies for moderators*. Madison, WI: Atwood Publishing.

DeBoer, G., Morris, K., Roseman, J. E., Wilson, L., Capraro, M. M., Capraro, R., et al. (2004, April 12–16). *Research issues in the improvement of mathematics teaching and learning through professional development*. Paper presented at the American Educational Research Association, San Diego, CA. Retrieved on April 26, 2006, from http://www.project2061.org/publications/articles/IERI/aera2004.htm

Dörner, D. (1996). *The logic of failure: Why things go wrong and what we can do to make them right* (R. & R. Kimber, Trans.). New York: Holt, Rhinehart, & Winston.

Ericsson, K. A., Krampe, R. T., & Tesch-Römer, C. (1993). The role of deliberate practice in the acquisition of expert performance. *Psychological Review, 100*(3), 363–406.

Falk, B. (2001). Professional learning through assessment. In A. Lieberman & L. Miller (Eds.), *Teachers caught in the action: Professional development that matters* (pp. 118–140). New York: Teachers College Press.

Feldman, A. l., Konold, C., & Coulter, B. (2000). *Network science a decade later: The Internet and classroom learning*. Mahwah, NJ: Lawrence Erlbaum Associates.

Ganesan, R. (2005). *Perceptions and practices of expert teachers in technology-based distance and distributed learning environments*. Unpublished doctoral dissertation, Syracuse University, Syracuse, New York.

Goodyear, P. (2000). Online teaching. In N. Hativa & P. Goodyear (Eds.), *Teacher thinking, beliefs and knowledge in higher education* (pp. 79–102). Dordrecht, The Netherlands: Kluwer.

Goodyear, P., Salmon, G., Spector, J. M., Steeples, C., & Tickner, S. (2001). Competences for online teaching: A special report. *Educational Technology Research & Development, 49*(1), 65–72.

Hativa, N., & Goodyear, P. (Eds.). (2002). *Teacher thinking, beliefs and knowledge in higher education*. Dordrecht, The Netherlands: Kluwer.

Hiltz, S. R., & Turoff, M. (2002). What makes learning networks effective? *Communications of the ACM, 45*(2), 56–59.

Hislop, G. W., & Ellis, H. J. C. (2004). A study of faculty effort in online teaching. *The Internet and Higher Education, 7*(1), 15–31.

Jonassen, D. H. (2000). *Computers as mind tools for schools: Engaging critical thinking*. Englewood Cliffs, NJ: Prentice-Hall.

Jonassen, D. H. (Ed.). (2003). *Handbook of research on educational communications and technology*. Mahwah, NJ: Lawrence Erlbaum Associates.

Jones, E. T., Lindner, J. R., Murphy, T. H., & Dooley, K. E. (2002). Faculty philosophical position towards distance education: Competency, value, and educational technology support. *Online Journal of Distance Learning Administration, 5*(1). Retrieved on May 1, 2004 from http://www.westga.edu/~distance/ojdla/spring51/jones51.html

Kanuka, H., Collett, D., & Caswell, C. (2002). University instructor perceptions of the use of asynchronous text-based discussion in distance courses. *American Journal of Distance Education, 16*(3), 151–167.

Kearsley, G. (1999). *Online education: Learning and teaching in cyberspace*. New York: Wadsworth Publishing.

Klein, J. D., Spector, J. M., Grabowski, B., & de la Teja, I. (2004). *Instructor competencies: Standards for face-to-face, online and blended settings*. Greenwich, CT: Information Age.

Ko, S., & Rossen, S. (2001). *Teaching online: A practical guide*. Boston: Houghton-Mifflin.

MacKinnon, G. R. (2002). Practical advice for first time online instructors: A qualitative study. *Journal of Instruction Delivery Systems, 16*, 21–25.

Merrill, M. D. (2002). First principles of instruction. *Educational Technology Research & Development, 50*(3), 43–59.

Moore, M., & Kearsley, G. (2005). *Distance education: A systems view* (2nd ed.). Belmont, CA: Wadwsorth.

National Research Council. (2002). *Scientific research in education.* Washington, DC: National Academy Press.

Peterson, C. L., & Bond, N. (2004). Online compared to face-to-face teacher preparation for learning standards-based planning skills. *Journal of Research on Technology in Education, 36*(4), 345–359.

Popper, K. (1963). *Conjectures and refutations: The growth of scientific knowledge.* London: Routledge & Kegan Paul.

Reigeluth, C. M. (Ed.). (1983). *Instructional-design theories and models: An overview of their current status.* Hillsdale, NJ: Lawrence Erlbaum Associates.

Richey, R. C., Klein, J. D., & Nelson, W. A. (2004). Developmental research: Studies of instructional design and development. In D. H. Jonassen (Ed.), *Handbook of research on educational communications and technology* (2nd ed., pp. 1099–1130). Mahwah, NJ: Lawrence Erlbaum Associates.

Rosenberg, M. J. (2001). *E-learning: Strategies for delivering knowledge in the digital age.* New York: McGraw-Hill.

Sales, G. C. (2002). A quick guide to e-learning: A "how to" guide for organizations implementing e-learning. Andover, MN: Expert Publishing.

Schön, D. A. (1983). *The reflective practitioner: How professionals think in action.* New York: Basic Books.

Simonson, M., Smaldino, S., Albright, M., & Zvacek, S. (2003). *Teaching and learning at a distance: Foundations of distance* education (2nd ed.). Upper Saddle River, NJ: Pearson Education.

Spector, J. M. (2002). Foreword. In C. Steeples & C. Jones (Eds.), *Networked learning: Perspective and Issues* (pp. xiii–xvii). London: Springer.

Spector, J. M. (2005). Time demands in online instruction. *Distance Education, 26*(1), 3–25.

Spector, J. M. (in press). What makes good online instruction good? New opportunities and old barriers. In J. Visser (Ed.), *Learners in a changing learning landscape: Reflections from a dialogue on new roles and expectations.* Berlin: Springer.

Spector, J. M., & Anderson, T. M. (Eds.). (2000). *Integrated and holistic perspectives on learning, instruction and technology: Understanding complexity.* Dordrecht, The Netherlands: Kluwer.

Spector, J. M., & de la Teja, I. (2001, December). *Competencies for online teaching.* ERIC Digest EDO-IR-2001-09. Syracuse, NY: ERIC Information Technology Clearinghouse. Retrieved on April 26, 2006 from http://www.eric.ed.gov/ (search on ERIC # ED456841).

Spector, J. M., Doughty, P. L., & Yonai, B. A. (2003). *Cost and learning effects of alternative e-collaboration methods in online settings* (Final report for the Andrew W. Mellon Foundation Cost Effective Use of Technology in Teaching Initiative). Syracuse, NY: Syracuse University.

Spector, J. M., Klein, J. D., Reiser, R. A., Sims, R. C., Grabowski, B. L., & de la Teja, I. (2006, April 17–21). *Competencies and standards for instructional design and educational technology.* Paper posted for discussion on ITFORUM. Retrieved on April 25, 2006 from http://it.coe.uga.edu/itforum/paper89/ITForumpaper89.pdf

Stacey, E., & Rice, M. (2002). Evaluating an online learning environment. *Australian Journal of Educational Technology, 18*(3), 323–340.

Steeples, C., & Jones, C. (Eds.). (2002). *Networked learning: Perspectives and Issues.* London: Springer.

The Contributing Student: Philosophy, Technology, and Strategy

Betty Collis
University of Twente

Jef Moonen
University of Twente

We often surprise our instructional-design colleagues by saying that our approach to course design is to start with the course Web environment as empty as possible. Instead of designing a course around what we will present to the students, we spend most of our time devising and setting up the activities that the students will be doing. Based on this, we plan the support that we, the instructors, can offer, and in particular, we plan the assessment procedures. The key to this approach is the idea that the learning activities are based on what we call the *contributing student* approach (Collis & Moonen, 2002, 2005, in press). Through the process of their learning activities, the students contribute resources of various types to the course Web environment that are built on by all in subsequent learning activities and that result in a contribution that can be used by others. Sometimes the contributions are simple, for example, the students together build an internet links collection to be used as a resource for the rest of the course and updated by the students in subsequent cycles of the course. Other times, the contributions involve developing a report or product of some kind that represents an analysis from the student's own experiences or research. The individual contributions become part of a collection that is then used by the students for subsequent comparisons or other types of learning activities. Most interesting is when the contributions are integrated together into a resource that will be useful to an audience outside of the course itself. In the contributing student approach, the course Web site may start out being relatively empty, but it fills up quickly with the work and imagination that is shown in the contributions of the students. Assignments are not something to be put into a drop box in order to get a grade from the instructor; they are contributions that become learning resources for others.

The contributing student has both educational and strategic motivations. From an educational perspective, learning by acquisition and learning by participation (Sfard, 1998) are embedded within the idea of learning by contributing to a shared knowledge base. The contributing student principles are similar to Kearsley and Shneiderman's (1998) *Engagement Theory*, and to *Action Learning* (Dopper & Dijkman, 1997; Simons, 1999). Table 2.1 contrasts these approaches with the key ideas of the contributing-student pedagogical model.

The contributing student approach also has a strategic motivation. The need for participation and contribution reflects current developments in society. Internationalization, the world becoming a global community, the fact that individuals can expect to work in different settings and as members of multifaceted teams, and the need for social skills and communication skills: All are commonly described as characteristics of living and working in a knowledge economy that are rapidly gaining in importance (World Bank Group, 2003). In corporate settings, global networks and other forms of knowledge-sharing communities are key tools in learning from the tacit knowledge of others in the corporation. This learning comes from finding relevant examples and resources, from asking others in the community for help or clarification, or by joining in debates and discussions on how to generate solutions for workers' real problems. In professional contexts, for learning communities or communities of practice, digital workbenches increasingly serve major roles in the ways in which people in a common company or professional group interact and learn from each other (Wenger, 2005). Thus the contributing student approach is also preparation for the professional workforce.

EXAMPLES FROM PRACTICE

In simplest form, there are two categories of learning activities for a contributing-student pedagogy; finding and contributing, or creating and contributing (where creating usually involves some elements of finding). The following are examples of how a contribution approach can steer course design. They also show how Web technology is an important facilitative tool.

TABLE 2.1

The Contributing Student contrasted with similar approaches

"Participation-oriented" (Sfard, 1998)	"Action Learning" (Dopper & Dijkman, 1997; Simons, 1999)	"Engagement Theory" (Kearsley & Shneiderman, 1998)	"The Contributing Student"
Key definition of learning: Learning as participation, the process of becoming a member of a community, "the ability to communicate in the language of this community and act according to its norms" (p. 6); "the permanence of having gives way to the constant flux of doing" (p. 6) *Key words:* Apprenticeship, situatedness, contextuality, communication, social constructivism, cooperative learning; Belonging, participating, communicating *Stress on*: "The evolving bonds between the individual and others" (p. 6); "The whole and the parts affect and inform each other" (p. 6) *Role of the instructor:* Facilitator, mentor, expert participant	*Key characteristics:* (a) Practical problems are central: Learning is based on workin on problems from one's own work situation (b) When there are contacts among learners, these are focused on stimulating self-reflection and learning from others (c) Instead of "lectures," learners use contact times for activities *Stress on*: Learning to learn, to collaborate, to self-regulate *Role of the instructor:* Leader, motivator, and guide of the learning processes; giving feedback on evolving phases of the problem-oriented project, and evaluator of the final submission. Must ensure that learner contact is more that the sharing of experiences but also that experiences are related to theory	*Key idea:* "students must be meaningfully engaged in learning activities through interaction with others and worthwhile tasks" (p. 20) *Key characteristics:* Learning activities that (a) "occur in a group context (i.e., collaborative teams) (b) are project-based, and (c) have an outside (authentic focus)" (i.e., are meaningful to someone outside the classroom) *Role of instructor:* Supporting and screening the initial definition of projects and formulation of teams, provide guidance in working in teams, provision of criteria to evaluate projects *Role of technology:* "To facilitate all aspects of the engagement" (p. 23)	*Key ideas*: Learners contribute to the learning materials via contributions made available to others in a Web-based system. The others may be others in the same group or others at other times. *Key characteristics:* (a) the Web site is largely empty at the start of the learning experience; the learners and the instructor will fill it via the process of many activities during the course (b) Learners learn from realistic materials as well as peer-created materials as much as or more than professionally developed materials (c) Learning materials contributed by students are reused in other learning settings *Role of instructor*: Designer of activities and of feedback and monitoring strategies for activities. *Role of technology*: To facilitate all aspects of the activities

Note. Adapted from Collis & Moonen, 2001, p. 88.

- In a course taught by one of us on the topic "Online Learning" that ran from January–April 1994, the main activity for the students was to communally create a book on the potential of the Web for education. As Web technology was new, there was no textbook available; the students and instructor needed to build on what had been learned in the past about technology and learning, and then extrapolate this to the new affordances available via the Web as a workbench. Together they identified a set of chapters for the book, which would not only be about the Web but would also be a Web-based product jointly created by all in the course for an audience beyond the course. The students worked in groups of three; each group chose one of the chapter themes, and each was paired with a colleague of the instructor's somewhere in the world who had agreed to serve as a mentor for the chapter. The book was then revised by students in the following cycle of the course.
- In a graduate course in project management, the students worked in groups to develop a proposal and prototype solution for online materials for one of a local corporation's product lines. In the final presentations, the representative of the corporation, along with the instructor and the students themselves, rank ordered the presentations, which were then given to the corporation to use as it wished (Merrill, 2000).
- In a course in computer science, teams of students each had the responsibility of developing coaching and self-study and testing materials for their classmates on one of the topics of the course. They had to become "experts" in that topic in order to answer questions relating to the exercises and model answers that they developed.

In corporate and professional situations, similar ideas to these can extend the contributing-student approach to a contributing-professional approach. In these contexts, the benefits of extracting and building on the tacit knowledge within the corporation or professional group can be easily seen. Examples from a corporate-learning setting for engineers in the oil industry (Margaryan, Collis, & Cooke, 2004) include:

- A course on health-risk assessment in the workplace in which participants arrange a visit to a site of their choice in their workplaces, diagnose it in terms of potential health or safety hazards, and develop a plan for reduction of the risks. Each step of the process involves interactions with a team in the actual workplace, summarized via the course Web environment, and used by the other participants as resource materials for analyzing their own work. The activities in this course progressively build on one another, the final product being a health-risk assessment plan for each participant's own workplace, ready to put into action.

- A course that involves challenges that occur with the application of new technologies in oil-production plants in which the participants submit detailed analyses of a problem situation in their own workplaces to the course Web environment before the classroom session. The activities involve the participants interacting with others in their own workplaces and using knowledge-sharing groupware tools for the creation of the analyses. Once physically together, the learners form small groups based on their interactions via the Web site, and tackle each others' submitted problems by peer-assisted activities (Collis, Waring, & Nicholson, 2004).

In a course designed in such a way, traditional approaches to organizing the course need to be adapted. Students need to begin specialized study of their assigned part of the contributed resources early on. The instructor needs to shift attention away from linear lecture-to-lecture presentation of material to supporting self-study, working with the groups of students to help them to help others in the course through what they produce. Also, network technology plays a critical supporting role. A Web-based system with appropriate upload, collaborative, and communication functionalities provides the common medium into which contributions are placed for further sharing as well as for feedback and assessment. The resources contributed can become new content objects in themselves, depending on how they are used in subsequent activities and other course processes.

FROM THE TRENCHES: THE CONTRIBUTING STUDENT, FROM THE INSTRUCTOR'S PERSPECTIVE

We have included contribution-type activities in our courses since long before the days of the Web and online learning, but the activities had to be limited in scale and logistics to what could be created and shared in the classroom, using media such as printouts from stand-alone computers that then had to be photocopied for sharing. Now, we have used the approach in more than 30 of our own courses since 1994 with Web tools and since 1997, with a Web-based course-management system. In addition, we have worked with instructors in other universities and corporate-learning settings on the design and management of the approach in their own courses. We also have supervised a 4-year research project, in which the time- and task-management issues encountered by the instructor when managing courses using a course-management system and involving student contributions have been studied in detail (Gervedink Nijhuis, 2005). From all this we have learned many lessons the hard way, as well as seeing many positive results confirmed again and again. First, we discuss the lessons learned the hard way.

Lessons Learned the Hard Way

The lessons we have learned the hard way can be grouped around categories relating to management burdens, assessment-related issues, intellectual-property considerations, mindset-change conflicts, and, running through all of these, time burdens.

Management Burdens.   A key characteristic of contribution-type activities is that the instructor does not know in advance what the students will contribute. Thus, if instructions are not clear and explicit about what is expected in terms of scope, origin, criteria, length, and presentation, the management burden can become enormous. Students contact you by e-mail at all hours of the day and night asking for clarification or asking you to look at what they have so far to see if they are on the right track. If they submit something that turns out to be inappropriate, then they will want to redo the assignment, meaning another round of feedback from the instructor. All these communications have to be kept track of, somewhere, or else students send you an e-mail sometime later saying "But you said that I could do it again." This becomes even more of a managerial nightmare if there is more than one instructor involved in the course. The risk develops that one of the instructors will say "OK, I will give you another chance" but forget to tell the other instructor.

As soon as the students are working on a project that involves developing something for an outside audience or client, then a new layer of management tasks occurs. Contacts with the outside party have to be carefully managed, as do differences of opinion as to the amount of time that the students will have to do the project. The instructor now has to manage the contacts that the students have with outside parties in order to assure that appropriate professional behavior is followed.

When students are working in groups, the instructor must find a way to manage group processes so that all students have roles and do a fair balance of the work, so that group members who fulfill their tasks are not disadvantaged if others in the group fail to fulfill their responsibilities. Managing dysfunctional groups who are meant to be carrying out an assignment with a contributing-student approach is a burden for the instructor.

A major management problem occurs when students are late in submissions that are meant to be building blocks for the next learning activity. Then the instructor must manage the concerns of worried or annoyed students who can't get on with the next phase of work because of others who have not yet submitted what is needed to proceed.

From all of the management issues we have encountered, we have learned the following lessons:

- Be crystal clear in the written instructions on the Web site for any contribution-type activity. Indicate clearly how much and in what form the contribution should be and where in the Web environment it should be submitted. If it is a group submission, make it clear who should submit on behalf of the group. Provide a model or example. If possible, include a template to download, fill in, and upload with the contribution.

- Be clear and firm about submission dates and the policy for late submissions. Indicate these in your course Web site at the start of the course and point them out in your communications with the students. Indicate the consequences of late or inappropriate contributions, again in writing in the course Web site. Design follow-up activities in a way that allows the rest of the students to continue if some are behind.

- Keep a folder in the instructor's area of the course Web site where you place copies of all e-mails or records of agreements with students about extensions, changes in planning, resubmits, time limits, and anything else that a student may challenge you on later. If there are multiple instructors, make sure you develop as a team a procedure for keeping this shared folder orderly and up-to-date. Never contradict each other on what you say to students about their contributions.

Other lessons learned with respect to management are discussed in connection with assessment and intellectual-property issues.

Assessment-Related Issues.   Assessment is a major challenge for the instructor in a contributing-student approach. By definition, there are no predetermined "right" answers, but instead there will be different degrees of appropriateness on different dimensions. Students are, understandably, highly sensitive to potential ambiguities in grading and marking. Most of the management issues that were just discussed become stressful for all involved when they affect students' grades. The more open-ended or complex the contribution, the more conflict can develop around the grade. Students will argue that "I did what you said. Why shouldn't I have full marks?" Grading of group work is a particular minefield; not only in the occasions where students did not all contribute to the group at the same level but also in other cases where the group works together so closely that it is difficult to untangle what the individual may not really understand. All this contributes to a headache for the instructor. Our major lessons here include:

- Provide a scoring sheet or rubric in your Web environment along with the instructions for any contribution-type activity. Present categories of generic criteria, such as "appropriate choice of source documents" and "effective presentation of conclusions," which do not constrain creativity but still make it clear how you will grade. For each such criterion, indicate a point range (for example, 1–5) and what the difference is between the points, for example, between a 3 and a 4. Use a model submission from a previous year to illustrate the top of the point ranges.

• For complex contribution activities, split the activity into stages and give marks for each stage, such as three submissions of 5 points, 10 points, and 20 points instead of one final score of 35 points. In this way, students will better understand what you are looking for and can incorporate your feedback into the next stage of the work. This is particularly important for group projects.

• Make your policy clear as to how a late submission will be scored, if revisions and resubmissions will be allowed, and if so, what the effect on the marks will be.

Intellectual-Property Considerations. A strength of a contributing-student approach, particularly in preparation for workplace knowledge sharing, is the aspect of learning from each other and building on each other's experiences. However, in the university setting, issues of intellectual property make the processes more complicated than is the case within a company. Students need guidance and coaching on how to properly use and cite the work of others, a particular problem when the cutting and pasting of work in digital form is technically so simple. In our own experience, despite repeated attempts to provide examples and guidance, there are typically one or two students who, realizing it or not, make improper use of the work of others (with or without citations). How to manage this in terms of marking the assignment, and even of the student continuing in the course or program is a major headache. In some institutions, students may need to give consent before their work is seen by other students; managing this can be tedious for the instructor. Within course-management systems, there are often technical restrictions on access to the submissions of other students. These issues lead to the following lessons learned.

• Be clear in the Web site about how to refer to and provide examples from the work of others. Insist on appropriate citations and referencing. If a student includes pieces of work, such as blocks of text, a table, a figure, originating from others without proper referencing, give one warning, but after that, indicate what the implications are for a grade (or for continuing in the course).

• If an assignment involves adding to another student's previously submitted work, find a way to differentiate the work of the different students and maintain both students' names on the resulting product.

• For subsequent cycles of a course, only reuse contributions that are particularly good examples. Obtain the student's consent for reuse of his or her work.

Mindset-Change Conflicts.   It is our experience that if the contribution activity is well chosen so that students can see its value to themselves, if it is well managed (see previous lessons), and if the assessment is perceived as fair, then students are very positive about the approach. But this may not be the situation at the beginning of the course, or if those "ifs" are not positively carried out. Students have said to us "Why don't you just give us what we are supposed to learn? That would be much more efficient" and even more sharply, "It's your job to teach us." These sorts of comments reflect a mindset about the role of the teacher as the one responsible for the flow of quality-assured study materials, and the students as the ones responsible to know what is in those study materials in order to pass a test or do an exercise. Many course-evaluation forms in higher education, and also in corporate learning, emphasize the instructor's performance in terms of presenting and testing. With the contributing-student approach, there is a mindset change needed in the role of the instructor, away from presenting quality-controlled content, toward monitoring and guiding the students as they make decisions themselves about the quality of what they find or what they produce. The role of the instructor still involves quality control, but more of the products produced by the students than of the materials presented to them. The role of the instructor still involves careful preparation and clear presentation, but of learning activities and their instructions and expectations for assessment rather than of lecture delivery. The role of the student changes from being a consumer of what is delivered to a prosumer, both producing and consuming, and in addition, producing for others. Instructors and students become co-learners and share responsibility for the value of the course. These mindset changes have taught us lessons such as the following.

- Explain the reasons for the contribution approach in a way that motivates the students. Indicate clearly in the course Web site why this approach is being used, and what affect it has on the roles of those involved.
- Ensure that the students see you as a fellow learner. Pick up on ideas in their contributions and build on them in your reflections in the course Web site. Show that you are excited by what they find, for example new Web links, and what they produce as new resources for others.
- Be professional in your own part of the process: provide feedback to all submissions promptly in the course Web site, be systematic in your communications and in the ways that you monitor the students' ongoing work.

Time Burdens.   In our experience, a contributing student approach takes more time than a traditional course. Not more time before the course, but certainly more time during the course. Even when applying all of the lessons learned, it takes more time to manage and assess contributions that bring in new ideas and experiences than it does to manage and assess assignments where everyone does the same exercises and should come to the same result. Over time, we have become quite efficient about managing our time as instructors with the contributing student approach. Some of the lessons we have learned follow.

• First, follow all the lessons that have already been mentioned in the previous sections.
• Second, block time each week for communication, feedback, and management. Treat this time with the same seriousness as you would treat a scheduled lecture. Indicate in the course Web site when you will be active with the course each week and when you will provide feedback, for example, "By each Friday at 17:00 I will mark all submissions that have been uploaded since the previous Friday." Do not get behind in feedback and marking, or in communicating with students; but at the same time, let them know that they cannot expect you to provide 24/7 responsiveness.
• Third, be clear about your own time planning. For example, we say to students that if they choose to submit later than the deadline, then we will provide a mark but will not be able to provide personalized feedback. Have some sort of final moment in the course, with presentations (face to face if possible; submitted by a clear date and time if only online), and then wrap up the course with a feeling for all that the course is now over. In the Web environment, add a news item that serves this purpose. Round off all marking within a short time period; we aim for one week after the close of the course.
• As part of the course wrap up, select the contributions that you will use as models in subsequent course cycles, and make any adjustments needed to instructions, scoring sheets, or study materials while the course is fresh in your mind. Store any useful notes or ideas in a folder in the instructor area of the course site, as well as an overview of student marks and final grades. All of this makes launching the next cycle much more efficient.

Finally, for new courses, we have found that the following design sequence is efficient for us:

1. Design the contribution-oriented activities and what the students will need as support for the activities. (Oliver & Herrington, 2001, is an excellent resource for this.)
2. Design the assessment and its tools and processes.
3. Design the Web environment to support the approach.
4. Design the rest of the course.
5. Design to avoid problems in practice; communicate clearly in the course Web environment, ahead of time, what your commitment will be to the students and what you expect from them.

As an overall lesson learned, we would not want to use the contributing student without good Web-based tools and a course-management system that allows for a flexible and contribution-oriented approach. If an online course environment was only oriented toward presenting lesson materials, for example, with quizzes and perhaps "drop boxes" for individual student assignments, we would not be able to function in the ways needed for a contribution orientation, so we would not want to be instructors for such courses.

Confirming the Positive

We have learned many lessons from our years in the trenches with the contributing-student approach. We also have had many cycles of confirmation about the positive aspects of the approach. We get great pleasure in seeing students become co-creators in a course, proud of their contributions and engaged through those contributions with others in the course. The students' contributions extend and enrich the course beyond what we could have produced ourselves. We pass (some) of the work onto students, in terms of bringing in new examples and insights and applications from practice. We learn with and from the students, becoming a minicommunity in the process. The value of the course for us is in what we can stimulate the students to produce. In the corporate context, we see the knowledge sharing that occurs as directly valuable to the business, both short and long term. In any setting, we believe the approach is consistent with what we see as key skills for productive functioning in a knowledge economy.

CONCLUSION: WHAT ARE OUR ONLINE VOICES IN A CONTRIBUTING-STUDENT APPROACH?

The matter of finding an online voice in a course that emphasizes a contribution approach is a process that has evolved for us over time. When we observe instructors who are new to the approach, we realize how much we have learned through our experiences.

The first observation is that there is not a single, stable online voice. Our tone and style of communication varies, depending on how our roles vary in the course. The voice we have for giving the instructions for contribution activities, the expectations for performance, the assessment procedures, are formal voices, in which we take care to write in a clear and unambiguous way. These formal expectations can be directly transferred into the university's printed course guides. The voice we use to monitor and stimulate students is much more like that of a personal coach, now and then stopping to say something to the group as a whole. Here the tone is personal, warm, friendly, and the more the students are contributing, the more we can make our coaching an opportunity for positive reinforcement. But when students are not performing appropriately, our tone and voice change to those of an evaluator and even someone who will have to make a tough decision on the student's status in the course. When all meshes well, our tone by the end of the course comes close to that of a peer community—close but never exactly, because the fact remains that we must be responsible for the assessment role and for the final say as to the acceptability of performance.

Another observation we have made, many years ago, is that talking online is a different form of communication, something between written and spoken words. Reflections as we are making here are typical of the way that we write reflective comments to our students. It's more personal and less formal than professional written communication (we won't use a contraction like "it's" in professional written communication, for example). But it is less personal than a face-to-face discussion. It is better structured than verbal flow. But it lacks the body language and eye contact and vocal intonations that characterize face-to-face communication. This is one of the reasons we recommend blended courses with some opportunity for face-to-face contact, even if only at the beginning and end of the course. We have found that establishing the chemistry of the course is much easier to do with a face-to-face launch session than without it. Once this has occurred, than the students can better hear our human voices as they read our words on their screens.

REFERENCES

Collis, B., & Moonen, J. (2001). *Flexible learning in a digital world: Experiences and expectations*. London: Routledge.

Collis, B., & Moonen, J. (2002). The contributing student: A pedagogy for flexible learning. *Computers in the Schools, 19*(3/4), 207–220.

Collis, B., & Moonen, J. (2005, September). *An on-going journey: Technology as a learning workbench*. Public address, University of Twente, Enschede, The Netherlands. Retrieved September 15, 2005 from http://www.BettyCollisJefMoonen.nl

Collis, B., & Moonen, J. (2006). The contributing student: Learners as co-developers of learning resources for reuse in Web environments. In D. Hung & M. S. Khine (Eds.), *Engaged learning with emerging technologies* (pp. 49–68). Dordrecht: Springer.

Collis, B., Waring, B., & Nicholson, G. (2004, October 21). *Learning from experience, for experienced staff*. Paper presented at Annual Conference of the AECT (Association for Educational and Communication Technology), Chicago, IL.

Dopper, S., & Dijkman, B. (1997). Action learning geschikt voor deeltijdonderwijs [Action learning appropriate for part-time students]. *Onderzoek van Onderwijs* [Research in Education], *23*, 57–59.

Gervedink Nijhuis, G. (2005). *Academics in control: Supporting personal performance for teaching-related activities*. Unpublished doctoral dissertation, Faculty of Behavioural Sciences, University of Twente, The Netherlands.

Kearsley, G., & Shneiderman, G. (1998). Engagement theory: A framework for technology-based teaching and learning. *Educational Technology, 38*(5), 20–24.

Margaryan, A., Collis, B., & Cooke, A. (2004). Activity-based blended learning. *Human Resource Development International*, 7(2), 265–274.

Merrill, M. D. (2000). *Write your dissertation first, and other essays on a graduate education*. Utah State University. Retrieved July 16, 2005 from http://cito.byuh.edu/merrill/text/papers/GraduateEducation.pdf

Oliver, R., & Herrington, J. (2001). *Teaching and learning online*. Centre for Research and Information Technology and Communications, Edith Cowan University, Western Australia.

Sfard, A. (1998). On two metaphors for learning and the dangers of choosing just one. *Educational Researcher*, 27(2), 4–13.

Simons, P. R. J. (1999). Three ways to learn in a new balance. *Lifelong Learning in Europe*, *IV* (1), 14–23.

Wenger, E. (2005). *Communities of practice: A brief introduction*. Retrieved May 16, 2005 from http://www.ewenger.com/theory/index.htm

World Bank Group. (2003). *Lifelong learning in the global knowledge economy*. Retrieved May 16, 2005 from http://www1.worldbank.org/education/lifelong_learning/lifelong_learning_GKE.asp

Online Learning—
For Better or For Worse?
A Reflective View

Jan Visser
Learning Development Institute

THE POWER OF VIRTUAL COMMUNICATION: A DEDICATION

I dedicate this chapter to David Wolsk.[1] I never met David face to face. Yesterday he died. I received the news this morning by e-mail from my friend Diana in Tucson, Arizona, whom I never met either. However, I had been able to bring her and David into contact with each other not so long ago when David happened to be in Tucson and had told me so, also by e-mail. So I mentioned Diana to him and he took the initiative to look

---

[1]David Wolsk was, at the time he died, associated with the Centre for Global Studies, University of Victoria, Canada. He spent his life as a neuroscientist and educator who championed self-directed, experiential/real-life learning. Above all, David was a man of wisdom and peace, qualities that are perhaps best described in the words of another friend, who responded to his death in an e-mail I just received. "David had achieved much of what he wanted to achieve in his life—although he could never have achieved everything that was in that incredible mind of his. And I know how happy he was in his kids and his grandkids. I will hang on to the memory of a sunny four hours sitting on a bench by the Thames in London, surrounded by trees in all their fall glory, sailing boats and swans on the river, and a couple of dogs running around as though they had to get all their fun in life into one day, and talking as though we'd known each other for years, instead of actually having met each other live just a week earlier" (personal communication, S. Lee, April 23, 2005).

her up. We would all meet a few weeks from now in The Netherlands—at least, that's what we had planned. But now it will never happen. I lost a friend whose face I never saw.

Such is the power of virtual communication.

Actually, I never called Diana "my friend" before. Somehow David's death drew us closer together. I also found myself this morning addressing the members of two lists that both David and I used to contribute to as "Dear Friends." Many of those list members probably never met David either, at least not face to face, but I felt we had all become friends because of this shared loss. Such is the power of virtual communication. People experience a real sense of loss when someone transits from the world of the living to that of those who lived, leaving it to others to build on their heritage. That sense of loss is apparently not determined by physical closeness but rather by the words they created, words on a screen, words on paper, vibrations in the air, resonances in the mind.

This is what explains the power of virtual communication. It allows us to separate the words people utter from their physical external reality. However, it does not detach those words from who and what those people were or are. The words they utter that appear on our screens "are more than 'just words on the screen' for behind those words are love, care, support, interaction [and] growth" (Y. L. Visser, personal communication, April 23, 2005).

Four years ago Francisco Varela died. He was a member of a small transdisciplinary research community in which I also participate. On the day he died, the coordinator of our small community sent out a message to all members suggesting that "we all meet in mind and spirit at his Web site http://web.ccr.jussieu.fr/varela/index.html and discover the extent of his undying genius" (B. Nicolescu, personal communication, May 30, 2001). As I am writing these words, I just checked that Web site (Varela, 2000) again. It is still available, including Francisco's phone and fax numbers and his e-mail address. Such is the power of virtual communication that the mechanisms through which we used to communicate with those who are no longer with us remain a reality that transcends their bodily existence. So great is that power that it led me to defy any rational thought and copy my message about David's death to David's own e-mail address.

A VISION OF LEARNING AND TEACHING
AND WHAT IT MEANS TO BE AN (ONLINE) EDUCATOR

This book, according to its subtitle, compiles the stories of experienced online educators. I don't normally think of myself as an online educator. I have a certain experience, though, as an educator, having engaged in interaction with learners—both face-to-face and at-a-distance—for more than four decades; I started teaching while I was still a graduate student of physics. In addition, I have been a parent for some 35 years. Interacting with my own children, initially in the immediate family environment and later on, as we spread around the globe, increasingly online, has significantly contributed to my perceptions of what it means to be a good educator.

Being a good educator implies, in the first place, being a good listener. The voice required for being a good listener is that of someone who knows when it is better to be out of the way of the other person's learning and when one should be involved. It's also the voice of someone who is able to make the other person feel comfortable and welcome. It is often a soft and tender voice, one that includes moments of deliberate silence and that respects the intricate emotional substrate of the conversation. It is a voice that invites the learning individual to awaken in him or herself the lure of learning (Liston, 2004).

At times, the professional activity of teaching was my main job, but most of the time it has been something that I love to do on the side of other things. That same love is still there. It has not changed since the advent of online communications, nor has my style of educationally interacting with people greatly changed as a consequence. I think I would find it difficult to teach if I were not engaging significantly in things other than just teaching. Anchoring the teaching–learning dialogue in the shared but different realities of teacher and learner is for me an essential part of my voice as an educator. This implies more than the occasional reference to real-world examples. It means developing a dialogue that is meaningfully connected to the lives of two people who communicate with each other with the aim to grow, both of them, beyond where they were when the dialogue started. A precondition for this is the disposition to be vulnerable.

I became an active and dedicated user of e-mail and the Internet in 1990 and have been using the ever-increasing variety of online facilities of communication and knowledge processing, now also including voice interaction and collaborative authoring, ever since. Compared to my pre-online life, the volume and diversity of my communications with other people has dramatically increased. However, although my writing style in general has evolved over the years, there is no marked difference in tone between the letters I used to write and put in the mail in the past and the electronic communications I now prepare sitting in front of my computer screen, sending them out via the Internet. In other words, my voice as an educator has been more influenced by my experience-based views of what it means to learn and to teach than by the technological means that carry my voice.

I see learning and teaching as intimately and inseparably interwoven. I define both these concepts in much broader ways than do most people generally. Briefly formulated, learning is what one does to generate intelligent behavior that enhances one's constructive presence in the world (for a more elaborate discussion, see J. Visser, 2001). This includes the acquisition of specific competencies but is in no way restricted to it. Teaching means being present in the learner's environment in such a way that learning is facilitated. Because learning is an essentially social and dialogic phenomenon, teaching is best done when the teacher is also willing to be a learner. Consequently, my voice as an educator is one that suggests openness to the kind of dialogue in which both communicating parties accept to be equally vulnerable. Communicating such a disposition is more than making a statement to that effect. Usually it is not making a statement at all, but rather a showing over time of one's preparedness to engage with problems the same way one expects one's students to do. There is no fundamental difference between how one does this online or in a face-to-face context. In both cases it is important that student and teacher have agreed, often implicitly, to be interacting with problems and that doing so is a serious matter. It assumes that problems are real and relevant and that the student is genuinely interested in learning (rather than in grades and degrees) and the teacher is equally interested in learning, both his or her own learning and that of the student (rather than being motivated by the salary it generates and the tenure or promotion opportunities tied in with the teaching task).

STORIES OF LEARNING—LEARNING FROM STORIES

A few years ago, my attention as a researcher was drawn to the stories of learning that people were able to generate about their experiences as life-long learners (e.g., Y. L. Visser & J. Visser, 2000; sample stories are available at http://www.learndev.org/LearningStories.html). Those stories were invariably fascinating. I collected hundreds of them. Those were not only stories of learning; they were also stories *for* learning, stories one could learn from. In fact, we learned from those stories that, generally, the learning that impacts people most takes place outside the formal contexts that are specifically designed for the purpose of helping them to learn, such as schools and universities. Indeed, experiences of life and death, love and despair, care and exclusion were found to be the powerful prompts for people to change course and to start interacting with their always changing environment—the heart of what it means to be learning—in crucially different ways (J. Visser, 2001).

ONLINE LEARNING: A DIFFERENT KIND OF LEARNING?

I recently concluded a chapter for a book on the future of higher education asking myself and my readers the question whether it would be useful to continue to treat distance education as a field in its own right? I concluded it was not. Among other considerations, I had the following thoughts:

> I consider questions about the technologies, mechanisms and processes used to facilitate the kind of learning demanded by the challenges…[of our time] largely irrelevant. It is not irrelevant, though, that we have those technologies and that more sophisticated ones will become rapidly available, and that knowledge exists about mechanisms and processes through which technologies are being used. However, the key challenge is to the imagination to reinvent, and continue to reinvent…education using all means available and inventible. While doing so, it will become increasingly irrelevant to try and reserve a special place for what we used to call distance education. (J. Visser, 2006)

It matters little in the previous context that we now often refer to online learning or e-learning when previously we used the term distance education. The crux is that, from the learner's perspective, learning, in the full sense of the word, is usually much richer than what is provided for by the instructional context. The competent learner will complement the affordances of the deliberately designed learning environment with whatever else is at hand. Thanks to developments in information and communication technology, the variety of complementary resources from which to choose is tremendous. Some such resources involve the online voice of others. I discuss a few examples in the next section, deliberately choosing instances that fall outside the realm of formal educational settings.

THE INCREDIBLE WEALTH OF VIRTUAL SPACE

24 Hours on the Net

I look back at the last 24 hours. During it, I engaged in a variety of online activities that affected either my state of mind or that of the people with whom I interacted—in case the online activity was interactive—and probably both. In other words, learning has taken place. I and those other people are no longer the same, thanks to our neural plasticity. In what follows, I mention several of the online activities I engaged in and discuss them in terms of their potential significance for human learning and their implications for finding one's voice.

Instant Text Messaging

Chatting With a Teenager   Early today I had a brief chat with a 14-year-old girl (Exhibit A). She usually adds a short personal message to the nickname she uses for the particular chat platform we both use and changes it frequently. As she is on my list of contacts, I can see when she comes online. Thus, whenever she signs in, I'm immediately being made aware of what mood she is in, at least according to what she has decided to broadcast to her circle of friends and acquaintances. This time it said "Broken...." It had done so a couple of times before, usually when she had been disappointed in establishing an emotional relationship with someone she liked. The rest becomes clear from reading the sidebar (Exhibit A).

There are probably zillions of conversations like these being conducted around the globe every day. They have their own flavor, so different from a face-to-face or telephone conversation that they are usually not interchangeable with those other modalities of communication. I think of them as an enrichment of our communication environment, rather than as a reason to do away with those other and older ways in which we used to converse.

Why broken again?
Sounds like a flip-flop.
lol
no it's the name of a song
IC
Actually, I know.
ok
But I thought you also used it in the real sense, to express the mood you are in. Everything alright?
yeah i'm good
great!
going to paint i think, i feel like it
What's on your mind? (regarding what to paint)
well i feel like learning to draw hands
so i'll look up a tutorial online
and try to learn
then i'll paint something like my avatar
with a hand
Hope you'll find something like this online. Would be interesting. Let me know if and how it works.
Okay
Alternatively, there are also books that are quite good.
Da Vinci had some interesting sketches
yes but i'm a little low in the money
department at the moment.... i spent
80 euros on art supplies last week :S
i love DaVinci...
i don't know all of his work but while i
read the DaVinci Code i was obsessed
with him
Wow. But it's probably money well spent. I love him too. Great guy.
^^
yeah
too bad we missed him by a few
centuries....
indeed
But with some luck someone like that may emerge again in our era. It may be you. :)
haha
i doubt it will be me i don't spend that
much time on my art
but it could happen
^^
Never underestimate your abilities and opportunities!
good advice
i'll stick to it!
OK. Have to go again. Love you.
bye
me too

Exhibit A.   Chat via MSN Messenger with 14-year old girl.

Finding One's Instant Messaging Voice—Speaking the Language.
Finding one's voice in such an environment is not difficult; it is almost automatic. It works mostly by trial and error. Using one's intuition, one finds out how to express oneself, when to take turns in the conversation, and how to prompt the other side into responding, thanks to the fact that conversations, including ones online, follow definite patterns (Mazur, 1996). Familiariza-

tion with the special lingo and abbreviated phraseology used in instant text messaging also occurs largely through exposure and getting involved.

Actually, the example given in Exhibit A is a very mild case of such usage. Text messaging lingo is hardly used in it. Had it been used, it would rather have looked like Exhibit B. The use of text messaging lingo is prominent among teenagers, particularly in Europe, thanks to the ubiquitous use of the cell phone in conjunction with the limitations of the usual cell phone keypad for inputting text, prompting users to economize whenever they can on the number of characters that have to be keyed in. In a brief journalistic article largely written in the lingo in question, Batista (2002) referred to this as "gnr8n txt" (generation text). Becoming familiar with the medium requires being sensitive to the other person and the context of the communication. If in doubt, one can of course always ask the user of a particular acronym or shorthand about its meaning, but it may require some courage to reveal one's ignorance in an environment in which a new language seems to be emerging not only for reasons of economy of communication but also because using the lingo is a way of expressing one's group identity. Luckily, there is always the Web, that huge haystack in which, thanks to the technology of search engines, even a needle can be found. A Google search for the exact phrase "text messaging lingo" currently results in 9,600 instances found, including entire dictionaries as well as Web-based translation facilities, such as http://www.transl8it.com and http://www.lingo2word.com.

```
Y brkn 'gen?
swNdz llk a flip-flop.
    lol
    n itz d nAm of a song
lC
Actually, l knO.
    k
bt l thawt U also Usd it n d real senS, 2
express d mood U R n.
evrtng aiight?
    yyssw im gud
gr8!
    goin 2 p8nt i tink, i fEl llk it
wot's on yor mind? (re: wot 2 paint)
    weL i fEl llk LernN 2 draw h&z
    so i'll L%k ^ a tutorial on9
    & try 2 Lern
    thN ill p8nt somTlN llk my avatar
    w a h&
hOp UL find somTlN llk DlS on9. wud b
intRStN. lt me knO f & how it worx.
    k
Alternatively, ther R also bukz dat R quite gud.
Da Vinci had som intRStN sketches
    yS bt im a ltl low n d monE department
    @ d momNt.... i spent 80 euros on art
    supplies last wk :S
    i luv DaVinci...
    i dun knO aL of Hs wrk bt whll i rED d
    DaVinci Code i wz obsessed w him
Wow. bt it's problE monE weL spent. I luv him
t%. gr8 guy.
    ^^
    yyssw
    t% bad we msD him by a few
    centuries....
indeed
bt w som luk SOME1 llk dat mA emerge 'gen n
our era. lt mA b U. :)
    haha
    i doubt it wiL b me i dun spNd dat much
    tym  on my art
    bt it c%d hpn
    ^^
nevr underestimate yor abilities & opps!
    gud advice
    ill stiK 2 it!
k. hav 2 go 'gen. luv U.
    bi
    me t%
```

Exhibit B. Chat in exhibit A translated into text messaging using Lingo (see http://www.transl8it.com).

Not surprisingly, different kinds of lingo develop also in languages other than English. They are as different as the languages from which they derive are diverse. I am somewhat familiar with text messaging lingo in French and Dutch. Development of all these different kinds of lingo seems to follow similar rules in all three languages. Some of the character combinations (such as on9 = online or h& = hand) are reasonably good intuitive prompts for discovering the phonetic equivalent of particular words in the language in question. You say them aloud and hear something that resembles the original word. French speaking teenagers have developed the capacity to shorten words and phrases to a particularly high level, undoubtedly because the French language in its canonical form is rather uneconomical from the point of view of the number of characters required to express a particular thought. Examples are such expressions of affection and adoration as "jtm" (*je t'aime*) and "jtdr" (*je t'adore*), or a phrase like "tt ce kil te fo" [*tout ce qu'il te faut* (all you need = "aL U nEd" or "ll u nd" in English, depending on the variety of lingo used)]. Another kind of character combination stands for series of words. Btw (= by the way) and g2g (= got to go) are examples. It is not difficult to get used to reading text messages expressed in text messaging lingo. With only a little practice, one is readily able to read them; using the lingo for one's own writing requires somewhat more practice.

Finding One's Voice—Sensing the Specificity of the Communication Environment.   The use of specific lingo is not what makes communication via short messages so particularly interesting. In fact, it's only a minor detail of little significance with which one simply has to become familiar if one wishes to communicate effectively. There are three far more relevant aspects that I like stressing because they make this mode of communication stand out among alternatives.

In the first place, participants in an exchange of instant messages often display a level of spontaneity they would not normally show had the conversation taken place face-to-face, via letters or e-mail, or by telephone. Participants are generally much more playful in the text messaging mode. They inject jokes, laugh out loud (lol), communicate basic feelings (via a growing range of emoticons) and often seem to be on the lookout for opportunities to tease or challenge each other intellectually, not always in an entirely subtle manner.

A second interesting aspect of text messaging is the fact that such exchanges of brief statements force the minds of the communicating parties into a dialogic mode. No way that a question like the one raised in Exhibit C would be answered through a lengthy explanation. By nature of the use of this technology, the style is entirely conversational and interactive. This is a wholly different dialogue than if the same question had been raised in a face-to-face context, whether formal or informal. How easily, then, would the experienced educator have reverted to the lecturing mode! "Look here. Let me explain this to you. This is how it works." And there you go, chalk or pencil in hand.

A third interesting aspect, possibly a corollary of the conversational nature of this way of communicating, is that it so easily branches out into seemingly unrelated—but not necessarily irrelevant—issues. Exhibit C is only a small excerpt (about a quarter) of a much longer conversation that opened with remarks about the weather at the two places from which the communicating parties were "talking" to each other. From there it moved into a couple of jokes about the use of the metric system versus the use of the U.S. customary system of units. That led to the discussion of weight and mass excerpted in Exhibit C. Without any logical connection with anything that had come before, the conversation then switched to a lengthy and profound discussion of the life and thinking of St. Augustine, whence it moved into the contemplation of ethical considerations originally entertained by the Bishop of Hippo but equally relevant for our time, before the conversation had to close because other business started claiming priority. Such varied digressions would likely not have occurred had the mode of communication been e-mail.

> ....
> **Isn't it true that I would weigh 500 kg (or is it 5000?) on the moon, instead of 50 here?**
> No. You wouldn't. The gravitational pull on the moon is much smaller. So you would feel lighter. Your weight on the moon is less than on earth. But your mass is the same. A balance with two scales, which you use to compare masses, would measure the same mass as on earth. But a spring balance would tell you that your weight is less, I think about a sixth of that on earth.
> **spring balance?**
> Yes. A device that determines your weight by comparing the pull of gravity on your body with the elastic force caused by deforming a spring (compressing or stretching it, for instance).
> **Ah. Now I understand how that spring system works. Never thought of it that way. So it's kind of a counter force to gravity. Why then did they tell me in school that somewhere (I forget where) I would weigh ten times as much?**
> No idea.
> **Could it be that gravity has a 10x relationship with something else? (trying to remove the cobwebs from the back of my head to bring it all to the fore again).**
> **Now that I think of it, it's quite obvious you'd weigh so little on the moon. Why, otherwise, would astronauts behave so ballerina-like? :-)**
> Since Newton, everyone knows that two masses attract each other with a gravitational force that is proportional to those masses. The factor 10 is the acceleration (in m/sec) an object undergoes when it falls freely in the gravitational field of the earth.
> **If it wouldn't be for the widespread lack of scientific understanding, the media effect on body image of women would long have caused them to go to the moon. "Men are on earth; women on the moon" instead of "Women are from Venus..." :-)**
> meters per second squared, I meant.
> I guess women are more concerned about their mass than about their weight...
> **Got it. But I recall that it has something to do with weighing, not acceleration. Perhaps the teacher mixed it up.**
> Might he have said something about expressing a force in either kilogram-force or Newton? There is a difference of a factor 10 (approximately) between the two.
> ....

Exhibit C. Excerpt of chat with 30-year-old female on Newtonian gravity.

Being Educational Without Being Didactic.

Note that almost everything in the conversations of Exhibits A and C had educational value, both in the sense that understanding of some phenomenon improved, such as is demonstrated in Exhibit C, and that motivation to advance beyond one's current state of growth was being reinforced, as is the case, more in particular, of Exhibit A. However, none of it had been planned and none of it was in any way strongly linked to a formal educational setting in which one person is teaching the other. The parties involved in the two examples knew each other face to face before they initiated their online conversation. However, this is largely irrelevant to the quality and depth of the dialogue. I have had many online conversations with people I knew exclusively online—sometimes even exchanging thoughts and feelings with them for the very first time—and such conversations were in no way inferior to the ones of the two examples previously given.

Whereas the previously referenced chats occurred spontaneously, instant messaging can very well be used in a deliberately planned manner, such as in a formal educational context. Relevant practical reasons can call for the inclusion of text messaging in a formal educational setting, such as that of a distance education course or program. L. Visser and West (2005) argue for such use in the case of developing countries where cellular telephone networks, whose operators usually offer Short Message Services (SMS), often penetrate when other channels of communication, including the Internet, are not at all or less well accessible. Messages transmitted via these networks are limited in size—usually around 150 characters, including spaces—but they are ideally suited for communicating short motivational prompts. Motivational messaging has been shown to be crucially effective for improving learning performance in both instructor-led face-to-face contexts (see J. Visser & Keller, 1990, for print-based messaging) and in distance education settings (see L. Visser, Plomp, Amirault, & Kuiper, 2002, for print- and e-mail-based messaging). The immediacy and the sense of proximity associated with the cell phone can only add to the effectiveness of this particular aspect of educational communication.

It should be noted that, although text messaging via any medium—such as the Internet, cellular telephone networks, or postal services—can significantly enhance the effectiveness of educational processes, whether deliberately planned or spontaneously engaged in, it does not automatically do so. There must be an intention among those who partake in the conversation to educate each other and to be willing to learn from each other. If that is not the case, then, what can potentially be an opportunity for "inspirational interaction" can easily degenerate into "idle talk" (Van der Spa, 2004, p. 97). One sees examples of such idle talk not only in the cyber-communities analyzed by Van der Spa, but also in many a threaded discussion in a formal online course environment in which students are motivated by the mere requirement to mark their presence in order to make the grade. This uninspired participation by some can easily turn off fellow students who are genuinely interested.

Exchanging E-Mail

A portion of my online activity during the 24-hour timeslot arbitrarily chosen as a basis for reflection on my online behavior had to do with managing and exchanging e-mail. Part of that process now includes circumnavigating and eliminating the uninterrupted bombardment with junk mail and virus-infected messages. My typical e-mail day thus starts off checking the accuracy of my spam control software, usually deleting all e-mails in my spam and junk mail boxes and occasionally salvaging one that was erroneously identified as spam. In addition, I have to manually identify as spam some of the e-mail that escaped the attention of my software. As I manage a couple of e-mail addresses that forward automatically to my main e-mail address, I receive most spam messages at least two or three times. Thus the proportion of spam received is, in my case, around 90%. The total number of spam messages I have to delete after some 6 hours of sleep is currently around 60. During the day, spam continues to come in and I normally take care of it on the fly.

This is more than a mere technical nuisance. One also has to put up with the frustration caused by loss of precious time and attention, and has to face up to being addressed in ways that can be outright insulting, having to read language one rather stays away from. This is a serious problem when appreciated across cultures and age groups. I have met people in Islamic countries who told me that they gave up their e-mail addresses because they could no longer cope with the onslaught on what they considered dear to their culture. I also realize that the 14-year-old girl with whom I had the conversation of Exhibit A and all her online friends sooner or later receive the same junk e-mail I receive.

Finding one's online voice in such circumstances is, at times, difficult. It is like coming out of a meeting room in which you have been verbally abused and shouted at for no justifiable reason whatsoever and immediately thereafter, having to receive a guest in your office with whom you are expected to interact as if you are totally unaffected by what happened only a moment ago. Most people, and I include myself among them, are able to do exactly that, but it adds to the daily stress one experiences. As long as the problem has not been solved, it should be seen as a significant downside that diminishes the tremendous benefit we can all derive from leading part of our lives online.

A Question of Response Time and Power Law Relationships. The voice one uses while exchanging e-mail is different from the one used in short message exchanges. Expectations about response time, in combination with the psychological pressure this puts on the communicating parties involved to respond, is a likely factor of influence. In the case of instant text messaging, the responses are "almost immediate," rather than "immediate" as in the case of a face-to-face or telephone conversation, where silences of more than a few seconds tend to be perceived as embarrassing. The "little extra time" people will allow themselves in preparing their responses while conducting a conversation via the exchange of short text messages—in combination with the need to express oneself succinctly—is just enough to make this mode of communication distinct from instant voice communication.

For the same reason, the exchange of e-mail is distinct from both instant voice communication and instant text messaging. Not only is the average response time significantly longer, the range over which response times vary may go from instantaneous to more than a year. In that sense the way today's users of e-mail manage their interactions with others does not differ significantly from that of prolific letter writers of the past. Oliveira and Barabási (2005), who analyzed the correspondence patterns of two prolific letter writers of the past whose correspondence has been preserved, Darwin and Einstein, concluded that "although the means have changed, the communication dynamics have not: Darwin's and Einstein's patterns of correspondence and today's electronic exchanges follow the same scaling laws" (p. 1251). What is different, though, is the scaling exponent, providing evidence, according to these authors, "for a new class of phenomena in human dynamics" (p. 1251).

Assuming that Darwin and Einstein were not essentially different in their letter writing behavior from today's academics who communicate mainly via e-mail, the comparison is of interest, including the fact that the scale is different. According to the cited article, Darwin and Einstein sent during their lifetime more than 7,000 and 14,000 letters, respectively; they received more than 14,000 and 16,000 letters, respectively. This compares of course favorably with the thousands upon thousands of e-mails today's academics receive and send every year. Nonetheless, prioritizing today's e-mail conversations and letter-based exchanges in the past is a comparable challenge. It is no wonder, therefore, that the same power law applies to the probability $P(\tau)$ that either a letter or an e-mail gets responded to within a particular response time τ, namely $P(\tau) \gg \tau^{-\alpha}$, with $\alpha = 3/2$ in the case of Darwin's and Einstein's letter writing behavior.

In another study, Barabási (2005) argued that, contrary to current models of human dynamics, the patterns according to which we engage in such actions as sending e-mails are not randomly distributed in time. They can thus not be approximated by Poisson processes. Instead, the waiting time between such events is "better approximated by a heavy-tailed or Pareto distribution" (p. 208). Leaving the mathematical detail aside, what matters is the striking phenomenon that, while under a Poisson distribution "consecutive events ... follow each other at relatively regular time intervals" (p.

208) virtually excluding very long interevent times, by contrast, events that follow the Pareto distribution "allow for very long periods of inactivity that separate *bursts of intensive activity*" (p. 208, my emphasis).

Varying One's Online (E-Mail) Voice. Because of the previous phenomenon, our voice in e-mail exchanges should allow for variation. Some issues, usually the majority, get responded to immediately. Other matters, those that require serious thought or extensive work, need to wait until a next "burst of intensive activity" occurs. Looking back at my 24-hour timeframe under consideration, there were e-mails that I responded to briefly, merely to recognize that I received them. This could either mean the conclusion of a conversation, or the announcement that I would attend to the matter at a later moment. Alternatively, other e-mails received a brief and immediate response because all I was expected to do was communicate some level of agreement or disagreement; level and nature of appreciation; or provide some piece of factual information. Because of the wide variability in response time that e-mail users have grown used to and are aware of, such brief responses, even though they contain not much issue-related content, are important in order not to leave the party with whom one corresponds in limbo about where one stands in the *process* of conducting the correspondence. Considering the dramatically expanded load of exchanges allowed by using e-mail, keeping each other abreast of where we stand or what we intend to do following receipt of a particular message greatly diminishes the stress and distraction from creativity that surrounds this mode of communication (Fried, 2005).

There also are those e-mails one receives where it is not immediately clear how and in what manner one will respond. For such cases, I have developed the habit of flagging the message in question for follow-up by a specified date, when I think I will have had sufficient time to think about how to handle the matter at hand. My self-chosen target date for follow-up may on occasion be different from the expectations of the sender, resulting, in such cases, in a request like the following one:

"Could you confirm having received my e-mail of September 26?"

which would typically trigger an immediate brief reply, such as:

Thanks for checking.

Yes, I received your e-mail as well as the attached document a week ago, but I'm swamped and haven't yet had a chance to even glance at it. I will read the attachment, though, hopefully before long. I've marked your message as "unread" and flagged it so that I will be reminded. Don't hesitate to ask me again later.

   In this example, I added the last sentence as I had meanwhile decided I would indeed follow-up.

   Thus, my online voice while using e-mail is one that gets distributed over time in a nonrandom fashion with typical bursts of intensive activity that focus on the serious issues, usually with a long breath. Accordingly, the way in which I use my voice adapts to the varying circumstances. Within the 24-hour timeframe under analysis, in addition to the many messages that could be responded to briefly, immediately and usually informally, there were two that related to more serious matters. One concerned my participation by e-mail in a collaborative authoring effort; the other one requested my advisory feedback regarding a research proposal (someone's dissertation work) into the development of collective mindsets among communities of problem solvers. I postponed responding to the latter and informed the sender accordingly. As to the former, I wrote the equivalent of several pages of single spaced text.

   My voice in such much more extensive and serious e-mail messages is usually that of discursive writing, a form of art less and less practiced in the context of today's digital communications and wrongly so. A portion of the use of e-mail opens excellent opportunities for engaging in the kind of discursive writing that one can still come across when exploring the volumes of collected letters of some well-known people (e.g., Born & Müller, 1986; Feynman, 2005; Van Gogh-Bonger, 1955). The fact that such writing is so little engaged in any longer is probably largely due to the attitude to consider all e-mail the same, and thus respond to it in a similarly relaxed fashion whatever the nature of the correspondence. As I previously argued, there are solid reasons why we should discriminate between different uses of e-mail with, on the one extreme, those messages that allow responses of a few words or at most a couple of quick lines and, on the other end, those that invite deep thinking and careful crafting of a response. It would be one of the roles of the school system to prepare the generation that comes of age in today's world for the technologies it may encounter—that is, for the uncertainty surrounding new forms of technology that will undoubtedly emerge—and particularly to instill among its members the capacity to critically discriminate between different ways and opportunities to use emerging technologies. As most school systems don't do so (yet), it remains a challenge to the online educator to lead in this area both by example and, when appropriate, through instruction.

   E-Mail-like Communications.   I include a few remarks here about forms of digital communication that are somewhat related in my mind to e-mail, such as blogs, listservs, and discussion boards. Their subscribers, assuming they set themselves up appropriately, often receive new postings (or alerts to new postings) via e-mail to which they can then respond, if they so wish, either by e-mail or via a Web-based platform. With blogs and listservs, there is normally no definite expectation as to whether a specific recipient should respond, unless he or she is expressly addressed in a particular post. Therefore, there is normally less urgency surrounding these forms of communication. This may be different for a discussion board, at least in cases when one has signed up for the deliberately agreed purpose of participating in a planned discussion with a clearly defined timeline. Considering all these various options, I argue that, just like in the case of regular e-mail communications, there are different degrees of urgency that will determine if, how, and when one responds. This leads to a similar pattern of online activity as discussed earlier, distributed in time according to a power law, thus comprising bursts of intensive activity separated by long periods of inactivity. Relating this to my personal experience, I offer the following observations.

I subscribe to lists populated by a limited number of people—usually between 10 and 20—who are all focused on the same set of issues. Because the size of such groups is small and thanks to the shared focus, all individual members contribute regularly with responses and original postings that are typically short and more or less immediate. So are mine. My voice in these cases is usually businesslike.

Other lists to which I subscribe bring together hundreds or occasionally thousands of people interested in some broad area of concern. Here the size of the group and the lack of focus on any specific issue within the area of concern lead to an entirely different communication behavior. I intervene from time to time, conditioned by my interest in a particular upcoming topic and by the possibility for me to make time available for composing a well-crafted response. My response might be immediate or delayed, depending on whether I find myself in one of those "bursts of intensive activity." My voice will typically be that of the discursive writer as I will be motivated by the consideration that I am coming across an opportunity that I shouldn't miss. By taking advantage of it, I can engage in an interaction through which not only I but all those who participate, can grow.

On discussion boards, at least in those cases where the discussion was previously agreed on and planned for, my postings and responses will be a mix of short businesslike communications and longer discursive ones. Typically, such discussions are themselves a mix of procedural events—such as to establish consensus regarding a particular point—and exploratory dialogues—such as to deepen understanding or to become aware of all the different angles of an issue. Discussions that I generate myself, whether in formal educational settings or in less structured contexts in which people communicate in order to learn something, will almost always be of an exploratory nature, aimed at understanding something better after the discussion is over. I believe creative exploration to be one of the most important ways for people to advance beyond their present state.

The previously mentioned propensity for discussions of a creatively exploratory nature probably explains why, in the sphere of blogs, I selectively choose to interact with only those blogs where I sense that the interaction may help discover new horizons. A good example is Ron Burnett's Personal Weblog on "Critical Approaches to Culture + Communications + Hypermedia" (Burnett, 2005). My participation in providing contributing comments to postings on such blogs follows the already mentioned pattern of bursts of intensive activity that characterize my digital communication behavior in general. According to the studies by Barabási (2005) and Oliveira and Barabási (2005), I am not alone in following such patterns in the dynamics of my interaction with my fellow human beings, although my choice of creatively exploratory blogs and emphasis on discursive writing may be idiosyncratic.

Finding the Voice I Want to Listen to

The third and last instance of spending my 24 hours online on which I wish to reflect in this chapter has to do with finding a different kind of voice—not my own, but rather that of someone else to whom I wished to listen. Like most other examples in this chapter, the context is again informal learning, my own. During the timeframe in question, I downloaded a podcast about "Learning and Memory," an interview by Ira Flatow with Eric Kandel (Science Friday, 2004), from the relevant Web site onto my MP3 player and went out for a walk in order to listen to it. Learning on the go? M-learning? No, just learning, but I happen to like walking and have learned by experience that certain of my mental processes, like stimulating my creativity, benefit from such rhythmic bodily activity as walking (J. Visser, n.d.).

A multitude of interesting audio programs with important value for one's learning are now available on the Web. In the category to which the previously mentioned Science Friday program pertains, there are for instance The Naked Scientists Online (n.d.); Nature Podcast (n.d.); and Universe Today (n.d.), to mention but a modest scoop out of what comes up if one does a simple Web search for "science podcasts." Audio files are available on the Web in a wide variety of areas of interest. Some are free of charge, such as the previously mentioned science programs; other programs, such as those of The Teaching Company (n.d.), have to be paid for. Given the programs I have immediate and free access to, why do I choose one over the other? What characterizes the voice I want to listen to? Why do I have those preferences? What is the voice I recommend to others to listen to? Following are some of the thoughts that come to mind as I try to answer these questions.

When listening to someone, not having the opportunity to interact directly with the person in question—such as is the case of a podcast of a radio program like Science Friday, even though in its original version there was the possibility to interact with it by phone—one is at risk of being left only passively involved. To become actively involved, which is what I prefer because it improves the depth of my learning, the voice one hears must somehow prompt a dialogue that one conducts inside one's own head. What kind of voice is that?

Dreyfus (2001) argues that embodiment is key to effective learning. In the literal sense, this means that without the bodily presence in each other's proximity of the people who participate in the learning dialogue, no effective learning—learning that results in expertise, mastery, and practical wisdom—can take place. Dreyfus argues that learning develops according to seven stages, namely those of novice, advanced beginner, competence, proficiency, expertise, mastery, and practical wisdom. The first three stages can adequately develop in the distance education mode. However, says Dreyfus, reaching proficiency and expertise requires "emotional, involved, embodied human beings" (p. 48), something that he fears the online environment is incapable of accommodating. Moreover, apprenticeship, which is necessary for the last two stages, calls for the physical presence of experts of flesh and blood whose "style is manifest on a day-to-day basis" (p. 49), allowing it to serve as a model, to be emulated, to be inspired by, to become a bridge to the culture of which one gradually becomes part and in which one develops one's own style. Dreyfus thus concludes that what he calls "the dream of distance education" (p. 49) can only be achieved if and when "the bodily presence required for acquiring skills in various domains and for acquiring mastery of one's culture [can] be delivered by means of the Internet" in the form of telepresence that enables human beings to be present at a distance "in a way that captures all that is essential about bodily presence" (p. 49).

Considering these observations, what I look for and what particularly attracts me in the voices I decide to listen to (both literally, or figuratively, when I hear them while reading), is the space they leave me to do my own thinking, to conduct my own mental and emotional explorations, to add questions, those that are relevant to my entire being, to those already asked, allowing me to feel bodily, that is, emotionally and intellectually, part of a community of people who advance from question to question, driven by their unending curiosity and embodied presence in a world of which I am also part. For it to be relevant and real, it is also crucial that I am convinced that those voices I let into my life come from people whose expertise and wisdom I respect and admire. A program that simply does an excellent job of informing me about the current state of research—and I access those as well—is therefore less satisfying than one that explores, that takes current achievements not as an endpoint but rather as a beginning, a prompt for asking the next set of questions, questions that get asked by those who are courageous enough to explore, to put themselves at the frontier of a particular development.

The beauty of a program like Science Friday is that it never gives the impression of having been scripted, at least not in detail. While the dialogue I am listening to develops, I become aware of emotions, uncertainties, and ambiguities among those who participate. They start resonating with my own, even though I am separated in time and space from those others. I realize that the experience is similar to what happens when I listen to music composed—and, assuming the music is recorded, also often performed—by people whose lives I no longer share in the immediate physical sense of the word. I can't resurrect the body of Chopin, but his virtual presence becomes an embodied one when I listen to his music performed by others, dead or alive, and, even more so, when my hands touch the keys of a piano on which I play, hesitatingly, as I rediscover for myself the original emotions from which his music emerged.

CONCLUSIONS

In this chapter, I have tried to give a reflective view of what it means to be learning at a time when the environment in which such learning takes place is conditioned, among other factors, by the pervasive availability of computing technology and associated ways for human beings to be in touch with each other. At the back of my mind was a further question: Is it for better or for worse? I have no definitive answer to the latter question. It is probably too early to expect such an answer, but it is not too early for the question to be asked.

Prompted by the challenge posed by the title of this book, I have particularly asked myself how I want to sound to others as I interact with them and influence their learning and they mine. Toward the end of the chapter, I transform that question into one that looks at what it is in me that makes me prefer one voice over the other. In making that digression, I considered that teaching and learning always go together and that, therefore, I shouldn't put myself outside the equation.

As a basis for my reflections, I considered that learning in the context of premeditated learning events, such as courses, training interventions, and educational curricula that stretch over timeframes of multiple years, is only a small part of the learning we engage in along and across our lifespan and the broad range of experiences that integrate our lives. I thus deemphasized formal settings, considering also that in all likelihood, many of my colleagues would tackle that area, choosing instead informal events and settings as my examples.

Looking back at what I wrote, I conclude that the voice I have gradually found and am in the process of still further developing, as well as the one I seek in others, is the voice that explores; that asks questions; is uncertain, yet fully and comfortably aware of and knowledgeable about where we stand. It is a voice that expresses a listening attitude, that invites the other person to speak, and that is grounded in personal experience. Such a voice communicates both cognitively and, above all, affectively.

REFERENCES

Barabási, A.-L. (2005). The origin of bursts and heavy tails in human dynamics. *Nature, 435*(7039), 207–211.

Batista, E. (2002). *Euro teens understand this* [Online]. Retrieved on November 20, 2005, from http://www.wired.com/news/wireless/0,1382,53659,00.html

Born, J., & Müller, M. (Eds.). (1986). *Briefe an Milena*. Frankfurt: 1986. [An English translation of these letters by Franz Kafka appeared in 1990 as *Letters to Milena*, translated and with an introduction by Philip Boehm.] New York: Schocken Books.

Burnett, R. (2005). *Personal Weblog on "Critical Approaches to Culture + Communications + Hypermedia"* [Online]. Retrieved on January 4, 2006 from http://www.eciad.ca/~rburnett/Weblog/

Dreyfus, H. L. (2001). *On the Internet*. New York: Routledge.

Feynman, M. (Ed.). (2005). *Perfectly reasonable deviations from the beaten track: The letters of Richard P. Feynman*. New York: Basic Books.

Fried, I. (2005). Driven to distraction by technology. *CNET News.com*, July 21, 2005 [Online]. Retrieved on January 2, 2006, from http://news.com.com/2100-1022_3-5797028.html?tag=st.prev

Liston, D. (2004). The lure of learning in teaching. *Teachers College Record, 106*(3), 459–486 [Online]. Retrieved on November 14, 2006, from http://www.tcrecord.org/content.asp?contentid=11524

Mazur, J. M. (1996). Conversation analysis for educational technologists: Theoretical and methodological issues for researching the structures, processes, and meaning of online talk. In D. H. Jonassen (Ed.), *Handbook of research for educational communications and technology* (pp. 1073–1098). New York: Simon & Schuster.

Nature Podcast. (n.d.). *Nature Podcast* [Online]. Retrieved on January 6, 2006, from http://www.nature.com/nature/podcast/index.html

Oliveira, J. G., & Barabási, A-L. (2005). Darwin and Einstein correspondence patterns: These scientists prioritized their replies to letters in the same way that people rate their e-mails today. *Nature, 437*(7063), 1251.

Science Friday. (2004). *SciFri podcast 2004070224 – Eric Kandel on Learning and Memory* [Online]. Retrieved on December 18, 2005, from http://www.sciencefriday.com/pages/2004/Jul/hour2_070204.html

The Naked Scientists Online. (n.d.). *Internet science radio show PODCASTS & naked science live events* [Online]. Retrieved on January 6, 2006, from http://www.thenakedscientists.com/

The Teaching Company. (n.d.). *The teaching company* [Online]. Retrieved on January 8, 2006, from http://www.teach12.com/

Universe Today. (n.d.). *Universe today* [Online]. Retrieved on January 6, 2006, from http://feeds.feedburner.com/universetoday/podcast

Van der Spa, M. (2004). Cyber-communities: Idle talk or inspirational interaction? *Educational Technology Research and Development, 52*(2), 97–105.

Van Gogh-Bonger, J. (Ed.). (1955). *Verzamelde brieven van Vincent van Gogh* [Complete letters of Vincent Van Gogh]. Volumes 1 and 2. Amsterdam, Antwerp: Wereldbibliotheek.

Varela, F. (2000). *Francisco Varela's home page* [Online]. Retrieved on April 23, 2005, from http://web.ccr.jussieu.fr/varela/index.html

Visser, J., & Keller, J. M. (1990). The clinical use of motivational messages: An inquiry into the validity of the ARCS model of motivational design. *Instructional Science, 19*, 467–500.

Visser, J. (2001). Integrity, completeness and comprehensiveness of the learning environment: Meeting the basic learning needs of all throughout life. In D. N. Aspin, J. D. Chapman, M. J. Hatton, & Y. Sawano (Eds.), *International handbook of lifelong learning* (pp. 447– 472). Dordrecht, The Netherlands: Kluwer.

Visser, J. (2006). Universities, wisdom, transdisciplinarity, and the challenges and opportunities of technology. In M. Beaudoin (Ed.), *Perspectives on of higher education in the digital age* (pp. 187–206). Hauppauge, NY: Nova Science Publishers, Inc.

Visser, J. (n.d.). *Walking: A way of being* [Online]. Retrieved on January 8, 2006, from http://www.learndev.org/People/JanVisser/Walking.html

Visser, L., Plomp, T., Amirault, R. J., & Kuiper, W. (2002). Motivating students at a distance: The case of an international audience. *Educational Technology Research and Development, 50*(2), 94–110.

Visser, L., & West, P. (2005). The promise of m-learning for distance education in South Africa and other developing nations. In Y. L. Visser, L. Visser, M. Simonson, & R. Amirault (Eds.), *Trends and issues in distance education: International perspective* (pp. 117–129). Greenwich, CT: Information Age Publishing.

Visser, Y. L., & Visser, J. (2000, October 25–28). *The learning stories project*. Paper presented at the International Convention of the Association for Educational Communications and Technology, Denver, CO.

Chapter 4

How Scenario-Based Learning Can Engender Reflective Practice in Distance Education

Som Naidu
University of Melbourne

Mohan Menon
Commonwealth of Learning

Chandra Gunawardena
Dayalatha Lekamge
Shironica Karunanayaka
Open University of Sri Lanka

As educators, our goals and aspirations in relation to teaching are to engage learners in their learning processes. Furthermore and especially in relation to teacher education, we seek to provide opportunities for learners to critically reflect on their experience and professional practice. Our aim is to shift our learners' focus from the common tendency to master facts, principles, and procedures in isolation of the learning context. Instead, we seek to engage our students in problem solving and critical reflection on practice and their experience with the help of relevant facts, procedures, principles, as well as appropriate and timely feedback. In the case of learners with no prior work experience, such as preservice teachers or nurses, we could use contrived but authentic problems or cases to situate their learning activities. With adult learners who are already in service, we are able to get them to

53

draw on their own relevant work experience to situate learning. In adopting this approach to teaching and learning, our goal is to make learning more motivating, relevant, and meaningful for our learners, who are in-service teachers. In short, our aim is to make teaching for teachers an inspiring, challenging, and rewarding experience that will indeed help them find their teaching voices in a variety of settings.

The scenarios used in the *Master of Arts in Teacher Education—International (MATE-I)* courses offer opportunities for students to learn by doing, and critically reflect on their practice with the help of expert advice from their teachers and other relevant practitioners from the field. These opportunities include the design, development, implementation, and reporting on of various challenging *learning activities* in order to address or solve the problems in the scenarios with which learners are confronted. These *learning activities*, which are not formally assessed, are carefully crafted to develop teacher educators' competencies as opposed to simple mastery of processes, procedures, or theories. They are designed to engender and promote reflective practice by directing students to critically examine what they and their colleagues are doing on a regular basis as teacher educators. Their aim is to make learning relevant, meaningful, and motivating. These learning activities also serve as scaffolds for the interaction among the learners, teachers and practitioners in the field. They lead to the completion of several *assignment tasks*, which, unlike the learning activities themselves, are formally assessed. We first provide a context for how these courses were designed and then elaborate and discuss the scenarios that comprise the courses.

CONTEXTUALIZING LEARNING

Contextualizing learning involves placing learners in situations where they are engaged in learning by doing, problem solving, and critical reflection in and on their activities (Naidu, 2004; Pea, 2004; Quintana et al., 2004; Reiser, 2004). This approach represents a learner-centered focus, which is a significant shift away from conventional approaches to learning and teaching that tend to place a premium value on the mastery of facts, procedures, principles, and theories. It is an approach to learning and teaching that is founded on the belief that the social, interpersonal, and cultural surroundings within which learning occurs affect both the learning processes and its outcomes (Schank & Cleary, 1995). It also suggests that the knowledge and skills that we seek are most meaningful when they are closely connected to their contexts—that is, when they are seen as being situated (Lave & Wenger, 1991; McLellan, 1996).

Situated learning is based on the belief that learning is most efficient and effective when it takes place within the context of realistic settings in which learners are clear about the learning outcomes and assessment tasks (Brown, Collins, & Duguid, 1989; The Cognition and Technology Group at

Vanderbilt, 1990b). This concept has close connections with the notions of experiential learning (Dewey, 1933), goal-based learning and case-based reasoning (Schank & Cleary, 1995), and problem-based learning (Barrows & Tamblyn, 1980; Evensen & Hmelo, 2000). Such approaches to learning enable learners and teachers to immerse themselves in the context and ecology of their subject matter, much like an apprentice carpenter is immersed at a building site with an experienced carpenter. Learning activities in such settings are carefully designed to reflect authentic tasks and to engage learners in cognitive apprenticeships (Brown et al., 1989).

Approaches to situated learning require a redefinition of what is meant by learning, thinking, knowledge, and expertise (Naidu, 2004). The emphasis is not on memory and acquisition of facts, procedures, and principles, but on skill development and critical thinking. Knowledge is not seen as simply something stored in a learner's head—rather, knowledge comprises the ability to interact intelligently in a context. The learning context may include situations similar to those to which learners have been exposed. The acquisition of knowledge and skill is the outcome of an active engagement of the learner in a learning context with appropriate and timely feedback from tutors, teachers, and other expert practitioners (Brown et al., 1989; Vygotsky, 1978).

In this manner, as the nature of learning and teaching becomes more situated in a rich and meaningful context, conventional methods of assessment of learning outcomes generally become less adequate (Naidu, 2006). For instance, when learning changes from a focus on memory and recall to problem-solving ability and critical analysis, the focus of measuring learning achievement must also shift. The assessment of learning outcomes in such settings becomes an integral part of the learning and teaching process. Indicators of learning achievement such as critical thinking and problem-solving abilities of learners are hard to quantify and assess. As such, they need particular attention to defining their criteria so that learners are very clear about what they are required to do and why (Naidu & Oliver, 1996, 1999; Naidu, Oliver, & Koronios, 1999).

Furthermore, not any situation, problem, or scenario can afford the learning that is desirable or expected. Care and attention is required in the development of problems, scenarios, learning, and assessment activities that are authentic, that closely mirror professional practice, and that have the potential to produce the kind of learning that is required (see Naidu, Menon, Gunawardena, Lekamge, & Karunanayaka, 2005). Scenarios, cases, and problems that stand to afford such learning opportunities are called "authentic" and "anchored" because of their connectedness to the learning context (The Cognition and Technology Group at Vanderbilt, 1990a). A single problem or learning scenario may not be enough to offer the richness and complexity for the coverage of all the key

concepts in a subject. In such cases, such as in the study of law and medi-
cine, many scenarios or cases may be required to address all the issues
within in a single topic area.

SCENARIO-BASED LEARNING

A learning design that enables us to situate and contextualize learning most
efficiently and effectively is scenario-based learning. Other learning designs that are able to afford similar capabilities include problem-based
learning (Barrows & Tamblyn, 1980; Evensen & Hmelo, 2000) and
case-based reasoning (Schank, 1997).

Scenario-based learning comprises the use of authentic learning contexts (in the form of scenarios) to situate and anchor learning, teaching, and
assessment activities (The Cognition and Technology Group at Vanderbilt,
1990a). A typical learning scenario takes the form of a storyline within
which learners are required to play a key role to achieve a mission or goal
such as resolve a conflict and build consensus among individuals or groups
in conflict (Schank, Fano, Jona, & Bell, 1994). As a result of accomplishing
the tasks associated with this mission, it is expected that learners will accomplish the intended learning outcomes of the course or program.

The role that learners are required to play in such scenarios is carefully
selected to reflect those that they might actually confront in real life. In order to achieve their mission, students are provided with the necessary resource materials in the form of readings and experiences of expert
practitioners to point them in the right direction when required (Schank,
1990, 1997). Learners may also be required to work in small groups if the
development of collaborative problem-solving, learning, and working skills
comprises one of the learning outcomes. This scenario, including all learning and assessment activities that are a part of it, serve as essential scaffolds
for all learning and teaching activities. Together, they comprise the main
point behind the concepts of learning by doing and story-centered curriculum that has been popularized by Roger Schank and his team (Schank et al.,
1994). Schank and his colleagues argued that because stories are such an integral part of human lives, there is good reason to make powerful stories the
center of educational practices. Stories also provide a context within which
teachers can easily locate their own voice making the instruction also relevant and compelling for the teacher as well as for the learner.

This learning scenario and its accompanying learning and assessment
activities, serve to provide essential scaffolds for promoting and engender-
ing reflective learning and teaching activities. This is particularly useful in
online education settings where a greater degree of scaffolding is necessary
due to the distributed and asynchronous nature of much of the communication between the teachers and students. The learning scenario provides a

context within which learning and assessment activities can be discussed meaningfully by students and teachers. This context brings with it other participants who can serve as expert practitioners, from whom students can draw out rich experiences and stories of failures and/or successes to apply to problems or projects on which they may be working as part of their learning or assessment activities.

For online distance education students, this is critical because the learning scenario and its context offer relevance and meaning to learning activities. This tends to ensure a higher level of motivation and student engagement with their studies—motivation and student engagement comprise serious problems in conventional distance education settings where it is regarded as a major cause of attrition (Amundsen & Bernard, 1989; Bernard & Amundsen, 1989). For the online distance educator—or any teacher—the learning scenario and its embedded learning and assessment activities serve as opportunities for orchestrating and facilitating student engagement with the subject matter content. They also serve as opportunities for providing students with meaningful and timely feedback as they are engaged in learning by doing something, such as developing a strategy for resolving a conflict or solving a practical problem on site. In sum, scenarios provide a grounding for a teacher's voice.

Scenario Building

The development of good learning scenarios that offer the best opportunities to situate or contextualize learning and teaching is a complex design task. Although the construction of the scenario is, to a large extent, a creative process, it needs to begin with the identification and clear articulation of the learning outcomes. Clearly articulated learning outcomes will almost suggest the nature and the scope of the scenario that is required. Appropriate scenarios will reflect reality as much as possible, which means that they are authentic. Furthermore, they will have the richness and requisite variety in them that mirrors reality—otherwise they would fail to offer the opportunities for learning that students would need. More importantly, such scenarios will be interesting and motivating so as to retain student engagement. A simple set of steps in the process could look like the following (Naidu, 2004).

1. Clearly articulate the learning outcomes for your learners.
2. Identify key events in the life of a person who has accomplished these outcomes.
3. Identify the main steps or processes that they might take/follow to work through these and similar sorts of events.
4. Develop a scenario with the richness and variety that will offer scope for the steps and/or processes outlined in 3.

5. In light of the intended learning outcomes, develop the learning tasks and assessment activities that learners will be required to complete within the context of this scenario.

THE MASTER OF ARTS IN TEACHER EDUCATION (INTERNATIONAL)

Our major contribution in the development and implementation of scenario-based learning is in the Master of Arts of Teacher Education—International program of the Open University of Sri Lanka. This program was developed with financial support from the Commonwealth of Learning. It is currently offered only in the print-based distance education mode and in the English language. However, some of the courses in the program are making use of online discussion groups (Karunanayaka, Lekamge, Gunawardena, Naidu, & Menon, 2005). One of the subjects (ESP 2242) in the program is being developed as a fully online subject. The intent is to make this program available online to an international student audience.

Students in the program possess postgraduate diploma level qualifications and are working as teacher educators in teachers' colleges, national colleges of education, universities, or are engaged in similar teacher development related capacities (MATE-I, 2004).

The goal of the MATE-I program is to develop among teacher educators competencies and practices in relation to the following areas:

• Teaching and learning strategies, including assessment of learning outcomes.
• Design, development, and use of educational technologies in teaching and learning.
• Design, development, and evaluation of curricula and curriculum related activities.
• Management and leadership in teaching, learning, and related educational activities.
• Research and evaluation of teaching, learning, and related educational activities.
• Teaching as a profession and the professional roles and responsibilities of teachers.

Program Structure and Learning Environment

The MATE-I degree program comprises six compulsory courses and a portfolio project that is carried out in lieu of a thesis (see Table 4.1).

The printed study materials comprise a study guide and a resource pack for all courses. Each study guide provides students with a very clear idea of how they will progress through each course. A detailed study schedule in

TABLE 4.1
MATE—I Program Handbook, 2004

Semester	Subjects on Offer	Portfolio Project
Semester 1	ESP 2240: Teacher educator as a teaching and learning specialist ESP 2241: Teacher educator as a curriculum developer	ESP 2646: Learning Portfolio
Semester 2	ESP 2242: Teacher educator as an educational technologist ESP 2243: Teacher educator as a professional	
Semester 3	ESP 2244: Teacher educator as an educational manager ESP 2245: Teacher educator as a researcher	

each study guide specifies the week-by-week learning activities that students are expected to complete for that course. All assessment requirements are also described in this study guide. Readings and other core study material (including multimedia resources) compiled in the resource pack are designed to support students in carrying out the specific learning and assessment activities in the learning scenario. Contact sessions with lecturers and local tutors provide further opportunities for closer interaction. Students are also able to communicate with the academic staff and their tutors via email (MATE-I, 2004).

In one of the courses in the program—ESP 2242: Teacher Educator as an Educational Technologist—in addition to the printed study materials, students are provided with an interactive multimedia development CD in their resource pack that also contains a CD with course information and linked resources. This course also makes use of online discussion forums to support and facilitate student interaction and online collaborative learning activities that are closely related to student assessment tasks. Local study centers provide students with computer and Internet facilities, library and video-viewing facilities.

Learning Design

A critical and unique feature of this program is its use of authentic learning scenarios to situate and contextualize learning and assessment activities in each subject. These learning scenarios have been developed to reflect the kinds of situations that students are likely to confront as teacher educators. These situations are used to orchestrate the learning and assessment activities in each subject. They appear in the form of stories in which students are required to assume key roles. Each scenario presents students with challenges of various sorts. Each challenge relates to the one before and builds on it. Students are required to work on each one of these challenges and tasks in order to proceed to the next one.

This story-centered approach represents a dramatic shift away from a traditional master's degree curricula, which tends to be content driven. As students work through the story to achieve the missions it puts forth, they will be able to develop the critical skills and acquire the knowledge that is covered in the subject. This approach to learning and teaching seeks to focus students' attention on critical reflection and problem-solving activities. It aims to promote a more learner-centered focus, which represents a dramatic departure from content-based approaches to learning and teaching (Naidu et al., 2005).

What follows is a selected scenario. We have attempted to depict sufficient detail to convey a sense of how the scenarios were used and how they influenced learning and teaching activities. Following the scenario, we identify some persistent problems and conclude with lessons learned from this effort.

A SELECTED SCENARIO FROM THE MATE-I PROGRAM

The Teacher Educator as a Teaching and Learning Specialist

We present a selected scenario from the MATE-I curriculum so as to illustrate our scenario-based approach to teaching and to provide a concrete example of how this approach facilitates learning and provides a context for finding one's voice (ESP 2240 Study Guide, 2004, pp. 9–18; used with permission. Copyright: ONSL (The Open University of Sri Lanka).

Learning Scenario: What are Learner Characteristics?

Tania is a relatively young teacher who has been appointed as a lecturer at the National Teachers' College. She was teaching Social Studies at a secondary school when she got this new appointment. She is very excited about her new appointment. However, she is not so confident about her capabilities in interacting with an adult student group. While introducing her to the rest of the staff, the Principal of the Teachers' College inquired about her experience in working with a group of adult learners of this kind. She admitted that she had no experience in working with a group of adult learners. However, she thought that she should take this as a challenge and try to adapt to the new learning situation.

After several months on the job, and having tried several methods of coping with a group of adult learners, Tania was becoming increasingly frustrated with many of her initiatives. Her attempts to enthuse and retain students' interest in her classes were seemingly ineffective. Many of her students wanted to have lengthy discussions about their prior experiences rather than listening to her views. Furthermore, she found that the student teachers preferred group projects to individual projects as a part of their learning activities. Tania was clearly very disappointed with her early experiences and she was eager to find what was wrong with her approaches. Tania discussed her problems with the Principal of the Teachers' College and was advised to develop a deeper understanding of the characteristics of adult learners to experience success in the teaching/learning processes at the college, and in order to be able to maintain a close interaction with them. The Principal of the College advised her to get the necessary support from senior colleagues in the institution.

Your Role: As one of her experienced colleagues, how would you help Tania improve her understanding of the characteristics of adult learners?

Learning Activity 1.1
• Prepare a list of adult learner characteristics that Tania can use to improve her understanding of her student group.

Learning Scenario continued … An Observation

After going through the list of adult learner characteristics, Tania realizes that the characteristics of adult learners are completely different from the characteristics of secondary school students. She had continuous discussions with some experienced teacher educators in her institution about the characteristics of adult learners. Their opinions were that: "The list shows only the ideal characteristics and student teachers may or may not possess those characteristics." They advised her to observe her students' characteristics more carefully herself, and in different teaching/learning situations to find out more about them. Therefore, Tania decided to carry out a number of observations in different teaching/learning situations of student teachers.

Tania comes to you for advice on preparing an observation schedule.

Learning Activity 1.2
• Prepare an observation schedule using the characteristics you have listed, identify suitable situations for observation, and provide necessary guidelines for Tania on how to use them.

Learning Scenario continued … A Supporting Hand

Tania has been using the observation schedule you developed for observing the characteristics of student teachers in different teaching and learning situations such as group-based and individual learning situations. In order to get a clearer understanding of the characteristics observed, she has had lengthy discussions with you and wanted to consult additional reading material on the subject. The Principal of the Teachers' College was very keen to find out more about Tania's experience because he wanted to improve the support provided for newly appointed lecturers in light of her experience. Therefore, he asked Tania to prepare a report on her observations, which he hoped would provide insights for new lecturers to understand the characteristics of adult teachers.

Your Principal puts the same request to you.

Learning Activity 1.3
• In order to prepare your report, observe a group of student teachers in your institution in different teaching and learning situations (as listed in the scenario).
• Prepare a summary report on the learning characteristics of your student teachers.

Assignment 1: Part I
1. Prepare a short report indicating the gaps in student teacher attributes and competencies justifying the schedule used in the observation.
2. Propose strategies (giving a brief rationale) that can be used to develop desirable attributes and competencies in your student teachers.

Learning Scenario continued … Similarities or Differences

When Tania submitted the report to her Principal, he inquired about her overall understanding of the general characteristics of student teachers. Tania said that she observed differences among the characteristics. The Principal suggested that learning is an individual activity, and as such there are likely to be differences in the way each student teacher approaches learning. In reflecting on the Principal's remark and on her own experiences gained by observing student behavior, Tania realizes that there are indeed individual differences among student teachers. Some student teachers learn complex concepts very quickly while others do not. Some want to have discussions with their peers or tutors to conceptualize concepts, whereas some attempt to relate their learning experiences to real life situations.

Tania would like to collect more information on the learning styles of student teachers but she is unsure of the usefulness of such information to a new-comer like her. She comes to you for help and advice.

Learning Activity 1.4
• Collect information on the learning styles of a group of student teachers using Kolb Learning Styles Inventory.
• Analyze the information collected and prepare a report on the learning styles of your student teachers for Tania.

Assignment 1: Part II
Submit a brief report on the following:
• Prominent learning styles of adult student teachers.
• Similarities and differences between different categories of student teachers.
• Usefulness of understanding students' learning styles for a teacher educator—illustrate with examples.

- The usefulness of having an understanding of the learning style of students to newly appointed teacher educators.

Learning Scenario continued ... Other Factors

Due to your help, Tania has a much better understanding of the general learning characteristics of student teachers and their individual approaches to learning. Now she is very anxious to engage in a teaching/learning situation with her group of student teachers. Yet, she is not certain if the identified student characteristics and approaches are the only factors that should be considered in a teaching and learning situation. What other variables other than students' learning styles, should be taken into consideration by her when developing a teaching/learning activity?

Tania is back and looking for your support in identifying different factors that may have an influence on student learning.

Learning Activity 2.1
- Go through Additional Reading 3—*Variables* - to be considered in a teaching/learning situation - and prepare a short report for Tania (with examples), indicating all variables other than student characteristics that should be considered in a teaching/learning situation.

Learning Scenario continued ... Teaching/Learning Methodologies

Tania has come to realize that along with students' learning styles, other factors that influence the development of teaching/learning transactions include the subject content and the teacher. She is now ready to design a new learning activity with all these factors in mind. She selects an interesting theme from the subject of Educational Psychology in the preparation of a plan for suitable teaching and learning methodologies. While engaged in this task, she realizes that some of the teaching and learning methodologies that are suitable for secondary school children do not suit the characteristics of her student teachers.

Given your experience in a teacher education institution what teaching-learning methodologies would you recommend to Tania for her adult learner group?

Learning Activity 2.2
- Go through Essential Reading 4—Teaching Methods for Adult Learners - to complete this activity. Identify the teaching and learning methodologies suitable for student teachers.

Learning Scenario continued ... Lesson Plan

Having considered all the variables that might have an impact on a specific teaching and learning situation, Tania completes her task by incorporating some of the teaching and learning methodologies suggested by you. She discusses her plan with other teacher educators in her institution. From this discussion, she discovers that there are several limitations in her plan. Her colleagues recommend that she should consult a model plan as an essential requirement for improving her plan.

Learning Activity 2.3
• Develop a model lesson plan for a teaching and learning situation that Tania will be able to use. In developing this model plan, consider all the variables that could influence the selection of appropriate teaching and learning methodologies suitable for student teachers. You must follow the steps indicated below in the preparation of your model lesson plan.

Step 1   Select a topic or subject for your model plan.
Step 2   Prepare a draft plan considering all variables and suitable teaching methodologies.
Step 3   Discuss this plan with some experienced teacher educators.
Step 4   Modify the plan based on their comments and feedback.
Step 5   Discuss with your tutor and colleagues at the contact session 1 to get more feedback.

Assignment 2
Submit a model plan (to help Tania) using the following format:
• Objectives of the teaching and learning situation you selected.
• Variables considered in relation to the specific teaching and learning situation identified.
• Suggestions for the use of teaching and learning methodologies in different stages of the teaching and learning situation and your justification for their use.
• Explanation of the learning environment.
• Your reflections on the comments made by the experienced teacher educators on your plan.

Learning Scenario continued … Assessment

Tania now has a model plan to follow. As you would know, it focuses on the most suitable teaching and learning methodologies for her student group and subject matter content. Tania's colleagues at the Teachers' College ask her about her plans for the assessment of learning outcomes and provision of feedback, as they are two essential components of a lesson plan. They suggest that she should analyze the significance of the assessment of learning outcomes and feedback strategies as a preliminary step in the process of identifying suitable assessment procedures and feedback strategies.

Learning Activity 3.1
• Analyze the significance of the assessment of learning outcomes and feedback strategies in the context of teaching and learning.

Learning Scenario continued … Assessment in Your Institution

Tania goes through your analysis of the significance of assessing learning outcomes of student teachers and giving necessary feedback using appropriate strategies. Many of your suggestions were unfamiliar and were some-what different from those used at the Teachers' College. Tania decides to explore the assessment procedures and feedback strategies practiced by teacher educators in her institution with the aim of identifying suitable pro-cedures for her plan.

Learning Activity 3.2
- Give a brief overview to Tania about the assessment procedures and feed-back strategies practiced in your institution.
- Review your model lesson plan, which you developed for the specific teach-ing–learning situation (Assignment 2) and develop procedures for assess-ment and provision of feedback, which suit student teachers. You must seek the views of experts before finalizing your plan.
- Present your plan to your local tutor and fellow students at the contact ses-sion 2 and improve it.

Assignment 3
Submit an assessment plan for the teaching and learning situation you had identified in your model lesson for Tania. This plan should incorporate the following:
- An analysis of the significance of the assessment of learning outcomes and feedback strategies in relation to the context of the specific teaching and learning situation.
- Assessment procedures and feedback strategies planned with reference to the specific teaching and learning situation. Indicate what, when and how.
- Your reflections on the comments made by the experts.

Learning Scenario continued … Evaluation

Tania now has a complete plan of the teaching and learning situation to try out with her student teachers. As she is less experienced in interacting with adult learners, she is cautiously optimistic that her plan will work. Her col-leagues suggest that she should seek help from an experienced teacher ed-ucator for feedback on the effectiveness of her plan. Tania requests you to help her with the evaluation of the plan following implementation with a group of students. She is interested in your independent assessment of her plan, feedback from students as well as the views of a selection of experi-enced teacher educators.

Learning Activity 4
- Make necessary preparations for implementing the lesson plan.
- Implement the plan with a group of student teachers in your institution.
- Obtain feedback from the students on the teaching and learning method-ologies, assessment procedures, and feedback strategies (you may have to develop a survey for collecting this data).
- Discuss your findings and observations with your colleagues.
- Reflect on your experiences with regard to the whole teaching/learning process.

Assignment 4
Submit an evaluation report of the implementation of Tania's lesson plan. Based on the feedback received from student teachers, experienced teacher educators, and your own reflections reflect on the following:
- How relevant were the objectives to students and the subject matter content? Explain.
- How effective were the teaching and learning methodologies?
- How motivating was the learning environment? How effective were the assessment procedures?
- How effective were the feedback strategies?
- What is your overall evaluation of the whole teaching and learning process?
- Give your suggestions for improvement of the teaching and learning situation.

PROBLEMS ENCOUNTERED AND WHY SOME PERSIST

We encountered numerous problems and issues with the implementation of scenario-based learning in the MATE-I program, many of which persist. These could be categorized as those that we confronted at the start of the design process and those that we faced during the design and development process.

A major challenge that we confronted very early on as part of the design process was ensuring that the full faculty group bought into and accepted scenario-based learning as a viable pedagogical model for the MATE-I program. When the full faculty group met for its first instructional and course design workshop, several critical decisions about the scope and coverage of the MATE-I program had already been taken. As part of our efforts in this workshop to engender and promote reflective practice in the program, we realized that several of these decisions needed revisiting and revising. In doing so, the scope and coverage of the courses in the program had to be revised. The most significant decision in this regard was a dramatic shift in their focus from the teaching of theories, principles, and procedures of teacher education to problem solving and critical reflection within contrived but realistic teacher education settings.

A clear articulation of the concept of scenario-based learning, and how it would be operationalized and implemented was another major challenge we confronted at the start of the design process. Although we knew where we were heading and what we wanted to achieve, at this stage we did not have a clearly articulated model of scenario-based learning that we could emulate. A clear model of what we understood by scenario-based learning emerged much later, and only after much thinking and several unsatisfactory attempts. This was not helped by the lack of clearly articulated design expectations; this deficiency initially led team members to focus their attention on the teaching of theories, principles, and procedures as opposed to problem solving and critical thinking skills.

Once a clear understanding of the shape and form of scenario-based learning was achieved, work on course development progressed with speed and much ease. Nevertheless, the development of appropriately rich and resourceful scenarios and related learning and assessment activities was by no means a simple process or an easy task. Learning scenarios had to have the requisite variety and a sufficient level of complexity to be able to serve the full range of the intended learning outcomes for a course. This required a good deal of inspiration and creative thought on the part of course team members and was a challenging and time-consuming task for very experienced teacher educators, especially in the absence of any prior experience with this kind of course design and development activity.

The development of appropriate learning scenarios was invariably an iterative process. Course team members worked persistently in groups to develop these scenarios and to refine them with constant feedback from their peers and other collaborators. The development of these learning scenarios also comprised development of all learning and assessment activities in the course and very clear guidelines to students on how they would progress through the course in terms of the things they would be required to do as part of their studies in a course, with what resources, and in what kind of a timeframe.

Development of rich and resourceful learning scenarios did not ensure that the learners necessarily found this learning experience any easier than what they had been used to in the past. Learners expected to find in these courses what they had been used to before. Despite not finding that here, many set about to study these courses in much the same way they had successfully carried out their study in so many other subjects over all these years. Moreover, they tended to reproduce material from their textbooks and other resource materials as part of their assignments, despite very clear directions in terms of the level of critical analysis and thinking that was required.

As a result of this, in the first few assignments that students submitted, there were several instances of students receiving failing grades. If this situation had been allowed to persist, several of these students may have had to leave the program. Therefore, alternative remedial arrangements and processes had to be promptly put in place so that students receiving failing grades could be given an opportunity to revise and resubmit their assignments to improve their grades and retain their place in the program. In a professional development program such as the MATE-I program, where most of the students are sponsored by their organizations, a failing grade would have meant loss of sponsorship. Along with such efforts, workshops at study centers and at the university had to be held that focused on educating students on the particular orientation of the MATE-I program. Unfortunately for the faculty members in the program, this meant an increase in their workloads that were already overloaded with various other commitments, not only in MATE-I program but others as well.

Faculty resources to support the MATE-I program continue to remain a major problem for the department, especially with several experienced faulty members due to retire in the next few years. It is extremely difficult to find faculty members who possess requisite professional qualifications, and those who are as familiar with either scenario-based learning generally, or with its use in the MATE-I program. It is clear that the Faculty of Education will have to put processes in place to familiarize other and new academic staff in scenario-based learning if they were to teach into this program.

Efforts to incorporate online learning and teaching activities in the MATE-I program is constrained by student's lack of access to the technologies, the cost of purchasing and using the relevant services, and a lack of their familiarity in the use of the technology. The majority of students in the current MATE-I cohort lack basic information technology skills, such as the use e-mail and Internet searches. For most students, online learning and the use of online discussion forums are totally new concepts. Although, once they were introduced to online discussions, they found it very exciting, motivating, and useful. In one of the courses where an online discussion forum was introduced, only about half the group logged in regularly. The others did not participate in the discussion either because of lack of access to technology, costs of the technology, or because of a lack of any compulsion to do so.

Such difficulties were not generally encountered by instructors who were more familiar with online discussions and found their voice more easily due to the familiarity of the learning scenarios. In this particular course, the online discussion forum was used to familiarize students with this facility and to enable them to communicate with each other in relation to their studies. It was also used regularly by the course coordinator to post notices to students.

PRACTICAL ADVICE AND GUIDELINES

Start at the Beginning to Avoid the Need to Undo and Unlearn

This means first and foremost, paying a great deal of attention to the conceptual design of learning and teaching activities. Whatever is your theoretical orientation, it is extremely important to be very clear about how it is going to be operationalized. This is important in order to be able to convince your stakeholders that it is a worthwhile and workable idea. A clearly articulated conceptual design would mean that less time and resources are wasted in undoing and unlearning what may have been already done due to a poorly articulated conceptual design. This is like saying that you do not want to start constructing a building without first having a validated building plan and a permit from relevant authorities to build it; otherwise you may have to tear it down if it did not conform to some sort of regulation or standard. In the same way, you would not want to start developing a course or a program without first developing and validating a design for learning and teaching transactions and activities.

Ensure Buy-In From Senior Management and Other Relevant Stakeholders

This means getting the support and sponsorship of all key stakeholders. It includes senior management and those who control the purse strings as well as those who will be involved in developing and implementing the program. Support and ownership of the concept and the program is critical from both higher and lower echelons. Without this kind of backing, the program is likely to suffer from a lack of funds and essential resources and from general inertia. If this is the case, the program is unlikely to succeed no matter how rigorous is its conceptual design.

Ensure That Staff Are Motivated, Enthused, Supported, and Adequately Rewarded

This means that your stakeholders are intrinsically motivated to be a part of the program, are enthusiastic about it, and are appropriately rewarded for their efforts. Without this, no matter how innovative the program, its novelty will wither away quickly, leading staff to feel uninterested, overburdened, and without enthusiasm. The trick is in ensuring that staff members see a tangible benefit for themselves, personally and collectively, in working on the program. Rewards come in several ways in academic settings. It is important to identify these clearly and make these available so that staff members feel compelled to put in more than their fair share—and they will if they feel that they own the program.

Ensure That Students Are Motivated, Enthused, and Adequately Supported

Just as for staff in the program, it is critical to ensure that the students in the program remain motivated and enthusiastic about the program. Your students are your clients, and if they leave, you do not have a viable program.

Student motivation and enthusiasm for the program will depend a great deal on the kind and the level of support that you are able to provide them. This is not always dependent on physical and financial resources. There are many creative ways for ensuring student support such as with the help of other students in the program and those who may have left the program (Collis & Moonen, in press).

Ensure That There Are Adequate Opportunities for Interaction Among Students and Between Teachers and Students

We know that students want the opportunity to communicate with their teachers and tutors as well as with other students in the program. Study groups, group projects, and online discussion forums are a great way to provide and support interaction among students and teachers. These activities can be carefully designed and implemented to require minimal input from teachers. Students, themselves, especially those who are mature and in the workforce already, can become conveners and moderators of such activities, provided they are adequately rewarded for such contributions in the learning and teaching process. An online discussion forum, for example, is unlikely to work if it is unclear what the students are expected to be doing and if participation is not going to contribute to grades and required competency development.

It is important to ensure that there is adequate staffing and resources to support student communication and infrastructure. In the case of online distance education, student support will need to comprise both maintenance of the online infrastructure and support of all communication on it. In such settings, the best pedagogy will be ineffective if the infrastructure is not up and running. The converse is also true—without sound pedagogy, a robust infrastructure is not going to be much use to anyone. The two must work hand-in-hand to ensure effective educational process. Especially in the developing world, maintaining the infrastructure often comes at great costs. In such settings, e-learning and online learning must be carefully thought through so that they support learning and teaching rather than becoming a deterrent for students and teachers.

Ensure That There is Adequate Staffing and Resources for Supporting the Program

It is critically important to ensure that there is adequate staffing to support the program. Sadly, in many cases and especially in developing world contexts, such resources are rarely sufficient. However, staffing and resource considerations should not comprise an afterthought. These considerations should form an integral part of the planning and feasibility processes. Failure to attend to these problems will jeopardize the success of a program and make it more difficult for both teachers and learners to find their voices in the context of meaningful learning experiences.

ACKNOWLEDGMENT

Funding and support for the development of the Master of Arts in Teacher Education (International) program has been provided by the Commonwealth of Learning and The Open University of Sri Lanka.

REFERENCES

Amundsen, C. L., & Bernard, R. M. (1989). Institutional support for peer contact in distance education: An empirical investigation. *Distance Education, 18*(2), 85–109.

Barrows, H. S., & Tamblyn, R. (1980). *Problem-based learning: An approach to medical education*. New York: Springer.

Bernard, R. M., & Amundsen, C. L. (1989). Antecedents to dropout in distance education: Does one model fit all? *Journal of Distance Education, 14*(2), 25–46.

Brown, J. S., Collins, A., & Duguid, P. (1989). Situated cognition and the culture of learning. *Educational Researcher, 18*(1) 32–42.

Collis, B., & Moonen, J. (in press). The contributing student: Learners as co-developers of learning resources for reuse in Web environments. In M. S. Khine (Ed.), *Engaged learning with emerging technologies*. Amsterdam: Springer.

Dewey, J. (1933). *How we think: A restatement of the relation of reflective thinking to the educative process*. Boston, MA: Heath.

ESP 2240 Study Guide. (2004). *The teacher educator as a teaching and learning specialist*. Sri Lanka: The Open University of Sri Lanka, Department of Education.

Evensen, D. H., & Hmelo, C. E. (Eds.). (2000). *Problem-based learning: A research perspective on learning interactions*. Mahwah, NJ: Lawrence Erlbaum Associates.

Karunanayaka, S., Lekamge, D., Gunawardena, C., Naidu, S., & Menon, M. (2005, May 22–22). *MATE (International) Program: A novel approach to developing global partnerships in teacher education*. Paper presented at the Asian Roundtable on Open and Distance Learning for attainment of Millennium Development Goals, Colombo, Sri Lanka.

Lave, J., & Wenger, E. (1991). *Situated learning: Legitimate peripheral participation*. New York: Cambridge University Press.

MATE-International. (2004). *Program handbook: Master of Arts in Teacher Education (International)*, Sri Lanka: The Open University of Sri Lanka, Department of Education.

McLellan, H. (Ed.). (1996). *Situated learning perspectives*. Englewood Cliffs, NJ: Educational Technology Publications.

Naidu, S. (2006). *E-Learning: A Guidebook of principles, procedures and practices, 2nd edition*. New Delhi, India: Commonwealth Educational Media Center for Asia (CEMCA), and the Commonwealth of Learning.

Naidu, S. (2004). Learning design as an indicator of quality in teacher education. In K. Rama & M. Menon (Eds.), *Innovations in teacher education—International practices for quality assurance* (pp. 65–76). Bangalore, India: NAAC.

Naidu, S., Menon, M., Gunawardena, C., Lekamge, D., & Karunanayaka, S. (2005, November 9–11). *Quality teaching and learning in the Master of Arts in Teacher Education program at the Open University of Sri Lanka*. Paper presented at the biennial conference of the Open and Distance Learning Association of Australia, Adelaide, South Australia.

Naidu, S., & Oliver, M. (1996). Computer supported collaborative problem-based learning (CSC-PBL): An instructional design architecture for virtual learning in nursing education. *Journal of Distance Education, XI*(2), 1–22.

Naidu, S., & Oliver, M. (1999). Critical incident-based computer supported collaborative learning. *Instructional Science: An International Journal of Learning and Cognition, 27*(5), 329–354.

Naidu, S., Oliver, M., & Koronios, A. (1999). Approaching clinical decision-making in nursing practice with interactive multimedia and case-based reasoning. *The Interactive Multimedia Electronic Journal of Computer Enhanced Learning* [Online]. Retrieved on November 3, 2005, from http://imej.wfu.edu/

Pea, R. (2004). The social and technological dimensions of scaffolding and related theoretical concepts for learning, education, and human activity. *The Journal of Learning Sciences: Special Issue on Scaffolding, 13*(3), 423–451.

Quintana, C., Reiser, B. J., Davis, E. A., Krajcik, J., Fretz, E., Duncan, R. G., Kyza, E., Edelson, D., & Soloway, E. (2004). A scaffolding design framework for software to support science inquiry. *The Journal of Learning Sciences: Special Issue on Scaffolding, 13*(3), 337–386.

Reiser, B. J. (2004). Scaffolding complex learning: The mechanisms of supporting and problematizing student work. *The Journal of Learning Sciences: Special Issue on Scaffolding, 13*(3), 273–304.

Schank, R. C. (1990). *Tell me a story*. Evanston, IL: Northwestern University Press.

Schank, R. C. (1997). *Virtual learning: A revolutionary approach to building a highly skilled workforce*. New York: McGraw-Hill.

Schank, R. C., & Cleary, C., (1995). *Engines for education*. Hillsdale, NJ: Lawrence Erlbaum Associates.

Schank, R. C., Fano, A., Jona, M., & Bell, B. (1994). The design of goal-based scenarios. *The Journal of the Learning Sciences, 3*(4), 305–345.

The Cognition and Technology Group at Vanderbilt. (1990a, August–September). Anchored instruction and its relationship to situated cognition. *Educational Researcher, 19*(6), 2–10.

The Cognition and Technology Group at Vanderbilt. (1990b, May). Technology and the design of generative learning environments. *Educational Technology, 31*(5), 34–40.

Vygotsky, L. S. (1978). *Mind in society: The development of higher psychological processes*. Cambridge, MA: Harvard University Press.

Chapter 5

Motivate and Manage:
Key Activities of Online Instructors

Zane L. Berge
University of Maryland

What advice one believes will help teachers do their jobs depends on what one thinks the purpose of teaching is. Simply put, the purpose of teaching is to facilitate student learning and the primary roles of the instructor are to motivate the student to learn and to manage the learning environment to maximize its potential as conducive to student learning. *Imparting knowledge* is not adequate as the purpose of teaching—the teacher bears a greater responsibility than that (Laurillard, 1993). Many prominent educational researchers argue that instructor-led approaches to training and education must be replaced with more active instruction, where each individual student constructs new knowledge for themselves through interactions and negotiations with others. Knowledge thus constructed by the learner can be used as a basis and a tool for future learning activities (e.g., Duffy & Jonassen, 1991).

BACKGROUND

Teaching online usually demands different technical skills, different approaches to teaching, and different teamwork than what has historically been educational practice. Teaching and learning online also means new roles for instructor and student, and what students expect of their instructors and their learning environment (Coppola, Hiltz, & Rotter,

2002; Phelps, Ledgerwood, & Bartlett, 2000). These new dimensions and functions usually require changes in how to promote student motivation and in how the online classroom is managed compared to in-person teaching and learning.

Changing Roles of the Instructor

As learners assume more responsibility for their own learning than in the past, thus changing the role they have in learning, the role of the instructor is changing, too. The faculty member's role shifts from sole expert to facilitator, coach, or mentor—in other words, to one who provides leadership and wisdom in guiding student learning. Various roles that the online instructor assumes such as chair, host, tutor, mediator, provocateur, observer, co-learner, community organizer, and even lecturer have been identified (Berge, 1992; Bonk & Wisher, 2000).

Probably the most important role of the online instructor is to model effective learning and accept "the responsibility of keeping discussions on track, contributing special knowledge and insights, weaving together various discussion threads and course components, and maintaining group harmony" (Rohfeld & Hiemstra, 1995, p. 91). Elsewhere I have categorized online instructor roles into technical, social, pedagogical, and managerial (Berge 1995). Not all of these roles need to be carried out in their entirety by the same person. In fact, it may be rare that they are. A brief description of those roles follows (Feenberg, 1986; Gulley, 1968; Kerr, 1986; McCreary, 1990; McMann, 1994; Paulsen, 1995).

Pedagogical Role.   Many of the most important roles of online instructors revolve around their duties as an educational facilitator. The instructor uses questions and probes for student responses in ways that focus discussions on critical concepts, principles, and skills.

Social Role.   Creating a friendly, social environment where learning is encouraged is also important for successful online learning. This suggests that promoting human relationships, developing group cohesiveness, maintaining the group as a unit, and helping members to work together in other ways for their mutual benefit are all helpful to the success of any online learning activities.

Managerial Role.   This role involves setting the agenda for the course; the objectives of the discussion, the timetable, procedural rules, and decision-making norms. Managing the interactions with strong leadership and direction is considered a *sine qua non* of successful online teaching.

Technical Role.   The online facilitator must make learners as comfortable as possible with the ICT (information and communication technology) hardware and software that is being used for the online learning environment. The ultimate technical goal is to make the technology transparent to the user. The closer to reaching this goal, the more the learner may concentrate on the academic task and activities necessary for successful learning. It is important to note that as online learning grows and matures, more of this role is handled by support staff and not by the instructor. Still, the instructor is often the first person that students call on for help when a technical issue interferes with their learning.

Interaction Involving Learning

Interaction is a significant factor in separating education from information transferal. Historically, in distance education before the advent of online technologies, interpersonal interaction had occurred almost solely between instructor and student. Today's technology increasingly allows interaction among students, even when geographically separated. Essentially, there are two types of interaction that are important in learning; interaction with content and interpersonal interaction. Both are critical in many types of learning. As an educator designs a course that is to promote higher order learning, with practice for the learner in such skills as analysis, synthesis, and evaluation, it becomes important to provide an environment in which both kinds of interaction can occur.

The point here is that different channels of communication can hinder or facilitate interpersonal interaction and interaction with content. It is a combination of technologies and media that provide an environment rich in various opportunities for interaction. The person designing the instruction must consider how to use the strengths and limitations of each technology within the learning environment (Berge, 1996). For example, designers of online instruction need to be aware that the greater the content density of the materials to be learned, the more the pacing should become the responsibility of the learner. High density content may be better delivered via recorded media such as printed text, videotape, or on a Web site—all of which can be revisited by the learner at his/her convenience and individual pace.

What types of interactions can teachers plan for students to motivate their learning? What are the critical roles that differentiate good instructors from not so good? Instructors need to have some expertise and experience in the subject matter for which they are teaching – this is what they are hired for. Because we all know highly proficient experts that are less than proficient at teaching others their subject matter, such expertise must be a necessary but insufficient factor in good teaching.

What Students Expect From Their Teachers

An important note to add here is that when adult students were asked what attributes they expect from their teachers, Donaldson, Flannery, and Ross-Gordon (1993) found a mixture of responses indicating characteristics associated with both teacher-centered learning (e.g., knowledgeable; to present material clearly) and student-centered learning (e.g., to show concern for student learning; to emphasize relevance of class material).

More recently, I have gathered responses from hundreds of adult students in researching barriers to online learning. Whereas the same attributes were mentioned by my respondents as Donaldson et al. found a decade ago, an additional characteristic that was mentioned most often by these students was that instructors must know how to teach online. I suspect student expectations of effective teachers and teaching may be changing, even if hard for students to articulate, in some part due to the use of technology in teaching. So in general, whereas online teachers should view themselves as facilitators of student learning rather than conduits to share their own expert knowledge, students expect to see expertise from their instructors and the competency to teach online.

MOTIVATING LEARNING

The learner-centered approach that is commonly used by online teachers is the confluence of several models. One model is the constructivist learning theory that asserts that knowledge is constructed by the learner using varied methods, both individually and collaboratively (Vygotsky, 1978). Another influential model from which the student-centered approach has derived is the experiential model in which teaching is seen as transformation of existing knowledge (Kohonen, 1992). The active learning model emphasizes that all learning activities involve some type of experience or dialog (Fink, 2002). Facilitators also encourage and support learners in reflecting deeply on their own experiences so they can generalize and transfer knowledge and skills (Curtis & Lawson, 2001; Fosnot, 1993). It has been my experience that both the roles and the approach that the teacher takes can help motivate students in their learning.

What is motivation with regard to learning? Should students always be eager to start something new? Should they willingly step up to the challenge of difficult tasks? Would motivated students be more likely to work harder or quicker than unmotivated students? Would motivated students show more persistence when they are having difficulty than students who are not motivated? Essentially Motivation = Expectancy * Value.

If learners have no reasonable expectation that they can accomplish the tasks before them, they are not likely to put forth the effort to try. Similarly, even if learners know they can do the task, but they judge the outcome to have little value to them, why should they bother? A teacher can increase learner motivation in one of two ways: (1) increase the value of what is to be learned to the learner or (2) increase the perceived expectancy of the learner for accomplishing the task (Ball, 1977; Keller, 1983; Vroom, 1964).

Much of online learning involves adult students. It is therefore useful to revisit some of the principles of andragogy, the learner-centered approach that treats learners as mutual partners in the learning enterprise, given that it drives much of the design to promote student motivation. Several assumptions underlie the andragogical model (Brookfield, 1986; Collins, 1995; Knowles, Holton, & Swanson, 1998; Ravitz, 1997):

- Adults tend to be self-directed learners.
- Adults have rich, varied experiences from which to draw and that serve as resources for their learning.
- Adults usually are motivated to learn by internal or intrinsic factors rather than through external or extrinsic rewards such as pay raises.
- Adult readiness to learn is often predicated on their need for increased knowledge or skill. Therefore, they tend to have a problem-solving orientation rather than being interested solely in content acquisition. Adults find authentic activities provide motivation and meaning in their learning.

Based on these assumptions, the online teacher often chooses to use a collaborative teaching model that involves the learners in teamwork or as partners. These assumptions also cause many online teachers to use a more asynchronous and self-directed learning approach. This is probably good in most cases. Historically, it has been in schooling where teachers have directed students in what to learn (and when and how to learn it as well). Students' motivation to learn is increased when they perceive their learning activities are practical and relevant and when they have some control over when, how, and what they learn (Kinzie, 1990). Most students involved in formal learning environments usually have little to say about when, how, what, and why they are to learn things. It has been my experience that all students, regardless of age, prefer more structure when faced with new or novel learning situations, with increasing levels of freedom as they become more familiar with their tasks. Still, I look at my teaching role as working myself out of a job. My overall goal is to help learners master not only content, but also how to approach future learning in a self-directed way.

Motivational and Affective Factors

Motivation influences what and how much is learned. Motivation to learn is influenced by the emotional state, beliefs, interests, and goals of the individual (APA, 1997). The following appears on the American Psychology Association Website under the title "Learner-Centered Psychology Principles:"

> The rich internal world of thoughts, beliefs, goals, and expectations for success or failure can enhance or interfere [with] the learner's quality of thinking and information processing. Students' beliefs about themselves as learners and the nature of learning have a marked influence on motivation. Motivational and emotional factors also influence both the quality of thinking and information processing as well as an individual's motivation to learn. Positive emotions, such as curiosity, generally enhance motivation and facilitate learning and performance. Mild anxiety can also enhance learning and performance by focusing the learner's attention on a particular task. However, intense negative emotions (e.g., anxiety, panic, rage, insecurity) and related thoughts (e.g., worrying about competence, ruminating about failure, fearing punishment, ridicule, or stigmatizing labels) generally detract from motivation, interfere with learning, and contribute to low performance. (http://www.apa.org/ed/lcpnewtext.html).

Students want to feel competent in their learning. This intrinsic motivation can be promoted by tasks and activities that are relevant to the students' interests and offer "just-enough" difficulty. While individuals vary in the amount of curiosity, insight, prior knowledge, and creativity, planning for activities that allow each student some choices in how or what to do, and that meet the individual's abilities regarding complexity and difficulty, will help that student optimize his or her intrinsic motivation. Without motivation to learn, students will be unlikely to exert the effort needed to acquire complex knowledge and skills. They will focus on the minimum expenditure of effort necessary to earn the grade, that is, unless sufficient coercion is introduced. Thus, the instructor needs to employ effective strategies to promote student motivation. These strategies include relevant learning tasks, feedback that is reinforcing, and promoting the learners' perceptions that each learning task may be complex or difficult, but it can be accomplished and does have value (Amigos Library Services, 2005; Bonk & Cunningham, 1998; Harasim, 1990).

Modeling and Mentoring Learning

A significant part of student motivation has to do with the instructor modeling learning behaviors, and mentoring the learner. The literature on cognitive apprenticeship discusses modeling as one important way that experienced practitioners can facilitate the acquisition of new skills and knowledge by novice learners (Brown, Collins, & Duguid, 1989). Modeling is essentially learning by observing others' behaviors.

Mentoring, coaching, or even peer support can provide an individual student with the motivation that is needed. If instructional content is available, even in a self-directed format, mentors, instructors, peers, or others who do not necessarily have expertise in the content area can be what is necessary to promote motivation in the learner. The primary role of the online mentor is to encourage, motivate, monitor, and provide feedback on the student's learning.

MANAGING THE ONLINE CLASSROOM

Managing the online classroom includes making sure students are ready for online learning and that they know what to expect of the technology and environment. Planning and preparation of the course needs to be done before the beginning of the class. The syllabus becomes one of the primary instruments for communicating expectations to the students regarding course goals/objectives, course materials (e.g., textbook), grading information, project and topics descriptions, course schedule, activities and assignments, academic policies, and any other expectations that are important to the operation and smooth running online class environment.

Managing learning here means creating and maintaining a safe, supportive, and challenging learning environment. It is characterized by the different procedures and tasks that the instructor does. Examples of processes are welcoming students to class, communicating what is expected of them, creating community, and managing communication. There are dozens of tasks that are involved with managing the learning environment, such as setting and maintaining a class schedule, showing students you care about their learning and their general well-being, and showing sensitivity to students' other responsibilities in the pacing and quantity of assignments. Managing the online classroom also means such things as increasing the interaction and participation of online students, managing the online assessment of learning, and tracking student progress and participation.

First and foremost, however, managing the online classroom means communicating expectations to the students. This includes expectations for student performance, setting topics for discussion, and links to external resources. Managing the classroom begins well before the class starts, and carries through the issuing of final grades. Effective online instructors establish and constantly maintain their presence in the classroom conferences. This is most often done through regularly posting topics, questions, follow-ups, comments, and responses to other postings (DE Oracle, 2003).

PROMOTING INTERACTION

It is also a key element in managing the online classroom environment for collaborative learning. As important as teamwork can be to online learning, the instructor must still maintain presence and support the teams' activities that are assigned. In order for teamwork to be successful, the instructor must establish and communicate explicit guidelines, timeframes, and expectations for student participation. Most activities can be effective as collaborative learning including group projects, case study analysis, role play, simulations, guest/expert visit, student-led presentation/discussion, and peer assessment applications.

In most asynchronous online classrooms, one of the major ways to promote interpersonal interaction is through discussion. This can be lead by the instructor or by students. Generally, questions that ask students to apply new theories and concepts to their own situation are the best. Doing so allows the topic to be opened to different ideas and insights regarding the content being learned (Whitesel, n.d.). It is usually more important for the instructor to generate good questions than to supply good answers to the conference (Berge & Muilenburg, 2000; Muilenburg & Berge, 2000).

CONCLUSIONS

No longer is the teacher looked upon to function as the sole knowledge provider, or even the main content provider. Therefore, the instructor's main roles are to motivate the learner and to manage the learning environment. The adult students' desire to influence the learning experience, their interest in the instructional pace, their ability to draw on past experiences, and their insistence that the content is relevant to them, makes the online environment an excellent place for learning to occur. Still, it is necessary for the instructor to motivate the students and manage the environment in ways that facilitate student learning. Students expect guidance, direction, and instructor-led activities at least some of the time.

As a rule, if an individual is motivated to learn, and if the instructional content is available in a self-directed format, most people can learn with only a small amount of interaction with an instructor. This "self-directed learning" model demonstrates the end-state for many teachers regarding their expectations and hopes for students at the end of a class or program of study. It also happens to demonstrate the greatest overall economies for online learning. Mentoring can also stimulate motivation in students and individuals who self-assess and reflect on their learning. Because self-reflection is central to mentoring (Hine, 2000), it can promote more conscious learners. Teachers and mentors who apply knowledge of learners' needs and who develop effective classroom management are in the best position to help facilitate learning.

REFERENCES

American Psychological Association (APA). (1997, November). *Learner-centered psychological principles: A framework for school reform & redesign.* Prepared by the Learner-Centered Principles Work Group of the American Psychological Association's Board of Educational Affairs (BEA). Retrieved December 31, 2004, from http://www.apa.org/ed/lcpnewtext.html

Amigos Library Services. (2005). *Lesson one: Introduction to distance learning research*. Retrieved July 23, 2005, from http://www.amigos.org/training/lessonone.html

Ball, S. (1977). *Motivation in education*. New York: Academic Press.

Berge, Z. L. (1992, October 27). *The role of the moderator in a scholarly discussion group (SDG)*. Posting to Interpersonal Computing and Technology List (IPCT-L). Retrieved December 29, 2004, from http://www.emoderators.com/moderators/zlbmod.html

Berge, Z. L. (1995). Facilitating computer conferencing: Recommendations from the field. *Educational Technology, 35*(1), 22–30.

Berge, Z. L. (1996). Changing roles in higher education: Reflecting on technology. *Collaborative Communications Review* (pp. 43–53). McLean, VA: International Teleconferencing Association.

Berge, Z. L., & Muilenburg, L. Y. (2000). Designing discussion questions for online, adult learning. *Educational Technology, 40*(5), 53–56.

Bonk, C., & Cunningham, D. J. (1998). Searching for constructivist, learner-centered and sociocultural components for collaborative educational learning tools. In C. Bonk & K. King (Eds.), *Electronic collaborators: Learner-centered technologies for literacy, apprenticeship, and discourse* (pp. 25–50). Mahwah, NJ: Lawrence Erlbaum Associates. Retrieved December 31, 2004, from http://www.publicationshare.com/docs/Bon02.pdf

Bonk, C. J., & Wisher, R. A. (2000). *Applying collaborative and e-learning tools to military distance learning: A research framework* (Technical Report #1107). Alexandria, VA: U.S. Army Research Institute for the Behavioral and Social Sciences. Retrieved December 28, 2004, from http://publicationshare.com/docs/Dist.Learn(Wisher).pdf

Brookfield, S. D. (1986). *Understanding and facilitating adult learning*. San Francisco: Jossey-Bass.

Brown, J. S., Collins, A., & Duguid, P. (1989, January–February). Situated cognition and the culture of learning. *Educational Researcher, 18*(1), 32–42.

Collins, M. (1995). Critical commentaries on the role of the adult educator: From self-directed learning to postmodernist sensibilities. In M. R. Welton (Ed.), *In defense of the lifeworld: Critical perspective on adult learning* (pp. 71–98). Albany, NY: SUNY.

Coppola, N., Hiltz, S., & Rotter, N. (2002). Becoming a virtual professor: Pedagogical roles and asynchronous learning networks. *Journal of Management Information Systems, 18*(4), 169–189.

Curtis, D., & Lawson, M. (2001). Exploring collaborative online learning. *Journal of Asynchronous Learning Networks, 5*(1). Retrieved July 23, 2005, from http://www.puc.cl/citeduc/datos/archivos/collaborative_online_learning.pdf

DE Oracle. (2003, March–April). *Helpful hints on effective teaching via WebTycho: Managing the online classroom*. Retrieved July 15, 2005, from http://info. umuc.edu/de/ezine/features/mar_april_2003/helpful_hints.htm

Donaldson, J. F., Flannery, D., & Ross-Gordon, J. (1993, Fall). A triangulated study comparing adult college students' perceptions of effective teaching with those of "traditional students." *Continuing Higher Education Review, 57*(3), 147–165.

Duffy, D. M., & Jonassen, D. H. (1991, May). Constructivism: New implications for instructional technology. *Educational Technology, 31*(5), 7–12.

Feenberg, A. (1986, March). Network design: An operating manual for computer conferencing. *IEEE Transactions on Professional Communications, 29*(1), 2–7.

Fink, L. D. (2002). *Active learning*. Retrieved December 30, 2004, from http://www.ou.edu/idp/tips/ideas/model.html

Fosnot, C. T. (1993). Rethinking science education: A defense of Piagetian constructivism. *Journal for Research in Science Education, 30*(9), 1189–1201.

Gulley, H. E. (1968). *Discussion, conference, and group process* (2nd ed.). New York: Holt, Rinehart & Winston.

Harasim, L. M. (Ed.). (1990). *Online education: Perspectives on a new environment.* New York: Praeger.

Hine, A. (2000). *Mirroring effective education through mentoring, metacognition and self-reflection.* Proceedings of the Australian Association for Research in Education Conference. Sydney. Retrieved July 23, 2005, from http://www.aare.edu.au/00pap/hin00017.htm

Keller, J. M. (1983). Motivational design of instruction. In C. M. Reigeluth (Ed.), *Instructional design theories and models: An overview of their current status,* (pp. 383–434). Hillsdale, NJ: Lawrence Erlbaum Associates.

Kerr, E. B. (1986, March). Electronic leadership: A guide to moderating online conferences. *IEEE Transactions on Professional Communications, 29*(1), 12–18.

Kinzie, M. B. (1990). Requirements and benefits of effective interactive instruction: Learner control, self regulation, and continuing motivation. *Educational Technology Research and Development, 38*(1), 1–21

Knowles, M. S., Holton, E. F., & Swanson, R. A. (1998). *The adult learner: The definitive classic in adult education and human resource development.* Houston, TX: Gulf Publishing.

Kohonen, V. (1992). Experiential language learning: Second language learning as cooperative learner education. In D. Nunan (Ed.), *Collaborative language learning and teaching* (pp. 17–32). Cambridge, England: Cambridge University Press.

Laurillard, D. (1993). *Rethinking university teaching. A framework for the effective use of educational technology.* New York: Routledge.

McCreary, E. (1990). Three behavioral models for computer mediated communications. In Linda Harasim (Ed.), *Online education—Perspectives on a new environment* (pp. 117–130). New York: Praeger.

McMann, G. W. (1994, April). The changing role of moderation in computer mediated conferencing. In A Yakimovicz (Ed.), *The Proceedings of the Distance Learning Research Conference: "Covering the world with educational opportunites"* (pp. 159–166). College Station: Texas A & M University.

Muilenburg, L., & Berge, Z. L. (2000). A framework for designing questions for online learning. *DEOSNEWS, 10*(2). Retrieved February 18, 2005, from http://www.emoderators.com/moderators/muilenburg.html

Paulsen, M. F. (1995). Moderating educational computer conferences. In Z. L. Berge & M. P. Collins (Eds.), *Computer-mediated communication and the online classroom. Volume 3: Distance learning* (pp. 81–90). Cresskill, NJ: Hampton Press.

Phelps, R., Ledgerwood, T., & Bartlett, L. (2000, August). *Managing the transition to online teaching: The role of project management methodology in the learning organisation.* Paper presented at the Moving Online Conference, Gold Coast, Australia. Retrieved July 26, 2005, from http://wwwdev.scu.edu.au/schools/sawd/moconf/mocpapers/moc24.pdf

Ravitz, J. (1997, February). An ISD model for building online communities: Furthering the dialogue. *Proceedings of the Annual Conference of the Association for Educational Communications and Technology.* Albuquerque, NM. Retrieved July 26, 2005, from http://www.bie.org/Ravitz/isd_model.html

Rohfeld, R. W., & Hiemstra, R. (1995). Moderating discussions in the electronic classroom. In Z. L. Berge & M. P. Collins (Eds.), *Computer-mediated communication and the on-line classroom in distance education* (pp. 91–104). Cresskill, NJ: Hampton Press.

Vroom, V. H. (1964). *Work and motivation.* New York: Wiley.

Vygotsky, L. (1978). *Mind in society: The development of higher psychological processes.* Cambridge, MA: Harvard University Press.

Whitesel, C. (n.d.). *Moderating conference discussions.* Retrieved July 23, 2005, from http://info.umuc.edu/de/ezine/archives/moderating_conference_discussions.htm

Chapter 6

Pursuing Interaction

Deborah K. LaPointe
University of New Mexico

Recently a doctoral student struggling to find her own research question asked me, "What question lies at your heart?" What a remarkable question she posed. According to Senge, Scharmer, Jaworski, and Flowers (2004), when one knows the question that lies at the heart and is reaching a state of clarity about and connection to such a question, "there is no decision making" (p. 89). The answers to the question and necessary actions to take become obvious. The question that I have sought to answer for nearly 10 years has been this: "How do I get learners to interact sincerely online with each other?" My story shows that I have made many decisions and pursued many paths in pursuit of an answer. Hopefully, clarity and connection are forthcoming.

First, let me explain what I mean by *interacting sincerely*. A learner interacting sincerely comes to class prepared, free from pretense in manner or actions. He or she has read and reflected on the assigned readings as well as on any additional readings he or she may have explored. The sincere learner is curious, ready to test tentative abstractions generated from the readings, and willing to engage others in discussing their ideas. This sincerity is a function of the time and effort an individual invests in a relationship or community (Pargman, 2000) for the ultimate measure of sincerity is our time and attention.

Attention has been studied widely and is an essential determinant of cognition as well as of the success or failure of any practical operation (Vygotsky, 1978). When many stimuli are simultaneously and naturally competing for learner attention today, taking the time and extending the effort to focus on learning means retreating from other stimuli. When instructor and classmates are sincerely interacting and devoting attention, they are genuinely prepared, keenly listen, earnestly inquire, and can more easily direct and inspire feedback, attention, and dialogue. Less uncertainty is felt as learners no longer linger online waiting for someone to respond to their postings, waiting to find out if they correctly interpreted other classmates' messages. There is less frustration as engaged learners do not encounter classmates unprepared for class or an instructor who fails to keep virtual office hours.

I have learned many valuable lessons from the learners in my online classes over the years. One learner recently broadened my understanding of sincerity. After attending a face-to-face session where small groups of learners presented progress on complex problems they were trying to solve, a learner related to me:

> This discussion has been amazing; I never again want to participate in a discussion where my classmates have skimmed—if looked at the assigned readings at all—and are merely reacting to the questions posed to them. I want to participate in discussions where groups of us have become experts or are at least well-informed novices who have spent time reading, organizing, synthesizing, reflecting, abstracting, and can present, answer questions, engage in discussion, and suggest applications for the information.

That is a description of the kind of interaction I have been trying to facilitate—a conversation of ideas, complete with recognition of their origins, applications, implications, and prospective consequences when plugged into an organization of one sort or another.

INTERACTION AND LEARNER AUTONOMY

Often unmet needs drive a person, including teachers. I myself had not experienced much interaction as a learner throughout my many years spent in classrooms. In fact, when I shared answers with my high school classmates, we all encountered various disciplinary measures for cheating. My undergraduate classes were filled with 200 plus students and a professor standing at the front podium. We listened, but we certainly did not set our own learning objectives, select learning resources, or evaluate progress. No one invited our thoughts.

Yet when I started studying distance education (DE) in the early 1990s, among the first articles I read were Moore's (1986) description of the *self-directed, autonomous learner*, Moore's (1989) explanation of three types of interaction—*learner–instructor, learner–learner,* and *learner–content*, and Moore's (1980) classification of distance education courses based on levels of interaction and degree to which learners had the ability to set learning objectives, select learning resources, and evaluate progress. It seemed to me that the growing phenomenon of distance education and the emerging computer-mediated conferencing (CMC) technologies would reform learning.

The distance education literature in the early 1990s was filled with the promise of higher quality DE courses and the potential for achievement of higher levels of learning due to CMC. Interaction with the instructor and peers could break down the distance among learners and instructor and permit learners to achieve sustained educational communication (Garrison & Cleveland-Innes, 2005) and higher levels of learning. CMC could foster the uniquely adult types of learning that Brookfield (1986) and Knowles (1980) described and the critical discourse espoused by institutes of higher education. Anderson, Rourke, Archer, and Garrison (2001) expanded the idea and suggested that CMC offered the potential to form communities of critical inquiry.

The four types of interaction, including *learner–interface interaction* (Hillman, Willis, & Gunawardena, 1994) offered the possibility for new voices to join the classroom. The new voices belonged to learners who had been unable to participate as they were previously unable to get to campus for a variety of reasons. But the new voices also included those who could and do attend every class session but never felt they could, wanted, or chose to speak in class. CMC also gave voice to the reticent, hesitant, reflective, and shy. CMC gave voice to the parents physically sitting in class but whose minds were preoccupied, filled with uncertainties about family safety and well-being while they attended classes. Their preoccupations and worries also had previously kept them silent as well. Pursuing CMC discussions was clearly relevant and vital.

Moore's concept of learner autonomy and the proficient, self-directed learner also seemed a significant idea. However, this concept seemed more relevant to earlier styles of DE when learners and instructors did not have immediate access to each other. With immediate access to an instructor, the online learner would not need to set goals, locate learning resources, and self-evaluate; the instructor would perform those tasks. Accordingly, I set aside and discounted the construct of learner autonomy initially.

PURSUING INTERACTION—LEVELS OF LEARNING

Early on, interaction was incorporated into my online courses as any good online course included interaction as a best practice. Many learners from a variety of majors took my online courses simply to experience the phenomenon of online learning. Those early online discussions in the mid-1990s were plentiful and rich with a variety of perspectives posted. Many voices were heard, just as the literature suggested. Guest speakers from the local community joined us. The discussion boards filled with text messages.

My experience corresponded with the literature emphasizing that CMC promoted topical discussions wherein learners reflect, share relevant experience and know-how, help one another remember, synthesize, and apply content in group learning situations (Siegel, Dubrovsky, Kiesler, & McGuire, 1986) with the potential to improve cognitive learning strategies (Verneil & Berge, 2000). Writing out thoughts before posting made learners conscious of their thoughts, increasing metacognitive awareness. As learners grounded and supported their statements, they found and addressed gaps in their thinking (Dillenbourg, 1999). Interaction among learners was motivating and gave the isolated learners gathered around computers in their homes a sense of participating in a class.

Midway through the 1990s, I conducted analyses of the computer transcripts produced from various online conferences to examine the anticipated higher levels of learning. Using Henri's (1992) content analysis examining three dimensions—cognitive, metacognitive, and social—I found unexpected data. The majority of student postings revealed (a) surface exchanges of opinions and (b) messages exchanged organizing and planning assignments, not the higher levels of cognition anticipated. These findings were similar to those of Rose and Flowers (2003) who found 41% of messages posted were of a cognitive nature whereas 36% were related to organizing learning activities. Deep processing was evidenced in 35% of the messages posted. A study by Kanuka and Anderson (1998) reported a majority of messages posted to an online conference showed low levels of knowledge construction. Gunawardena, Lowe, and Anderson (1997) created a transcript analysis model, the interaction analysis model, to evaluate the knowledge construction process that occurs in CMC. The phases of a computer conference were (a) sharing and comparing information, (b) discovery and exploration of dissonance, (c) negotiation of meaning, (d) testing and modification of proposed synthesis, and (e) agreement statements and applications of newly constructed meaning. The researchers applied the model to an international conference and discovered the majority of the messages posted involved sharing and comparing information. Murphy (2004), too, found only simple interaction wherein learners posted their ideas but rarely responded to questions raised by classmates when she analyzed class transcripts using her SPICE model.

Other literature as well as interviews I conducted started to show that learners were neither necessarily motivated nor supported by interaction with peers. Many voices were still quiet as many distance learners were preoccupied with too many other responsibilities. Busy distance learners seemed to take classes online that they would not have taken otherwise; busy lives contributed to online silence. Others expressed privacy and security concerns about posting comments or assignments on the Internet. Learners related they had nothing more to contribute after they posted their initial answer to a question. Others focused on posting the required number of postings rather than on the quality of their postings. Learners themselves expressed doubt about the value of mere surface exchanges of opinions that resulted when peers were neither required to elaborate nor examine assumptions underlying their postings (Andrusyszyn, van Soeren, Laschinger, Goldenberg, & DiCenso, 1999).

Other researchers investigating asynchronous CMC claimed that text-based communication could be interactionally incoherent, displaying a high degree of disrupted adjacency, overlapping exchanges, and topic decay (Herring, 1999). Without effective moderation, discussions strayed off topic as learners responded to the last message posted rather than to the discussion as a coherent whole (Hewitt, 2003). Many referred to the requirement to participate in online interaction as busy work with little return on investment (Gunawardena, Plass, & Salisbury, 2001). Learners who perceived online participation as not integral to course success soon chose not to participate (Vrasidas & McIsaac, 1999). Adding a discussion tool to the online class did not guarantee that meaningful interaction or high levels of learning occurred. In fact, Berge (1999) wrote that misuse or poor design led to learner boredom, information overload, frustration, and loss of attention. Clearly, I had to more diligently design for and encourage worthwhile postings as the years passed and learners lost the initial fascination with CMC.

PURSUING INTERACTION—COURSE REQUIREMENTS

The success of the online discussion is related to the value instructors place on discussion (Swan et al., 2000) as shown by the instructors' expectations of learner behavior in the discussion (Jung, Choi, Lim, & Leem, 2002) and grading criteria. The literature was clear—students can easily tell when the CMC discussion serves as an add-on course feature, indicating a fairly low level of importance to the students (Chong, 1998). Ungraded tasks and tasks that result in little feedback from peers and instructors are regarded as busy work and disregarded by learners (Bonk, Malikowski, Angeli, & East, 1998; Vrasidas &McIsaac, 1999).

Therefore, participation in my online discussions was required and was incorporated into the final grade for the course. However, I soon discovered that whereas some students would meet all course requirements without hesitancy or question in order to earn an A, other students would determine whether to participate in online discussions based on the value they held for (a) *talk* as a learning process and (b) the discussion topics as relevant to meeting their personal or professional goals. Some students still did not participate as they distinguished *talk* from getting something done (Mercer, 2000).

LaPointe (2003) found an extensive array of course requirements and instructions given to learners regarding participation in online discussions in a study of 30 online courses offered throughout the United States. Participation in peer interaction was required in 26 of the 30 courses (86.67%). Interestingly, 46.15% of the courses that required participation in the online discussion did not mention a requirement for the frequency or the nature of posting messages in the course syllabi or course outlines. Overall, course requirements to participate had no significant effect on learner participation in online discussion, although the finding could have been related to extreme variation in course requirements for participation (LaPointe, 2003).

PURSUING INTERACTION—LOOKING FOR PROCESSING

One young online learner enrolled in an associate degree course told me during an interview that he preferred online discussions over face-to-face (f2f) discussions. In online courses, he was able to *hear* not just a variety of thoughts and perspectives, but he had the opportunity to hear other people's thought processes. In the f2f classroom, he was usually exposed to approximately three to four thinking processes throughout the semester—his instructor's plus the other two to three classmates who usually spoke up. One classmate usually took a negative, argumentative approach to information presented. A second classmate always asked for clarification of the content for her personal use.

This young learner unknowingly broadened my understanding of interaction beyond the mere affordances of the technology to post messages. The learner's statement made me think back to Gagné's (1985) theories of instruction, emphasizing intellectual skills, cognitive strategies, and attitudes. If analyses of the computer transcripts of a computer-mediated conference showed high levels of learning were absent, then possibly we needed to teach and model those processes. Alternatively, maybe I needed to design tasks or assign topics that required sustained interaction and higher levels of learning or more sophisticated processing such as analysis, synthesis, evaluation, and problem solving.

My previous definition and fascination with interaction had been focused on learners posting messages to facilitate higher levels of cognition but did not include teaching the components of analysis, synthesis, evaluation, critical thinking, or problem solving. I also had not taught engagement in dialogue. Would other learners like me who sat through years of lectures be able to post comments at higher levels of cognition? Would they know how to engage in as well as invite others to engage in dialogue? Where would they have seen and heard discussion modeled?

A variety of resources also proposed that other learners from teacher-centered classrooms come unprepared for exploratory discussions and problem solving, critical thinking, and reflection necessary for the sincere discussions I had in mind. Our perceptions of and behaviors in learning experiences are the accumulation of a long, developmental history and reflect expectations set up by the years of previous experience in classroom roles and relationships (Bownds, 1999). Knowing, believing, and self-understanding have their origins in social interchange (Gergen, 1999). These statements suggest that human behavior within a specific setting is not random but rather represents a prescribed sequence of interactions and behaviors among people and objects (Blanchard, 2004) in an environment. Everyone stays trapped in his or her mental models and acts—or reacts—to circumstances based on prior programming especially when entering new learning environments (Senge et al., 2004). Learners then do not come to an online course, knowing how to invite others into a dialogue. Without engaging others to first learn about their perspectives, there can be no subsequent sense of common purpose or co-construction of knowledge or a product (Murphy, 2004).

PURSUING INTERACTION—SEEKING DIALOGUE

Under a socio-constructivist learning paradigm, the opportunity for learning results when learners negotiate and construct meaning through dialogue with others and are responsible for contributing to the learning of all. The challenge for teachers is to integrate opportunities for dialogue and collaboration as well as to be prepared to address the criticisms of learners unaccustomed to learning in an autonomous yet socio-constructivist learning environment.

Being self-directed in a socio-constructivist perspective means taking the responsibility to listen to others with respect, draw others out, build on one another's ideas, challenge each other to support opinions, review beliefs, share resources, accept responsibility to make sense out of the experience for the individual learner as well as help others construct meaning for themselves. Learning in a socio-constructivist environment depends on effective communication and a complex set of procedural skills that develop only through use.

Therefore, I next sought information related generally to dialogue and discussion and specifically to supporting and scaffolding learner movement toward dialogue. Littleton and Hakkinen (1999) discuss three different types of talk—(a) disputational, (b) cumulative, and (c) exploratory. Disputational talk is characterized as aggressive attacking, unproductive disagreement, and unsupported, oppositional, and challenging responses. Participants work to keep their identities separate and to protect their self-identities (Mercer, 2000). Cumulative talk adds uncritically to

what was said before without discussion or only with superficial amend-
ment (Littleton & Hakkinen, 1999). In cumulative talk, speakers build on
each other's contributions and add information in a mutually supportive
but uncritical way (Mercer, 2000). Cumulative talk is based on ground
rules that uncritically accept partners' contributions with no effort made
to synthesize or weave contributions.

In contrast, exploratory talk refers to discussions where classmates are
actively and jointly engaged with each other's ideas. They set the topic or
idea in the middle of their virtual space, and they examine the topic from all
sides, above, and below. The idea is separate from the personalities in the
class. Classmates support their opinions with appropriate justifications,
recognize their underlying assumptions, propose alternative hypotheses,
provide space for negotiation, and use critical thinking skills. Through exploratory talk, learners suspend the obvious, listen to alternative framings
of reality, grapple with comparative outcomes of multiple standpoints, and
recognize the legitimacy of other points of view (Gergen, 1999). Knowledge
is made publicly accountable, and reasoning is visible (Mercer, 2000). Classmates reflect back on their understanding of messages posted, and contributions are woven into new knowledge. Exploratory talk invites dialogue
that can lead to collaboration, liberates learners from past experience, and
provides the opportunity for future learning.

Another conceptual framework useful for designing and guiding interaction is Murphy's (2004) SPICE collaboration model. The SPICE model is
built on a hierarchy of six stages—(a) learners' creating their social presence as real people to their classmates, (b) articulating their individual perspectives, (c) accommodating and reflecting back others' perspectives, (d)
co-constructing new perspectives and meanings, (e) building shared goals
and purposes, and (f) producing shared products. The first three stages are
the prerequisites and foundations for the final three.

These models suggest dialogue requires a learner to know himself or
herself, be well informed with an initial perspective to articulate, understand assumptions underlying that perspective, and have the courage to
contribute those perspectives. As well, the online learner must make a commitment, be humble, invite others to contribute, and reflect back and engage with the ideas of others. They are then responsible to go further and
co-create new perspectives with others. Learners who can employ such social autonomy will better master the full range of discourse roles upon
which effective communication (Little, 2002) and learning depend.

PURSUING INTERACTION—TASK DESIGN

To generate participation as well as to create a sense of the value in interacting with peers, learners must perceive value in the discussion and sense that

the task or assignment is structured in a way that is relevant to their learning needs, fits the natural learning cycle, and promotes interaction. To generate tasks that require collaboration and evoke higher levels of cognitive processing informed by conscious metacognitive processes, the instructor can design tasks using the case difficulty cube (Erskine, M. R. Leenders, & Mauffette-Leenders, 1963) and McGrath's circumplex (1984). Regardless of the guide used, assigned tasks must be challenging and intended to achieve more than promote undirected, unreflective, random exchanges and dumps of opinions (Garrison, 2000) and be appropriately rewarded; otherwise, learners will not move beyond their current developmental level.

The complexity of tasks and discussion topics can be analyzed using Erskine's case difficulty cube (Erskine et al., 1963). The cube examines task complexity from three dimensions—(a) an analytical dimension, (b) a conceptual dimension, and (c) a presentation dimension. The analytical dimension contains three levels. In Level 1, a question is posed to the learners. The question itself provides both the problem and solution and merely asks the learners to discuss whether the posed solution was appropriate. With a Level 2 task or topic, the instructor poses a problem, and learners discuss and determine the appropriate solution. In a Level 3 task, the instructor provides a scenario without setting out the problem or the solution. The conceptual dimension also contains three levels. Level 1 provides a simple, straightforward concept, easily recognized by keywords. A Level 2 conceptual task provides a combination of concepts, and Level 3 tasks set out many complex concepts. The presentation dimension also contains three levels. Level 1 provides students with relevant facts only. Level 2 provides relevant as well as extraneous data the learners must sift. Level 3 provides a large amount of relevant and extraneous data and omits essential data. The case difficulty cube serves as a framework for creating and analyzing assigned tasks to match task complexity and cognitive processing levels with desired course objectives and goals.

Using McGrath's circumplex, Hollingshead, McGrath, and O'Connor (1993) offer a method for analyzing tasks according to the degree of intersubjectivity required to accomplish the task. Hollingshead and colleagues (1993) described four task types, which are (a) generating ideas or plans, (b) choosing the correct answer, (c) choosing a preferred answer, and (d) negotiating conflicts of interest. The first three task types may be cooperative or competitive, depending on the manner in which the group divides, shares, and accomplishes its work; the last is both competitive and cooperative. These four task types reflect successively increasing degrees of interdependence among members, making consensus successively more difficult. Generating ideas or brainstorming tasks requires the group to generate as many ideas or solutions as possible. Brainstorming does not require the group to reach consensus and is easily conducted within CMC.

Intellective tasks require that group members find a demonstrably correct answer. Any group member with the correct answer should have little difficulty convincing other members to adopt the correct solution. Decision-making tasks make consensus more difficult for groups as no demonstrably correct solutions exist. Group members must reconcile their different information, attitudes, and opinions to reach consensus. Negotiation tasks present the largest barrier to group consensus as members have to reconcile their conflicts of interest as well as their different information, attitudes, and opinions. Completing these tasks will be problematic if group members have not learned to engage in exploratory talk.

Authentic problem solving presents another effective framework for designing tasks for online groups. The literature suggests that learning is meaning making that results from the complex process of real-world experience when students engage in authentic problems from real-life events and develop problem-solving strategies (McLoughlin & Luca, 2002). Engaging in problem solving enables learners to develop declarative, procedural, and contextual knowledge, essential in the professions and characteristic of the cognitive flexibility required in lifelong professional learning (McLoughlin & Luca, 2002). Through applying and testing abstract hypotheses in concrete experiences, information is gathered, organized, and rearranged through reflection and evaluation (Kolb, 1983). Abstract ideas are refined and externalized when the solutions to the problem are proposed and tested, and participants are either directly communicating or operating in the shared activity space (Avouris, Margaritis, & Komis, 2004). Smith and Stacey (2003) have written that problem-based learning activities are more successful when problems are identified by and require the divergent thinking and input from all learners rather than by instructors. All students can raise and explore divergent issues and solutions rather than merely agree to the one correct solution expected by the instructor. When people care about the questions that they ask and when their conversations are truly alive, participants naturally want to organize themselves to do whatever has to be done, discovering who cares about what, and who will take accountability for next steps. Collaborative groups then define and negotiate (a) the problem relating to their practice that needs to be investigated, (b) their timetable, (c) their work product and revisions, (d) the matching of their work product with course assessment requirements, and (e) the look of the final product (McConnell, 2003).

Problem-based learning, however, is not a free for all. In addition to interaction with peers, problem-based learning groups require an instructor's or facilitator's guidance toward useful conclusions and reflection. Orrill (2002) noted that despite two groups receiving the same assignment under the same guidelines, one group concerned itself with due dates and deliverables whereas the second group focused on problem solving, presenting data and ideas, asking questions, clarifying details, and voting among themselves. The first group posted syntheses of lists whereas the second posted summaries that synthesized individual ideas into a group understanding of key ideas. Orrill proposed that the second group's summarizations helped students focus on their thinking, kept their ideas alive, moved the conversation forward, and served as milestones of the group's achievement.

A study by Painter, Coffin, and Hewings (2003) observed the impacts of three tutorial groups led by three different tutors and found that the activities of the tutor influenced learner participation. The tutor for Group A was given no instructions for moderating an electronic conferencing over a 15-week period. The tutor for Group B encouraged students to post valid arguments. The Group C tutor required specific types of postings. The student who posted the least amount of messages in Group C matched the most prolific poster in Group A.

Rose and Flowers (2003) found assigning roles to learners involved in problem-based learning situations influenced the function, level, and interconnectedness of the group interaction. The researchers organized learners into six groups controlling for group process skill, major, location, and gender of four individuals and assigned each group to conduct and report a technology assessment. Some groups were assigned roles; other groups organized themselves. A comparison of groups found that assigning roles and responsibilities gave learners a common focus and helped students focus upon learning issues rather than coordinating group work.

Instructors also must be involved in evaluation throughout problem-based activities. Learners need more than formative feedback and assessment at the conclusion of problem-based learning; they need feedback throughout the duration of the activity to promote reflection and gain insight (Nurmi & Lainema, 2003). Gibson (2003) proposed an assessment model that provides (a) a conceptual model of how students represent knowledge and competence in the subject domain, (b) observation of all components of students' performance, (c) a presentation model that specifies how tasks will be rendered, (d) an interpretation method for drawing inferences from the performance evidence obtained, (e) an evidence model that specifies how to identify and evaluate feasibility of the work or product, and (f) a method for assembling and delivering assessments that specify how an assessment will be assembled or delivered. These can be presented as rubrics to inform and guide learners throughout the activities.

PURSUING INTERACTION—SYNCHRONOUS TECHNOLOGIES

Despite many years of online teaching experience, reflecting, generating, and testing, and thinking that I had finally learned to facilitate a dialogue that would reach effective learning outcomes, further research revealed more steps to take. Learner interviews conducted at the end of the fall 2004 semester revealed learners' needs and desires to interact spontaneously with classmates, mentors, and instructors to solve the assigned complex problems. One learner expressed his frustration, stating,

> I am paying extra money to take this course at a distance, yet I have less direct access to my instructor and classmates. I am working with an instructor I have never met; that causes me to instinctively distrust the professor; I cannot be sure she will know my needs as a learner.

Another learner said,

> I don't know if I'm "getting it" when I read others' postings. So I just post to meet the course requirements. I never return to see if anyone responds to me.

A graduate learner further described the laborious process of reading, thinking, reflecting, composing, correcting, and trying to post his message before the university server logged him off. He added, "I feel like a lone wolf in a box." Those statements led me to explore adding synchronous technology to my online course in order to better meet learner needs.

The literature resonated with what my learners were telling me. For instance, Mitchell, Banaji, and Macrae (2005) wrote that the degree to which learners can imagine they are engaged in interaction with others in an imagined, shared space is dependent on their own reflective abilities to create their engagement with the minds of other people. Research suggests that learners use observation, logical inference, (Gergen, 1999) and self-knowledge to infer the mental states and intent of others when the task that they are involved in requires them to understand the minds of others (Mitchell, Banaji, & Macrae, 2005). Without reciprocal feedback, there is no opportunity to dynamically negotiate another person's intended meaning, and discussions soon fragment and dissipate (Ahern & El-Hindi, 2000).

Since 2005, my online classes have included synchronous voice discussions. Synchronous virtual voice settings are appealing as learners gain the advantage of voice plus the contextual information of tone, enthusiasm, inflection, speed, as well as hesitation and silence to provide richer information. Processing and attention are stimulated by voice; there is correspondence between the acoustic information and the sensory functioning. A sense of place and class are fostered, based on the co-presence of others, and a sense of interdependence requiring accountability on behalf of each member is created—unlike asynchronous settings. Protocols, roles, turn taking, speed of responses, and consideration of others become critical for effective communication in the synchronous environment. Taking time out of a busy schedule to gather with classmates, mentors, and instructors reflects interest and attention. The co-presence and time-out features of synchronous CMC may increase the perceived sincerity of learners engaged in the online dialogue and better create the sense of class.

Synchronous voice interaction meets learner needs as well as creates additional technical issues for learners and instructors to troubleshoot. Learners and I have learned to troubleshoot compatibility issues involved with microphones, headsets, browsers, pop-up blockers, firewalls, and low-speed connections. However, we have enjoyed spontaneous, inspired discussions more similar to those experienced in on-campus seminar courses. Recently, though, an interview with a learner brought forth this dissatisfaction with the synchronous voice discussions:

> I need to see you and my classmates when we're talking; I need to see your visual cues, facial expressions, and body gestures.

Unfortunately, at my university at this time, there is no video solution that allows a class of 20 or more to multicast at an affordable price. Additionally, the slow-speed connections available to learners located throughout the state of New Mexico do not consistently support voice communication and will not reliably support video presentations. At this point in time, I have come to the end of the journey with regard to what I can solve through technology and tasks designed for sincere interaction. I now realize that learners have to help facilitate their learning by making adjustments on their end. It has become clear that my journey of focusing on interaction, on dialogue, and omitting learner autonomy was problematic. It is time to pursue Moore's concept of learner autonomy and responsibility, the concept I had earlier discarded as irrelevant.

PROMOTING LEARNER AUTONOMY

Historically, content in online learning environments has been presented as a means to an end rather than an end in itself, requiring the learner to make many choices about which material to use and how to use it (Oliver & Herrington, 2001). To make those choices, the autonomous, self-directed, proficient learner needs to know about and be comfortable with one's self as a learner and be familiar with one's learning strengths and weaknesses, preferences and dislikes, learning orientation, need for interaction, and locus of control in a variety of learning situations. Cognitive science and recent advances in neuroscience confirm that the learners in our classroom vary in what, why, and how they learn, seek and manage information, set goals, learn and perform, and evaluate. The instructor alone cannot design and teach to meet all learner preferences.

Today's learning management systems, digital libraries, and learning object repositories can help facilitate learner proficiency as digital technologies can allow learners to control their choice of resources and adapt presentation of information to learner needs. Learning systems can adapt to learner needs by matching psychological factors (Santally & Senteni, 2005). These psychological factors are cognitive style, learning orientation and strategy, learning modality, and skills. The system is based on simple adaptation rules that match the learner preferences and that provide the student with a set of learning objects matching to these preferences.

However, another partner who can assess and match learner needs in order to customize learning environments is the learner. By being aware of their cognitive style, learning strategy, learning modality, and skills, learners can better represent ideas and convert content into media they prefer. Learners must be able to determine what they know, what they need to know, what resources they need, and where to find them. They must develop and improve sophisticated learning skills—creative thinking, critical thinking, problem solving, project management—as well as inquire about and engage others' ideas. Because learners will find themselves in a variety of learning environments during their educational endeavors and ongoing professional careers, they need to be aware that their needs and preferences will change and adjust accordingly.

Such a proficient, independent learner, who starts, stops, and learns at his or her own pace, has historically been an integral part of distance education. In the distance education literature, autonomy has several meanings. First, autonomy can be seen as a teaching methodology, as a way of organizing instruction to control the goals and activities of the learning process (Garrison, 2003) with the instructors guiding learners (a) to become self-directed (Garrison, 2003) and (b) to increase learners' responsibility for their own learning processes (Bender, 2003). Autonomy is what the instructor does pedagogically that determines the extent to which learners assume responsibility for their learning (Garrison & Anderson, 2003). In this light, autonomy concerns the degree of control the learner has over the proportion, execution, and evaluation of his/her learning (Moore, 1986) and has been called the second dimension of Moore's theory of transactional distance (Moore, 1991).

Second, autonomy has also been defined as a predisposition of the learners to take control of and responsibility for learning (Garrison, 2003). An autonomous learner can establish a learning goal when faced with a problem to be solved, a skill to be acquired, or information that is lacking. He or she can set learning goals and define achievement. The autonomous learner knows (or discovers) where and how to gather the information required, collects ideas, and practices skills. When content is presented as text, the autonomous learner can convert the content to the form he or she prefers to work with, possibly sound files and concept maps. A learner with an external locus of control (Rotter, 1966) can establish timelines and project management skills. A learner with an independent sense of self-construal (Oetzel, 1997) will take steps to focus on group over individual achievement. When a field independent learner (Jonassen & Grabowksi, 1993) finds themselves taught by a field dependent instructor, they will seek opportunities to apply and problem solve. A resistant learner (Martinez & Bunderson, 2000) will acknowledge that his or her conflict with goals set by others adds to obstacles he or she faces in learning. After converting information to preferred formats, exploring divergent perspectives and Web sites, the autonomous learner can then judge the appropriateness of the information and ideas, deciding if learning goals have been achieved or whether learning strategies should be abandoned (Moore, 1986) and continue to construct knowledge based on his or her own experiences (Moore & Kearsley, 1996). The proficient autonomous learner studying in a socio-constructivist learning environment also recognizes and values his or her classmates as learning resources and inquires into and draws out classmates' thoughts, experiences, and perspectives. To develop learner proficiency in communicating through dialogue, helping others learn, and thinking critically and creatively, learners can use Paul's four kinds of questions (1993) as scaffolding. His questions are frequently incorporated into my assignments to help learners suspend their views and judgments long enough to examine their own as well as inquire into another's point of view. Paul's questions are (a) What is the origin of this thought? (b) What are reasons for and assumptions underlying this thought? (c) How would you answer others' objections to your position? (d) What are the practical consequences and actions that stem from this thought?

Rubrics for problem solving, evaluating learning resources, and presenting information can be created to support learners while they acquire sophisticated learning skills. The rubrics can distinguish levels of behavior into bad, better, best. For example in problem-based learning, framing a problem once is *bad;* revisiting the problem a second time as more information is learned is better; however, iteratively framing and returning to the information and reframing the problem is best.

Third, some authors wonder whether learner autonomy is an attribute of the learner's disposition or of the technology (Wheeler, 2003). The early generations of distance education technology presented an emphasis on independent study (Garrison & Anderson, 2003) as there were no practical ways to connect learners (Clark & Mayer, 2003). Today's technology provides computer-mediated conferencing to connect learners, yet is frequently portrayed as "any place, anywhere," "at the learner's convenience," and "24/7," which promotes the solo nature of learning. Even with the advent of computer-mediated communication and its use designed according to socio-constructive learning theories, the very nature of the technology used in flexible, online learning environments promotes and requires learner autonomy. The hypertext, hyperlinked attributes of online learning environments are open and give learners the ability to move outside the online classroom and visit other sites on the Web as opposed to the closed nature of a CD (Astleitner, 2003). The device-, distance-, and time-independent nature of the online environment endorses learner autonomy and presents a fact of life and challenge for the designer of and teacher in online environments. The digital environment provides nonsequential, multidirectional activity in online environments (Raschke, 2003), requiring learners themselves to decide how to proceed through the content as well as through the infinite hyperspace of learning resources available on the Web. Whether a learner sincerely "shows up" prepared for class and ready for dialogue with others then also depends on the path he or she selected through the content and learning resources.

Whether learner autonomy refers to a teaching methodology, the predisposition, capacity, or behavior of the learner, or an attribute of the technology, there is broad agreement that autonomous learners are assumed to understand the purpose of their learning program, to take responsibility for their learning, to share in setting their learning goals, to take initiative in planning and executing learning activities, and to regularly review their learning and evaluate its effectiveness (Little, 2002). For some, this will be liberating; for others, confusing (Bender, 2003).

Finally, from an educational perspective, the quality of learning outcomes is not simply a question of learner autonomy and responsibility. Although learner autonomy means learners take responsibility for their own learning, it does not mean that online learning environment is a free for all. The communities of practice, of which learners are potential members, share knowledge, address issues, and solve problems of relevance to learners. Consequently, learners must acquire the common cultural and professional knowledge expected of a member of a professional community of practice. The teacher, therefore, remains responsible for clarifying goals, shaping learning activities, assessing learning outcomes, and ensuring worthwhile outcomes and continuing efforts to learn (Garrison, 2003). The instructor serves as a facilitator and resource person, providing guidance dependent on the learner's ability for critical thinking and reflective ability, self-monitoring, and behavior (Marzano, 2001; Peters, 1998). Learner autonomy is very fitting with any framework underlying the online course design, but works especially well with constructivist learning as learner autonomy and independence of thought are important for construction of personal meaning in a social context mediated by interaction and collaboration.

CONCLUSION

Learning is an active, constructive, reflective process. Learners have to interact with others as well as set their own learning goals, determine their own effective learning strategies, and assess their own progress and results. Online learning, more than traditional classroom learning, demands autonomous learners who can prepare, perform, regulate, and evaluate their own learning while maintaining their own motivation and concentration (Mandl & Krause, 2003). Learner autonomy has received the most attention in distance education theory (Huang, 2002) followed closely by interaction. Today, descriptors of learner autonomy include taking the social initiative to invite others into a dialogue. Because the level of responsibility and autonomy is initially problematic for many online learners, the success of distance learning seems to be related to the extent to which the institution and the individual instructor are able to provide the appropriate structure of learning materials and appropriate quality of dialogue between teacher and students, taking into account both the extent and the development of the learner's autonomy (Gunawardena, 2004).

Senge and colleagues (2004) wrote that when people have problems to solve, they do not necessarily see or want to see any possible relationship between them and what the problem actually is. Therefore, we wind up being unable to see the problem accurately and may unwittingly contribute to maintaining the undesired situation. Although I may have deliberately pursued answers to the question that lies in my heart regarding my desire to effectively facilitate sincere interaction online in contrast to finding clarity and connection, the answer lies near. I believe the answer tempers a respect for dialogue and interaction with a respect for the autonomy and freedom of learners to first better know themselves so they, in turn, can make proficient choices regarding learning and then we can all sincerely engage in dialogue.

REFERENCES

Ahern, T. C., & El-Hindi, A. E. (2000). Improving the instructional congruency of a computer-mediated small-group discussion: A case study in design and delivery. *Journal of Research on Technology in Education, 32*(3), 385–400.

Anderson, T., Rourke, L., Archer, W., & Garrison, D. R. (2001). Assessing teaching presence in a computer conferencing context. *Journal of Asynchronous Learning Networks, 5*(2). Retrieved on April 22, 2006, from http://www.aln.org/alnweb/journal/jalnvol5issue2v2.htm

Andrusyszyn, M. A., van Soeren, M., Laschinger, H. S., Goldenberg, D., & DiCenso, A. (1999). Evaluation of distance education delivery methods for a primary care nurse practitioner program. *Journal of Distance Education, 14*(1), 14–33.

Astleitner, H. (2003). Web-based instruction and learning. In N. Nistor, S. English, & S. Wheeler (Eds.), *Towards the virtual university—International on-line learning perspectives* (pp. 37–63). Greenwich, CT: Information Age Publishing.

Avouris, N., Margaritis, M., & Komis, V. (2004, September). *Modelling interaction during small-group synchronous problem-solving activities: The Synergo approach.* Paper presented at the meeting of the 2nd International Workshop on Designing Computational Models of Collaborating Learning Interaction, Maceio, Brazil.

Bender, T. (2003). *Discussion-based online teaching to enhance student learning.* Sterling, VA: Stylus Publishing.

Berge, Z. L. (1999). Interaction in post-secondary Web-based learning. *Educational Technology, 39*(1), 5–11.

Blanchard, A. (2004). Virtual behavior settings: An application of behavior setting theories to virtual communities. *Journal of Computer Mediated Communication, 9*(2). Retrieved December 9, 2004, from http://jcmc.indiana.edu/vol9/issue2/blanchard.html

Bonk, C. J., Malikowski, S., Angeli, C., & East, J. (1998). Web-based case conferencing for preservice teacher education: Electronic discourse from the field. *Journal of Educational Computing Research, 19*(3), 269–306.

Bownds, M. D. (1999). *The biology of the mind: Origins and structures of mind, brain, and consciousness*. Bethesda, MD: Fitzgerald Science Press.

Brookfield, S. D. (1986). *Understanding and facilitating adult learning*. San Francisco, CA: Jossey-Bass.

Chong, S. M. (1998). Models of asynchronous computer conferencing for collaborative learning in large college classes. In C. J. Bonk & K. S. King (Eds.), *Electronic collaborators: Learner-centered technologies for literacy, apprenticeship, and discourse* (pp. 157–182). Mahwah, NJ: Lawrence Erlbaum Associates.

Clark, R. C., & Mayer, R. E. (2002). *e-Learning and the science of instruction*. San Francisco, CA: Wiley.

Dillenbourg, P. (1999). Introduction: What do you mean by "collaborative learning"? In P. Dillenbourg (Ed.), *Collaborative learning: Cognitive and computational approaches* (pp. 1–19). New York: Pergamon.

Erskine, J. A., Leenders, M. R., & Mauffette-Leenders, L. A. (1963). *Teaching with cases*. Ontario, Canada: University of Western Ontario, Richard Ivey School of Business.

Gagné, R. M. (1985). *The conditions of learning and theory of instruction* (4th ed.). New York: Holt, Rinehart, & Winston

Garrison, D. R. (2000). Theoretical challenges for distance education in the 21st century: A shift from structural to transactional issues. *International Review of Research in open and distance learning, 1*(1). Retrieved November 2, 2001, from http://www.icaap.org/iuicode?149.1.1.2

Garrison, D. R. (2003). Self-directed learning and distance education. In M. G. Moore & W. G. Anderson (Eds.), *Handbook of distance education* (pp. 161–168). Mahwah, NJ: Lawrence Erlbaum Associates.

Garrison, D. R., & Anderson, T. (2003). *E-learning in the 21st century: A framework for research and practice*. New York: RoutledgeFalmer.

Garrison, D. R., & Cleveland-Innes, M. (2005). Facilitating cognitive presence in online learning: Interaction is not enough. *The American Journal of Distance Education, 19*(3), 133–148.

Gergen, K. J. (1999). *An invitation to social construction*. Thousand Oaks, CA: Sage.

Gibson, D. (2003). Network-based assessment in education. *Contemporary Issues in Technology and Teacher Education*. Retrieved February 2, 2004, from http://www.cite journal.org/vol3/iss3/general/article1.cm

Gunawardena, C. N. (2004). The challenge of designing inquiry-based online learning environments: Theory into practice. In T. M. Duffy & J. R. Kirkley (Eds.), *Learner-centered theory and practice in distance education* (pp. 143–158). Mahwah, NJ: Lawrence Erlbaum Associates.

Gunawardena, C. N., Lowe, C. A., & Anderson, T. (1997). Analysis of a global online debate and the development of an interaction analysis model for examining social construction of knowledge in computer conferencing. *Journal of Educational Computing Research, 17*(4), 397–431.

Gunawardena, C., Plass, J., & Salisbury, M. (2001). Do we really need an online discussion group? In D. Murphy, R. Walker, & G. Webb (Eds.), *Online technology and teaching with technology: Case studies, experience and practice* (pp. 36–43). Sterling, VA: Stylus Publishing.

Henri, F. (1992). Computer conferencing and content analysis. In A. R. Kaye (Ed.), *Collaborative learning through computer conferencing: The Najaden papers* (pp. 115–136). New York: Springer.

Herring, S. (1999). Interactional coherence in CMC. *Journal of Computer-Mediated Communication, 4*(4). Retrieved December 4, 2004, from http://jcmc.indiana.edu/vol4/issue4/herring.html

Hewitt, J. (2003, April). *Toward an understanding of how threads die in asynchronous computer conferences*. Paper presented at the meeting of the American Educational Research Association, Chicago, IL.

Hillman, D. C. A., Willis, D. J., & Gunawardena, C. N. (1994). Learner-interface interaction in distance education: An extension of contemporary models and strategies for practitioners. *The American Journal of Distance Education, 8*(2), 30–42.

Hollingshead, A. B., McGrath, J. E., & O'Connor, K. M. (1993). Group task performance and communication technology: A longitudinal study of computer-mediated versus face-to-face work groups. *Small Group Research, 24*(3), 307–333.

Huang, H.-M. (2002). Student perceptions in an online mediated environment. *International Journal of Instructional Media, 29*(4), 405–422.

Jonassen, D. H., & Grabowski, B. L. (1993). Field dependence and field independence (global vs. articulated style). In *Handbook of individual differences, learning, and instruction* (pp. 87–104). London, England: Lawrence Erlbaum Associates.

Jung, I., Choi, S., Lim, C., & Leem, J. (2002). Effects of different types of interaction on learning achievement, satisfaction and participation in web-based instruction. *Innovations in Education and Teaching International, 39*(2), 153–162.

Kanuka, H., & Anderson, T. (1998). On-line interchange, discord, and knowledge construction. *Journal of Distance Education, 13*(1), 57–74.

Knowles, M. (1980). *The modern practice of adult education: From pedagogy to andragogy* (2nd ed.). New York: Cambridge Books.

Kolb, D. (1983). *Experiential learning*. New York: Simon & Schuster.

LaPointe, D. K. (2003). *Effects of peer interaction facilitated by computer-mediated conferencing on learning outcomes*. Unpublished doctoral dissertation, University of New Mexico, Albuquerque.

Little, D. (2002). Learner autonomy and second/foreign language learning. In *The guide to good practice for learning and teaching in languages, linguistics and area studies*. LTSN Subject Centre for Languages, Linguistics and Area Studies, University of Southampton. Retrieved June 11, 2004, from http://www.lang.ltsn.ac.uk/resources/goodpractice.aspx?resourceid=1409

Littleton, K., & Hakkinen, P. (1999). Learning together: Understanding the processes of computer-based collaborative learning. In P. Dillenbourg (Ed.), *Collaborative learning: Cognitive and computational approaches* (pp. 20–30). New York: Pergamon.

Mandl, H., & Krause, U. M. (2003). Learning competence for the knowledge society. In N. Nistor, S. English, S. Wheeler, & M. Jalobeanu (Eds.), *Toward the virtual university: International online perspective* (pp. 65–86.) Greenwich, CT: Information Age Publishing.

Martinez, M., & Bunderson, C. V. (2000). Building interactive world wide web (web) learning environments to match and support individual learning differences. *Journal of Interactive Learning Research, 11*(2), 163–195.

Marzano, R. J. (2001). *Designing a new taxonomy of educational objectives*. Thousand Oaks, CA: Corwin Press.

McConnell, D. (2003). Action research and distributed problem-based learning in continuing professional education. *Distance Education, 23*(1), 59–83.

McGrath, J. E. (1984). *Groups: Interaction and performance*. Englewood Cliffs, NJ: Prentice-Hall.

McLoughlin, C., & Luca, J. (2002). A learner-centred approach to team skills through web-based learning and assessment. *British Journal of Educational Technology, 33*(5), 571–572.

Mercer, N. (2000). *Words and minds: How we use language to think together*. New York: Routledge.

Mitchell, J. P., Mahzarin, R. B., & Macrae, C. N. (2005). The link between social cognition and self-referential thought in the medial prefrontal cortex. *Journal of Cognitive Science*. Retrieved July 21, 2005, from http://webscript.princeton.edu/~psych/psychology/related/socneuconf/pdf/mitchell-banaji-macrae.pdf

Moore, M. G. (1980). Independent study. In R. Boyd & J. Apps (Eds.), *Redefining the discipline of adult education*. San Francisco, CA: Jossey-Bass. Retrieved November 2, 2004, from http://www.ajde.com/Documents/independent_study.pdf

Moore, M. G. (1986). Self-directed learning and distance education. *Journal of Distance Education, 1* (1). Retrieved December 11, 2005, from http://cade.athabascau.ca/vol1.1/moore.html

Moore, M. G. (1989). Three types of interaction. *The American Journal of Distance Education, 3*(2), 1–6.

Moore, M. G. (1991). Editorial: Distance education theory. *American Journal of Distance Education, 5*(3), 10–15.

Murphy, E. (2004). Recognising and promoting collaboration in an online asynchronous discussion. *British Journal of Educational Technology 35*(4), 421–431.

Nurmi, S., & Lainema, T. (2003, August). *Enriching business education with complex, real-time based business game simulation*. Paper presented at the meeting of the EARLI 2003 Conference, Padova, Italy.

Oetzel, J. (1997). Exploring the relationship between self-construal and dimensions of group effectiveness. *Management Communication Quarterly, 10*(3), 289–318.

Oliver, R., & Herrington, J. (2002). *Teaching and learning online: A beginner's guide to e-learning and e-teaching in higher education*. Perth, WA: Edith Cowan University.

Orrill, C. H. (2002). Supporting online PBL: Design considerations for supporting distributed problem solving. *Distance Education, 23*(1), 41–58.

Painter, C., Coffin, C., & Hewings, A. (2003). Impacts of directed tutorial activities in computer conferencing: A case study. *Distance Education, 24*(2), 159–174.

Pargman, D. (2000). *Code begets community: On social and technical aspects of managing a virtual community*. Unpublished doctoral dissertation, Linkoping Universitet, Sweden. Retrieved December 9, 2004, from http://esplanaden.lysator.liu.se/svmud/pargman/

Paul, R. (1993). *Critical thinking, moral integrity, and citizenship: Teaching for the intellectual values*. Santa Rosa, CA: Foundation for Critical Thinking.

Peters, O. (1998). *Learning and teaching in distance education: Analysis and interpretations from an international perspective*. London: Kogan Page.

Raschke, C. A. (2003). *The digital revolution and the coming of the postmodern university*. New York,: RoutledgeFalmer.

Rose, M. A., & Flowers, J. (2003, August). Assigning learning roles to promote critical discussions during problem-based learning. *Proceedings of the 19th Annual Conference on Distance Teaching and Learning*, Madison, WI.

Rotter, J. B. (1966). Generalized expectancies for internal versus external control of reinforcement. *Psychological Monographs, 80* (1, Whole No. 609).

Santally, M. I., & Senteni, A. (2005). A learning object approach to personalized web-based instruction. *European Journal of Open, Distance and E-Learning*. Retrieved November 28, 2005, from http://www.eurodl.org/materials/contrib/2005/Santally.htm

Senge, P., Scharmer, C. O., Jaworski, J., & Flowers, B. S. (2004). *Presence: An exploration of profound change in people, organizations, and society.* New York: Currency Doubleday.

Siegel, J., Dubrovsky, V., Kiesler, S., & McGuire, T. W. (1986). Group processes in computer-mediated communication. *Organizational Behavior and Human Decision Processes, 37,* 157–187.

Smith, P., & Stacey, E. (2003). Socialization through CMC in differently structured environments. In S. Naidu (Ed.), *Learning and teaching with technology: Principles and practices* (pp. 165–176). London: Kogan Page.

Swan, K., Shea, P., Fredericksen, E., Pickette, A., Pelz, W., & Maher, G. (2000). Building knowledge building communities: Consistency, contact, and communication in the virtual classroom. *Journal of Educational Computing Research, 23*(4), 359–383.

Verneil, M., & Berge, Z. L. (2000). Going online: Guidelines for faculty in higher education. *International Journal of Educational Telecommunications, 6*(3), 227–242.

Vrasidas, C., & McIsaac, M. S. (1999). Factors influencing interaction in an online course. *The American Journal of Distance Education, 13*(3), 22–36.

Vygotsky, L. S. (1978). The development of perception and attention. In M. Cole, V. John-Steiner, S. Scribner, & E. Souberman (Eds.), *Mind in society. The development of higher psychological processes.* Cambridge, MA: Harvard University Press.

Wheeler, S. (2003). Web-based learning and transactional distance theory. In N. Nistor, S. English, S. Wheeler, & M. Jalobeanu (Eds.), *Toward the virtual university: International online perspectives* (pp. 87–99). Greenwich, CT: Information Age Publishing.

Chapter 7

Online Teaching Experiences in Higher Education: Obstacles and Opportunities

Lya Visser
Learning Development Institute

As the title of this book "Finding Your Online Voice" already suggests, this chapter brings forward a personal voice and largely builds on personal online teaching and learning experiences. The focus of this chapter is thus on teaching and learning methods that I have found to work, that have made online teaching a pleasant (learning) experience for me, as the instructor, and that have contributed to apparently effective learning for my students. My claim to validity is, therefore, a modest one. I am not trying to prove anything; I limit myself to discussing my own experiences, backing them up by referring to what I have learned from my students and colleagues and from research in the field.

Distance education has grown considerably in the last two decades. Currently 60% of graduate schools that offer face-to-face programs also offer online graduate programs. This means that a sizable proportion of those who teach in these institutions (also) do so online. This is a trend that is expected to continue. Sharing experiences, discussing opportunities and challenges, and consulting the existing research will contribute to making it easier for us, the instructors, to become successful, efficient, and effective online facilitators. In this way we, as online instructors, will hopefully incorporate the positive experiences and lessons learned in our teaching and avoid the negative ones.

In this chapter, we first look at what motivates faculty to teach online, followed by a personal account about what motivates me to teach online. After this, we look at a number of experiences of both online instructors and online learners. Then we discuss the need for instructors to know what the learners expect from their online instruction. The last part then deals with student motivation, a practical application of influencing motivation, and the role of communication in online teaching and learning. A summary of the lessons learned ends this chapter.

The various sections are designed in such a way that each includes theory and research related to practical examples of problems encountered and solutions that have worked, or sometimes that have not worked.

WHAT MOTIVATES FACULTY TO TEACH ONLINE COURSES?

From 2003 to 2004, online enrollment in the United States increased from 1.98 million to 2.35 million (Sloan Consortium, http://www.sloan-c.org/resources/survey.asp), continuing a trend that has been established over the past decade. It is likely that more online instructors will continue to be needed and that increasing numbers of those instructors who previously taught in face-to-face settings may get involved in online teaching. In all probability, some will gladly accept the challenge, whereas others may do so only reluctantly.

Management theorist, Peter Drucker, predicted some 10 years ago that higher education institutions in their current form will be relics in a matter of a few short years. His message was clear: Change or die (Lenzer, 1997). Regardless of whether faculty consider online education a positive or negative development, they may have to adapt and change with the times. Teachers do need time to rethink the evolving traits, to examine the learning environment changes, and to redefine their roles in a changing learning community.

Some instructors have positive feelings about online instruction whereas others feel it as a threat or even hate having to do this. Table 7.1 shows how challenges may work out differently for different people.

The online instructors' motivation will, of course, be considerably influenced by whether their attitudes mostly fit in Column 2 or in Column 3. We have to show understanding and to take into consideration that most instructors nowadays already face a number of challenges such as decreased funding, increased workloads, and the more prominent role of technology, all of these may contribute to a lack of confidence and a decreased motivation to face the challenges ahead. Attitudes are not static and may change. Encouraging processes that make the change from tradi-

TABLE 7.1
Positive and Negative Feelings of Instructors

Challenge	Positive Feelings/Reasons	Negative Feelings/Reasons
Use of technology	Expanding horizons, learning more about technology, staying abreast	Frightening and frustrating, takes time to get accustomed to
Irregular work schedule	Gives freedom, allows for adaptation of personal life. No need to travel to campus all the time	Makes life more complicated, cannot be accommodated in personal life. May mean more work
Changing role of instructor from knowledge owner to facilitator	Sharing of knowledge and learning from students. Opportunities to try out innovative practices	Status of instructor's role may be at risk. Only the instructor knows what is good for students. More freedom adds to more chaos

Note. Adapted from McVay, 2002.

tional teaching to online teaching a smooth one, can considerably influence the attitude of the instructor.

WHAT MOTIVATES ME TO TEACH ONLINE?

What motivates me to teach online? The answer is a simple one. I teach first and foremost because I love people—I like to interact, learn from people, and share my experience of the world, the things that I consider to be important in becoming better human beings, more effective professionals, more efficient and effective communicators, in short conscientious humans who function well in a complex and ever-changing world. My principle intrinsic motivation is self-fulfillment—doing something that I like to do and working hard to do it better every time. A second motivator is that I would like to get a better understanding of how people learn, what causes certain people to do certain things and not to do other things. Is it possible to influence people, to help them to complete courses successfully, and to ensure that they stay motivated? In this context, I have sought to understand more about effective approaches to learning, including improved communication skills and effective motivational "tactics" to enrich the online experience.

Growing up in a school environment where asking questions was not encouraged, where having doubts (a form of critical thinking) was seen as negative, was not always a very positive experience. Later on, however, when getting the opportunity to teach, these experiences challenged me to try to do better, to encourage questioning and critical thoughts, to foster curiosity and to challenge opinions. Lastly, the possibilities and the particular attributes of online teaching appeal to me because I have worked for more than 20 years in countries where students are underserved and where the geographical and social distribution makes it difficult to participate in traditional tertiary education. In such contexts, distance education can be an important means of making education more accessible and of increasing equity.

My intrinsic motivation is closely related to the five intrinsic motives that Wolcott and Betts (1999) mention:

- Personal or socially derived satisfaction (working with people who otherwise may not get a chance to study).
- Personal/professional growth (learning more about a field that I do not know very well).
- Personal challenge (become a more versatile professional).
- Humane concerns (decrease problems of equity).
- Career enhancing motives (be better prepared for an ever challenging and changing job market and world of work).

In the next section, I look in more detail at the experiences of those teaching and learning online.

ONLINE INSTRUCTORS, ONLINE LEARNERS, AND ONLINE EXPERIENCES

Those of us who have become instructors in traditional settings may look back at their school days and incorporate their positive learning experiences in their teaching and carefully avoid what they have experienced as negative. Online teaching and learning is different from traditional teaching and learning. Students, who for the first time engage in online learning, may feel somewhat lost, may have an instructor they have never met, may have classmates that come from different states or even different countries, may encounter technology that may be a challenge, and may be expected to accept more responsibility for their own learning processes. Online instructors may share some of these same experiences, and advanced technologies may present specific challenges. Many online instructors have not, unfortunately, had the experience of having been an online learner. They may look at online learning from the perspective of an outsider and without some of the benefits that I argue come from the experience of having been a distance education student. It may thus sometimes be difficult for online instructors to imagine how online students feel if they, for instance, have to wait for feedback for weeks, for an answer to a simple question for days, or receive a reply that is ambiguous. In a face-to-face context, the instructor often has a strong physical presence during lectures (class instruction) and may actively encourage discussion and polemics. In the online context, however, instructors are often perceived as much more absent, quite a few students even experience an almost total absence of the instructor who may choose not to get involved. This may have important consequences, particularly given that research has shown that student satisfaction is highly correlated with interaction with the instructor (Shea, Fredericksen, Pickett, & Peltz, 2003; Trippe, 2001). "I have had online instructors who have constantly been absent, they only once or twice got in touch with us during the 16-week course," remarked one of my students recently when reflecting on the various experiences with online education he had had. Another student wrote: "The silence of the instructor depresses me."

There is a real challenge to studying alone and being isolated. Traditionally, isolation and distance education have been closely linked over the years. Isolation of the student can be the result of bad course design or of not fully exploiting the opportunities online learning offers (Harasim, Hiltz, Teles, & Turoff, 1997), but it can be compounded by instructors who are not very responsive or understandable and who react slowly. As a distance education student, I often felt isolated. There was hardly any contact with the instructor, feedback on assignments took a long time, sometimes up to 6 weeks. This was partly due to the reliance on traditional means of communication—that is to say, receiving and sending the assignments through regular mail—although this was in an era when e-mail communication was starting to become mainstream. With regard to that early distance learning experience facilitated by regular mail, the fact that I could not orally explain that I had not understood a topic, and indicate that for me there was another important issue, or say that an adequate solution to a problem had been overlooked, was frustrating.

I end this section by giving two examples of instructor interventions that made a real difference to me as a distance education student. Almost 30 years ago, I was living and working in Botswana and doing a bachelor's degree in English in a traditional correspondence program. In one of the courses, contact with the instructor was very poor, especially in the second year. It was only when this second year instructor became ill and was substituted by one of my first year instructors that I realized what a big difference a caring instructor makes. My first year instructor sent me my corrected paper back with some very basic suggestions as was then the custom: "check on page 18 of ..." and then came the name of the grammar book. She added one sentence that I will never forget: "Still going strong I see!" Even now, almost 30 years later, I recall these five words and my reaction "here is someone who cares."

In the beginning of the 1990s, I decided to enroll in a master's in education external program of a British University. It consisted of four basic courses/ modules of 250 hours each, three electives also of 250 hours each, and a research project. Student support was still very basic: Course materials in a box, supported by audiocassettes and the occasional videocassette. For each course, two assignments had to be submitted; at the end, there was a written exam to be taken at the British Embassy. Feedback on assignments, although often delayed, was generally good. There was no contact whatsoever with the other students and no other contact than through assignments with the instructor. Although I finished the program successfully and in time, it had been very hard. Here again, one instructor made a difference. Discussing some research I had done for one of my courses, he said: "You could use these data when you are doing your doctoral work." This seemingly small remark made a big difference at the time. I concluded that he was not only sure that I would successfully finish my masters degree, but also that he thought that I could go on for a doctoral degree, something that I, a few years earlier, never would have considered. It was this experience that led to my dissertation research in motivational communication, which I discuss later in this chapter.

It is encouraging to note that there is increasing recognition for the need to provide more effective support to students. One concrete example comes from the United Kingdom. There, to create more understanding for the position of online learners, a division of the Open University has mandated its instructors to enroll in at least one online course, so that they get the feeling of what it is to be an online student.

Feelings of isolation can be diminished and possibly overcome by providing ample opportunities for interaction with the students and among them. Here are some helpful ideas, some of them suggested by McVay (2002):

- Establish electronic office hours for the instructor.
- Send a personal welcome letter.
- Invite students to introduce themselves to each other and to you, and introduce yourself to them.
- Establish a communication style (formal or informal).
- Check in with students regularly and get them to show presence.
- Involve students in the teaching learning process.

To be effective as an online instructor, it is important to know the needs and wants of the students. The next section discusses ways and means to get to know these needs.

WHAT DO STUDENTS EXPECT
FROM THEIR ONLINE INSTRUCTOR?

The expectations online students have about the interaction with their instructor may differ considerably. In one of my courses, I sent out a questionnaire about the expectations of students as regards student support. The answers from the international students ranged from "keeping me on track" to "phoning me every 2 weeks."

Students clearly had, in some cases, different perceptions of student support than did instructors. Exploratory research, looking at the expectations of distance education students regarding student support and the instructors' perceptions of student support expectations, showed a divergence as is seen in Table 7.2.

Given that the numbers were small, we should consider the previous results merely as indications. This is, however, in my opinion clearly an area where more research should be done.

Cultural contexts may play a role as was demonstrated in an exploratory study involving online students from a university in the United Kingdom and a university in Hong Kong. Online students in Hong Kong expected the instructor to give explicit guidance, to tell them what to do, how to do it, when to do it, and to indicate where they could find the answers to problems they had to solve. There was less emphasis on initiative, creativity, and critical thinking. Their preference was to enroll in a "course in a box," with clearly defined chunks of teaching and applying, so that the students who

TABLE 7.2
Divergence of Student and Instructor Perceptions

Question	Students' Answers	Instructors' Answers
Who is the most useful source of student support?		
Instructor	76%	86%
Librarian	13%	0%
Peer group	11%	14%
Identify the most important type of student support in distance learning:		
Academic support	62%	51%
Administrative support	20%	16%
Motivational support	18%	16%
No answer		7%
Identify the area where you need most affective support:		
Staying/becoming motivated	32%	33%
Coping with the traditional isolation of the d.e. learner	39%	
Problems related to self-confidence	21%	35%
No answer	8%	32%

Note. L. Visser & Y. L. Visser, 2000.

did the required readings contained in the study materials and the assigned exercises, would most likely pass the course. Students in the United Kingdom, on the other hand, expected the instructor to give a high quality lecture online, and/or to provide printed notes, and to encourage them to engage in finding resources and using their own creativity to find solutions to set problems. Their dependence on the instructor only showed in their wish to get quick, efficient, and effective feedback (L. Visser & J. L. Visser, 2000). On the other hand, students from Venezuela enrolled in an online masters' program formed study groups right from the beginning and expected the instructor to set groupwork and then to give feedback to individual groups and only occasionally involve the whole class. Although the examples given earlier relate to an international audience, I have seen the same cultural differences in online classes in the United States, where, for instance Hispanic students were enrolled.

The different needs and wants of students can still be problematic even in a context where the instructor thinks they know the expectations of the students. Last semester's example illustrates this. Luc (not the student's real name) had sent in a draft of an assignment. The instructor made a number of observations and suggestions so that Luc could improve the assignment. A week later, Luc submitted the final version of his assignment. It was returned to Luc with a B+ grade. The latter complained immediately stating that the instructor had failed to indicate in the draft paper every small item that had to be dealt with. Referring to suggestions the instructor had made that could have enriched the assignment, Luc wrote: "Why was this feedback not included in my draft? I added and made all changed [sic] you mentioned in my draft document, however, the comments you made in my final were not all made in my draft paper. If they were I would have addressed those concerns to better show my comprehension of the concepts." On the other hand, Marlies (fictitious name), another student, had another opinion. After she received feedback on her draft assignment she wrote: "Thanks for putting me into the right direction—it was helpful."

THE ROLE OF MOTIVATION AND COMMUNICATION IN ONLINE TEACHING AND LEARNING

We have already briefly discussed the importance of motivation. Motivation refers to the choices people make and to the goals they want to realize and, of course, to the effort people are prepared to put into the realization of these goals. This section looks at the role of motivation and of communication in online teaching and ultimately leads us to the use of motivational messages in distance education.

Motivation plays an important role in course completion. This was recognized by Briggs (1980) who stated that our theories or models of design
do not sufficiently take motivation into account, by Bohlin (1987) who considered motivation the backbone of instruction, and by Keller (1998) who
sees motivation as one of the main influences on performance. We instructors can help learners to set and maintain their motivational levels by attending to their perceived motivational needs. In order to do so, it is crucial
that we have initial basic information about the students, that we put sufficient effort into staying in touch with them, and that we communicate with
them in a caring and affective way that shows real (not fake) interest. Students seem to be very observant as to whether the interest of the tutor is real.
A comment on an introductory letter I sent out at the beginning of an online
university course read: "Thank you for your caring letter – better than the
usual introductory letters, devoid of any real interest in the student." Showing real interest and care may be easier in a face-to-face instructional context than in online instruction. Body posture, facial expressions, and the
speaker's voice are not easily transmitted in an online context. The online
education environment is, in spite of the many technological advances, still
not effective enough in substituting social cues such as a pat on the shoul-
der, a wink, or an encouraging smile that can be so effective in face-to-face
teaching and learning situation. The absence of social cues, and the lack of
opportunities for small talk, so often used in face-to-face classes to get to
know each other better, may make our communication with the students
more limited and poorer. We often have to use written words to substitute
these affective contacts. For students, and equally for instructors, this is not
always easy, especially if they are new to online teaching and learning.
There is hope that with the increase of the use of computer mediated communication, both the student and the instructor will have better opportunities for interacting in such a way as to compensate for the absence of face-
to-face (social) communication patterns.

To overcome some of the previously identified challenges, my current
approach is to establish contact with my online students by asking them at
the beginning of a course to e-mail me a PowerPoint slide with their photo
and with a short description of their work and private life. I react, solicit additional information if useful, and encourage them to post the slide so that
classmates also have access to the information. Most of the time, this exercise works well. The photos often tell a lot and may give some social cues as
was the case with the photo of a student sitting at his desk surrounded by all
kinds of technology, indicating with arrows what he used the technology
for, or that of another student reading a story to one of his children. In turn,
I also post information about myself. For my own reference, I print the
PowerPoint slides and especially during the first month, I make sure that I
have them available in online discussions or when I give feedback so that I

can refer back to specific expectations or issues that the students raised in their initial contact with me.

In face-to-face classes, discussions with students mostly take place in real time, that is to say face-to-face in the classroom or during office hours. On-line communication, on the contrary, can be divided into two different modes; synchronous, where the people who interact are at the same time online and can type messages to each other and respond (real time or near real time), and asynchronous, where people who are interacting are not on-line at the same time (e-mail, threaded discussions, and listservs, for instance). The main difference is that asynchronous communication is delayed—the answer may come hours or days later. It can happen that Ben, who had sent an e-mail that he is struggling with his assignment and does not see how he can send it in on time, may get an answer from the instructor by the time that he is much more optimistic (he may have arranged for 2 days study leave). Or take the case of Lydga (fictitious name) who may write that the lecture was not clear to her: "I'm overwhelmed, overwhelmed, overwhelmed." The instructor may write a motivational message encouraging Lydga to read the lecture a couple of times, make notes and/or get in touch with a classmate. It turns out that by the time Lydga receives this e-mail, she has already contacted Miriam (fictitious name) and she feels much better about the lecture. These cases happen frequently and emphasize the need for the instructor to try to reply without delay. It could, however, also be useful to add a line in the answer to the student indicating that circumstances may have changed and/or the problem may already have been solved. "Although it is likely that you feel much better now, I think that it would be useful to…" Or in the second case "Even as re-reading the lecture and making notes may have been effective, I think it is helpful if I suggest that getting in touch with a classmate is often very useful."

AFFECTIVE AND EFFECTIVE COMMUNICATION

We have already recognized the importance of motivation and now discuss the role of communication in teaching learning processes, later on combining the two concepts in motivational communication.

Effective communication is results based and requires careful and profound reflection on how, when, and what to communicate. We should focus on communication processes that are conducive to learning, that encourage and foster learning processes. Rogers (1962) wrote a groundbreaking article in which he argued that the quality of the interpersonal encounter with the client, in our case the student, is extremely important in building a relationship and in allowing this relationship to grow in a mutually satisfying manner. He identified three behaviors that form the basis for successful communication; open disclosure, warm affirmation, and empathic comprehension.

Open disclosure means that the relationship is mutual and is based on more than the minimum information necessary to work together. In face-to-face classes it often happens that students have more information about the instructor than the bare minimum. Students may know where their instructors have studied, where they live, what kind of car they drive. They may meet their instructors at parties, seminars, and/or sport events. Creating an environment of open disclosure is a much greater challenge in online learning environments. The absence of face-to-face interaction creates a barrier that makes it difficult and sometimes undesirable to engage in nonacademic topics. This may cause the instructor and the student to stay, in the real sense of the word, at a distance. I experienced the same in one of the online courses that I recently taught. Students in one of the MA modules had to write a short assignment on performance improvement strategies, and then use their own professional environment to indicate how they thought that they could use certain performance improvement strategies effectively in their work environment. The first part of the assignment had to be a short description of their work situation. Michael (fictitious name) wrote a paragraph describing his work environment as not flexible and not open to change; his colleagues were traditional workers, not keen on challenges. I commented on the paper in a personal e-mail and wrote a short remark: "It looks as if you are a little bit depressed in the way you write about your daily tasks." Michael was deeply offended and sent me an e-mail complaining "I find your comment: 'It looks as if you are a little bit depressed in the way you write about your daily tasks' … egregious and trite. I love my job, where I work and those that I work with." As an instructor, I was shocked. I had advocated that it is important to build up a personal relationship with the student that goes beyond the academic context of the course or program, and here was a student who clearly had not appreciated this effort. I apologized in writing for adding a personal note that apparently had not been called for. This is an example that shows that open disclosure is desirable, but not in all cases. A first condition may be that there is rapport and a minimum insight in the background of the individual student. In a face-to-face situation, one has the opportunity to withdraw, or to correct a "mistake" as in the case of a nonverbal reaction, such as an annoyed facial expression. This is not the case in online communication; a written reaction that may be more harsh than it was meant to be can be perceived as "uninvitingly intruding the other's space."

The second behavior that is important in communication identified by Rogers (1962) is warm affirmation, which concerns the extent to which the student and the instructor feel at ease with each other, and how their relationship develops. Is the instructor facilitating or teaching because he or she has to do it, or needs to earn some extra money, or is there a real interest in the student and the wish to know the student better, not only as a pupil but also as a person in his or her own right? In the second case we may speak about warm affirmation.

The third behavior Rogers (1962) identified refers to the capacity of the "other" (i.e., either the instructor or the learner) to place him or herself in the position of the opposite party and be partial to his or her position. Rogers called this "empathic comprehension"—the feeling that the other knows what it is to be me. Rogers' three concepts are clearly aimed at reducing alienation and creating positive outcomes.

A study based on Rogers' communication behavior involving a large group of university level students (L. Visser & R. M. Visser, 2005) indicated, among other things, that:

- Communication in online courses is initiated by the instructor in 80% of the cases.
- Less than two-thirds (62%) of the students received timely information on how to contact classmates. This was also found to be a real concern by Hara and Kling (2000).
- The speed of reply of the classmates was better than that of the instructor.
- Most instructors provided some information about their personal/professional background, but also that it was considered to be less than in traditional learning situations. The information provided was perceived as being less personal.
- Students on the whole felt quite comfortable to discuss academic problems with their instructor. However, only one in 10 students felt at ease approaching the instructor with personal problems, even where these problems were clearly affecting their progress in the course (e.g., financial or time management related).
- Over two thirds of the students reported having experienced some miscommunication with their instructor. In just over half of these cases, this experience had negatively influenced their motivation.

The experience I had with Michael and his reaction to my effort to build a relationship that went beyond the academic context of a course or a program, alerted me to the fact that not all students have the same needs. This was clearly a case of a student who did not appreciate this attempt at a more personal relationship and I had not recognized this. At the end of that same course, I was copied on an e-mail another student in the same group, Pedro (fictitious name), had sent to the department head of the university: "I enjoyed a personal connection with Lya Visser that I have not previously experienced in distance education." In my effort to create that personal relationship, I had clearly failed to recognize that Michael had not been ready for it, whereas Pedro had appreciated such a relationship.

These different demands make it not always easy to create favorable learning situations and a close interaction with the students. The examples given clearly indicate that there is a difference in perception about the role of the instructor and the communication processes that are advocated. An audience analysis may be a useful tool to avoid complicated situations. I wonder if the miscommunication with Michael that I mentioned earlier would also have been taken equally serious in a face-to-face class. It is likely that the miscommunication would have been solved quickly. Imagine Michael complaining to the instructor (possibly in the corridor) and the instructor telling him that it was not her idea to offend him but to show some care for his work situation and that she apparently had misunderstood him. Most likely she would have apologized for her mistake with a convincing smile and a "see you later."

THE USE OF MOTIVATIONAL COMMUNICATIONS/MESSAGES

We have discussed the important role motivation plays in successful completion of courses and in ensuring long-lasting effects. We also saw that how we communicate is crucial to the effect of communication. The recognized importance of motivation and communication led to the development of motivational communication. This concept formed the basis for the design and development of motivational messages that were sent to online and traditional distance education students at specific moments during the course. The content of the messages was based on perceived and/or assumed motivational needs and based on the ARCS model of motivational analysis (Keller, 1983), a multiple case study where these motivational messages have shown to work (L. Visser, 1998). These motivational interventions not only resulted in a doubling of completion rates in the courses researched, but also in increased pleasure in doing the course/program.

It seems that even a simple thing like adding a picture of a flower to an e-mail message to a student, complimenting her on her perseverance, seems to be effective as the message I received yesterday showed: "Thank you again, especially for the flowers."

LESSONS LEARNED

I would like to end this chapter by discussing a number of techniques and exercises that I have used to address the issues outlined earlier.

The first one relates to the course content. Over the years, I have seen that one of the weaknesses of online learning and teaching is that there often is no common ground (experience). Examples students give from their daily work environment, for instance, are hardly ever relevant for all their classmates, who are not necessarily familiar with the various universities, the military, or the corporate world where these examples may originate.

Recognition of this reality has led me to design a practical case of an imaginary institution that experiences a number of (management) problems that are dealt with in the various lessons/sessions. For example, in the case of a course on management of online learning, it was an imaginary distance education institute that had human resource problems, but who was also losing its competitive advantage and who, on top of that, showed signs of nepotism. I try to ensure that there is a strong recognizable human element in the story. This turned out to be very useful to students as problem solving and conflict resolution was an important element of the course and it had the advantage that interaction among students was now based on a "real" case that they had all read and apparently enjoyed. The assignments also related to this "case." As the case (the institute) was based in a foreign country, they also learned something about taking into account cultural differences and proposing solutions for communication problems while not necessarily using the most advanced technology.

The positive reactions to this approach gave me confidence and I used a somewhat similar approach in a performance improvement class that I recently taught. In that case, I designed another "story" related to performance improvement in a university department, but I only wrote the first three installments.

In this class, one of the three assignments required that each week, two different students would prepare an online class in close cooperation with the instructor. The students had to come up with ideas, questions, discussion points, and creative contributions. These were then discussed with the instructor and allowed for a week of increased personal contact. After having received feedback, the students would contribute part of the lecture or propose questions for the discussion area. In the latter case, they also had to lead the discussion. Another option was to write a sequence to the case for which I had designed and posted the first three episodes. If one member of the student pair, or both, chose this option, they had to write an episode that, of course, had to relate to the course content of that given week. The case dealt with a university department that was involved in the restructuring of the university, and in this case conflict management, motivation, communication, sharing, and retraining played an important role. During the 16-week module, four students chose this option, so four episodes were added to the case.

To have information on how the students assessed this way of working and learning together, near the end of the course I set up an exercise where each student either had to interview a classmate or had to design five questions for a questionnaire and distribute these to a colleague. Learning how to conduct interviews and design questionnaires was part of the course design. The topic students should use for their work was student participation in the design of the course content. They would contact a classmate and then do the exercise. After this, they were required to send the interview or the five questions to me; they were not allowed to mention the name of the person they had interviewed. I then discussed the design of the interview or the questionnaire (not the content of the answers) and gave feedback. In this manner I was able to obtain, informally, some feedback on how students assessed their involvement in the case study/story and class preparation. Here are some quotes:

> Question: Do you feel that helping to prepare lectures or training materials for other students helps you to learn?
>
> Answer: Definitely! I think that when I am preparing lectures I look at the information more deeply and do a better analysis of the material. So I may be actually learning more when I help prepare the lecture.
>
> Q: Do you feel that preparing lectures for other students benefits your learning?
>
> A: I have to say that I am uncertain. In a way, it forced me to focus my efforts for [sic] the course, read ahead, and learn the subject independently. However, I learn better in a somewhat more guided environment.
>
> Q: What was your initial reaction upon learning that helping prepare a lecture would be an assignment for your course?
>
> A: I suppose I found it a little bit odd as I know a lot about some of the topics being covered and almost nothing about others.
>
> Q: Of the learning experiences that you have mentioned, which one experience was most valuable to you and why was it important?
>
> A: Assisting in the creation of lecture topic activities was valuable in that it forced me to be creative within the confines of the topic at hand, which meant, for really digging into the topic to find something appropriate to work with in a discussion or activity format.

Another intervention I tried out was to introduce a study buddy (peer support) system, meaning that two students would work together during the first 4 weeks of the course, and then decide whether they wanted to go on, change partners, or just work on their own. The suggested areas for working together were sharing information on the reading and proofreading one another's assignments. There was also the implicit hope that by working together in this manner, students would end up taking some responsibility for each other and in case of decreasing motivation, would offer help. At the beginning of this course, I requested that students send me a confidential e-mail with their preferred buddy, and I then tried to link them up. I had asked the students to copy me on their first three or four e-mail exchanges, so that I could make sure that this support system took off. The first 3 or 4 weeks, the system worked, but after that new groups formed and first groups were dissolved. Most students continued, however, to work in groups. At the end of the course there were still about four groups of two or three people working closely together. During the course, I also intervened a number of times to adjust groups. Unfortunately, I have no concrete data available to see whether this peer support system has been helpful, but I have doubts. It has been quite a lot of work for the instructor and there were no obvious results.

FINAL OBSERVATIONS

I have, over the years, increasingly enjoyed online teaching. The communication possibilities media now offer have made it easier and more rewarding to teach online. E-mail is still a favorite in that it is easy to build a relationship with the student, but discussion areas are also very useful. Students still appreciate it if instructors participate regularly in the discussions.

In general, I have experienced that designing exercises or projects that require students and the instructor to be actively involved are very rewarding. This way of working is especially beneficial for students who have not studied and learned online before because they find it difficult sometimes to get accustomed to having to take on more responsibility for their own learning. The change from participating in a face-to-face class to participating in a virtual classroom may not be very easy. I have learned that it is the task and the responsibility of the instructor to make this change smooth and motivating.

Specifically, I have identified a number of issues that, in my opinion and based on my experience, are crucial to successful online teaching and learning endeavors. These include:

- The importance of understanding the motivation of the instructor and the impact this has or can have on the interaction with the students.
- The importance of making sure that online instructors learn to put themselves in the shoes of the online learner in order to be better attuned to the latter's needs.
- Knowing and understanding the online learner's expectations as to academic and affective support and providing instructors with the skills to bring these expectations to the forefront and build on them.
- Awareness of the role motivation has on learning processes and on acquiring the skills to recognize and address the motivational needs of the students if and when needed.

- Recognition of the various dimensions of communication and how these dimensions affect the learning and teaching processes.
- The added value that research can bring into further understanding the previous issues and other issues affecting distance education in general and online teaching and learning in particular. There is a need for more careful investigation in communication and motivation processes in distance education.
- Awareness of the responsibility instructors have in helping students to get accustomed to, and embedded into, the online learning system, so as to prepare them for efficient and effective lifelong learning.

REFERENCES

Bohlin, R. M. (1987). Motivation in instructional design: Comparison of an American and Soviet model. *Journal of Instructional Development*, *10*(2), 11–14.

Briggs, L. J. (1980). Thirty years of instructional design: One man's experience. *Educational Technology*, *29*(2), 45–50.

Hara, N., & Kling, R. (2000). Students distress with a Web-based distance education course. *CSI working paper* [Online]. Retrieved on March 2, 2006, from http://www.slis.indiana.edu/CSI/wp00-01.html

Harasim, L., Hiltz, S. R., Teles, L., & Turoff, M. (1997). *Learning networks: A field guide to teaching and learning online*. Cambridge, MA: MIT Press.

Keller, J. M. (1983). Motivational design of instruction. In C. M. Reigeluth (Ed.), *Instructional-design theories and models: An overview of the current status* (pp. 386–431). Hillsdale, NJ: Lawrence Erlbaum Associates.

Keller, J. M. (1998). Motivational systems. In H. Stolovitch & E. Keeps (Eds.), *Handbook of human performance technology* (2nd ed.). San Francisco, CA: Jossey-Bass.

Lenzer, R. (1997, March). Seeing things as they really are. *Forbes*, *159*(5), 122–129.

McVay, L. M. (2002). *The online educator*. London: RoutledgeFalmer.

Rogers, C. (1962). The interpersonal relationship: The core of guidance. *Harvard Educational Review*, *32*(4), 416–429.

Shea, P., K., Fredericksen E., & Pickett, A., & Peltz, W. E. (2003). A preliminary investigation of "teaching presence" in the SUNY Learning Network. Retrieved September 23, 2006 from http//dspace.lib.rochester.edu/rerieve/6543/TeachingPresence.pdf

Trippe, A. (2001). Student satisfaction at the University of Phoenix Online Campus. In *Elements of quality online education* (Vol. 3). New York: The Sloan Consortium.

Visser, L. (1998). *The development of motivational communication in distance education support*. Unpublished doctoral dissertation, University of Twente, Enschede, The Netherlands.

Visser, L., & Visser, Y. L. (2000). Perceived and actual student support needs in distance education. *Quarterly Review of Distance Education*, *1*(2), 109–117.

Visser, L., & Visser, R. M. (2005). But first there are the communication skills. *Distance Learning*, *1*(4), 24–30.

Wolcott, L. L., & Betts, K. R. (1999). What's in it for me? Incentives for faculty participation in distance education. *Journal of Distance Education*, *14*(2), 34–39.

Chapter 8

Finding a Fulfilling Voice Through Interactions

Barbara L. Grabowski
Pennsylvania State University

"One of my greatest satisfactions in teaching is engaging my students with the content of my course" (Mathews & Spielvogel, 2005). Drs. Jonathan Mathews and Sarma Pisupati both teach online for the Penn State University Department of Earth & Mineral Sciences. What is amazing about these two faculty members is that each teaches a course with hundreds of online students. From conversations with these two faculty members, it is clear that both exhibit two important characteristics; a deep commitment and love of their content, and a deep commitment to engage their students in a positive learning experience about the content they love. One even gives out his cell phone number to answer questions about the course content (Pisupati, DeLuca, Gutkowski, & Mahan, 2005). The primary determinant of the quality of their faculty teaching experience is a sense of contribution that is made to their students' learning; that is, the voice they offer to students. Likewise for me, I judge the quality of faculty teaching on my ability to provide voice to experiences that help students learn new skills, enhance performance, or stimulate new ideas that change the way they view or understand the world. For Mathews and Pisupati, their voices challenge, cajole, guide, and direct students, empowering them to generate an understanding about the content under study.

FULFILLING AND TEDIOUS VOICES

As faculty try to balance the challenges of teaching, scholarship, and service, they want and need the time that is invested in teaching courses to be *quality* time as described earlier. The general goal is that time spent interacting with students about content will be meaningful for students and therefore fulfilling for faculty.

Often, faculty fail to realize that the choices of learning activities that are made to create fully engaging, challenging, and fulfilling online courses may have tremendous impact on faculty time, not all of which results in *quality* time. In short, teaching time intended to be fulfilling can all too easily become tedious. Sometimes these choices have technological consequences that actually diminish the time for interaction with students by adding time requirements for tinkering with the technology (Popp, 2003).

Finding a Balance

Benefits of making efficient decisions result in a positive impact on the quality of the faculty experience. It is important, therefore, to select interactive learning tasks based on course objectives and expected faculty/student engagement while bearing in mind the type of time commitment required by faculty, that is, tinkering with technology or engaging students with the content. Faculty voice about content and learning is found in these interactions. Faculty satisfaction is also found in observing positive interactions between students and when students engage in the content. Therefore, the following three premises provide the foundation of a framework for judiciously selecting course interactions.

- Quality time for instructors is measured by the degree of engagement learners have with the content.
- Quality time engaging with content and students and tedious time off task tinkering with technology for both instructors and learners, need to be balanced.
- This balance can be achieved by examining the cognitive requirements against a variety of engaging interactive strategies and technology options for accomplishing the course objectives.

THE BUSINESS OF DESIGNING INTERACTIONS

Duffy and Cunningham (1996) observed that most online distance education programs use technology to deliver instruction, emphasizing the transmission of the content rather than collaborative, socially constructive engagements. In effective online programs, like effective instruction, learning occurs only when students are actively engaged with the learning material or the content (Wittrock, 1974). Following this belief about learning, faculty as course developers of online courses need to build learning environments in which faculty and students collaborate to achieve course goals. As a result, faculty are, in essence, in the business of designing interactions.

Assumptions Behind Designing Interactions

Choosing interactions that foster faculty voice and faculty fulfillment is challenging. Decisions about how much and what type of interactions should be guided by the level of thinking required by the type of task and by the learning management system (LMS) tools available. In this way, the best mix of collaboration and active engagement among learners can be selected. To help manage these decisions, a framework for selecting interactions was developed that takes faculty through a three-step—task level by interaction type by LMS systems tools—decision-making process. The framework is based on three design assumptions:

- Quality time on task for learners means engaging them in challenging tasks that are relevant to the learning objectives.
- Effective instruction consists of three stages—presentation, practice and feedback, assessment and feedback, with interactions required for practice and assessment feedback loops (Merrill, 1994).
- Learning occurs when learners are actively engaged with the content (Wittrock, 1974).

Assumption 1: Quality Time on Task.   Quality time on task means that learners are meaningfully engaged in tasks that will help them learn the required content. "Meaningfully engaged" is defined differently here from authentic contextual learning (Kafai & Resnick, 1996) or learning that is student centered (Hannafin, Hill, & Land, 1997). Rather, "meaningfully engaged" is defined as being engaged in tasks that match the level of thinking required. When the objectives indicate that knowledge should be applied, students are meaningful engaged when they are involved in activities that require them to apply the content rather than simply to list items, for example.

Assumption 2: Effective Instruction.   The online environment provides a repository for resources in many forms to support and display content (Grabowski, Koszalka, & McCarthy, 1999; Hill, Hannafin, & Domizi, 2005). Hill and colleagues (2005) included content resources such as "databases, print textbooks, video, images, original source documents and humans" (p. 114). However, resources in this form are just information. Resources combined with practice provide an opportunity for learning. Resources with practice combined with feedback constitute instruction (Grabowski & Curtis, 1991). These resource/practice/feedback loops form the basis of interactions in effective instruction (Merrill, 1994). It is also important to note that for effective instruction, these interactions are intentional and cannot be left to chance as is often possible in an in-class informal lecture and discussion. Unlike face-to-face and blended learning environments, faculty in an online environment must overtly specify and preplan the types of interactions that need to occur for each objective.

Assumption 3: Active Engagement. Learning occurs when learners are active participants in the learning process and construct their own understanding about the content (Wittrock, 1974). Wittrock noted that learners must be challenged to draw relationships among ideas within the content for lower level thinking, and between the content presented and their own experiences for higher order thinking. From the course objectives, the faculty member selects activities that require knowledge to be constructed at the appropriate cognitive level.

FRAMEWORK FOR SELECTING INTERACTIONS

Inadequate interaction can result in shallow, inadequate, meaningless products created by the learners. Too much interaction can result in high faculty investment of time with few learning gains. The goal of the framework, therefore, is to help identify appropriate types of interaction in online instruction, then use the framework to select tools that minimize invisible tinkering with technology time burdens and that maximize fulfilling faculty voice. The format of the framework shown in Table 8.1 shapes a three-step process; specifying the level of task and required artifacts, specifying interaction types and sequences, and selecting the learning management system (LMS) tools.

The first column, Task Level/Artifact, categorizes the underlying thinking requisite to course objectives according to Bloom's (1956) taxonomy. The second column designates the type of interaction required to perform a task or to create an artifact that will engage learners in the level of thinking specified in column one. This column captures the interactivity necessary for presentation and practice in instruction. The third column specifies a second type of interaction, that is, a sequence of faculty/student engagements for assessment and feedback in instruction. This feedback loop completes the entire interaction for the specific task. Finally, the last column identifies three types of system tools that support the interactions.

TABLE 8.1
Framework for Selecting Interactions

Task Level/Artifact	Interaction Type: Task Engagement to Create Artifacts	Interaction Sequence: Assessment and Feedback	LMS Tools
Knowledge	Individual	S-T-S S-F-S	Transmission of Content Interaction
Comprehension	Collaboration	S-S-F	Interaction
Application	Individual	S-F-S S-P-S Ss-P-F	Transmission of Content Interaction
Analysis	Individual	S-F-S Ss-P-F	Transmission of Content Posting Interaction
Synthesis	Collaboration	S-S-F	Interaction
Evaluation	Collaboration Individual	S-F-S Ss-P-F	Posting Interaction

S = Student; T = Technology; F = Faculty

Step 1: Specifying the Level of Task and Required Artifacts

Content of the course is analyzed to determine the learning outcomes that should be expected; that is, the objectives are defined. With this analysis comes an understanding of the level of thinking, from low to high, required by the learner to achieve the objectives. Faculty should determine if students need to know terms, understand concepts, apply rules and principles, analyze situations, create new solutions, or evaluate alternatives. The level of thinking then helps specify the type of task the learners should perform and the artifacts they should construct to demonstrate that they have accomplished the required objectives.

Six levels of thinking are used to classify the course requirements; (a) knowledge, (b) comprehension, (c) application, (d) analysis, (e) synthesis, and (f) evaluation (see Bloom, 1956). The levels show a progression of thinking from a lower level—knowledge—to a higher level—evaluation. Knowledge implies the acquisition of information. Comprehension requires the learner to pull ideas together to develop understanding about those ideas. Comprehension is a consequence of formulating connections among ideas rather than a function of placing information in or retrieving information from memory (Grabowski, 2003). Analysis requires the learner to pull ideas apart to see the underlying component parts. Synthesis requires the learner to bring together ideas to form new ones. Finally, evaluation requires learners to make judgments about the value of ideas.

Faculty need to reflect on these levels of thinking and choose tasks and require artifacts that match course outcomes. For example, a student learning a concept may create a concept map to develop comprehension. A student learning to make a decision about statistical procedures engages in analysis and synthesis to create a knowledge base for an expert system.

Step 2: Specify Interaction Types and Sequences

Following the basic instructional design strategy suggested by Merrill (1994)—presentation, practice, feedback—there are two interaction decisions. The first is called interaction type for task engagement to create artifacts. The second is called interaction sequence for assessment and feedback.

Interaction Type for Task Engagement to Create Artifacts.   In this step, the teacher-designer chooses one of two types of interactions for students to create the artifact specified in Step 1. Interactions for task engagement can occur in two ways—individually or in collaboration with others.

Individual interactions occur by self-with-self, or self-with-content (Moore & Kearsley, 1995). In a self-with-self-interaction, learners reflect specifically and intentionally about what they know and create an artifact based on what they already know, such as a story or lesson plan. In a self-with-content collaboration, the learner can simply relate the ideas from the material together, such as creating an outline or a concept map. They can also integrate information from the material with what they already know, such as creating analogies or making predictions (Grabowski, 2003).

Collaborations occur between or among students when they create a joint product. In a collaborative interaction, learners engage with the materials, with themselves, and with others. Collaborations aid in comprehension through the process of socially constructing understanding. Collaborations also enable learners to gain multiple perspectives and new ideas from outside themselves.

Interaction Sequence for Assessment and Feedback.   Interaction sequences for assessment and feedback close the learning loop by enabling the learner to obtain feedback on their artifacts. Without feedback, instruction does not occur. Learning can, of course, occur without instruction, and vice versa; however, providing an appropriate sequence of interactions that provide feedback increases the probability that learning will occur from the instruction. Four types of interaction sequences are included in the framework; student–technology–student; student–faculty–student, student–student–faculty, and students–peers–faculty.

In the student–technology–student sequence, students create a response and enter it into a computer that provides automated feedback. If incorrect, the student can reply again. An example of this sequence is an online quiz.

In a student–faculty–student sequence, the students create an artifact that is submitted directly to the faculty member for feedback. The student then can respond back to the faculty for clarification or revision. An example of this is an artifact submitted to a faculty member via e-mail, who in turn replies with feedback via e-mail and so forth.

In a student–student–faculty sequence, the students interact among themselves discussing the product prior to submitting it to the faculty member. A good example of this type of interaction is that which occurs in an online learning community, often within a forum or a bulletin board.

In a students–peers–faculty sequence, students create the artifact in collaboration and submit it for peer review. There is an interaction triggered by the feedback provided by the student when it works well. The teacher provides feedback to the peers for their review.

Step 3: Selecting the Learning Management System Tools

Online learning tools must support the three key features of an instructional sequence, that is, presentation, practice, and feedback. Presentation tools are those that provide the means for the faculty to convey information to the group. In other words, these tools allow for the transmission of content. Examples of these types of tools includes Web pages, links, portable document format (PDF) files, downloads of example files, databases of examples, and so on. Except for databases, the others function similarly; however, tinkering with the technology time goes up when downloading is involved. It is important to choose the fastest means possible for information transfers to and from the Internet. Databases of examples, on the other hand, offer additional payback in terms of enabling strategic, individualized selection of materials.

Practice and feedback require tools for interaction and posting. Examples of interaction tools include online quizzes, private communication via e-mail, public or learning community bulletin boards/forums, chat rooms, instant messaging, and forms-based automated replies. Each needs to be considered in terms of their affordances that facilitate the four identified types of interactions. For example, e-mail provides an efficient means of interaction between faculty and individual students; bulletin boards create online learning communities to facilitate multiple member communication, be they faculty or student. They also enable peer reviews and topic discussions.

Posting tools include student presentation spaces for student-created artifacts, templates for submission to the student presentation space or other databases, attachments, embedded e-mail, embedded posts to the bulletin board.

Posting tools can be the most problematic in terms of contributing to tinkering with technology time. Problems arise from the number of clicks it takes to get to the individual student submissions, combined with Web page refresh rates, downloading time, number of students, and number of required artifacts to be posted! Consider all of these factors in selecting the most efficient tool.

BRINGING IT ALL TOGETHER

The goal was to create a framework that could be used to identify appropriate interaction types and sequences for different task levels or artifact types, then use the framework to consider the types of technology tools that would enable fulfilling faculty voice.

The important operative in this assumption is that different levels of thinking are required for different types of learner artifacts, and that different types of interactions foster different levels of thinking. As suggested previously, inadequate interaction can result in shallow, inadequate products created by the learners. Too much interaction can result in high faculty investment of time with little learning gain. Either of these situations results in a tedious voice rather than a fulfilling voice from the teacher's perspective.

The logic behind each row in the framework is presented next. At the knowledge level or lowest level of learning, learning can occur with individual interactions, self-with-self, or self-with-materials. Elaborate interactions with others can, of course, occur, but they are not needed to support this level of learning. This would be an example of high faculty investment of time with little learning gain. Next, the most efficient means of task engagement and feedback should be selected. Between the two possibilities, student–technology—student or student—faculty—student, using technology for assessment is likely to be the most time efficient for the teacher.

Comprehension, on the other hand, requires an individual to pull ideas together to develop understanding. This is best accomplished through collaboration. Engaging students in groups through the use of forums will increase understanding. While students are interacting with each other creating a socially negotiated understanding, they provide feedback to each other. The faculty member completes the loop by providing feedback to the group (student—student—faculty). A colleague once remarked that pooled ignorance is still ignorance. This statement emphasizes the importance of expert feedback being provided to the learning group once they have pooled their ideas.

Application requires an individual to consider how information can be used in a personally meaningful way. An individual task is recommended for this level of learning. Feedback, in this case, would come directly from the faculty (student—faculty—student), or through peer assessment, followed by faculty assessment (Students—peers—faculty). The most efficient content transmission, posting, and interaction tools are needed to support this level of learning.

Analysis is also seen as an individual task. Analysis requires pulling ideas apart to see the underlying component parts. Feedback from the faculty member (student—faculty—student) or from their peers completes the assessment loop (students—peers—faculty). Technology to support this level of task includes all three types, content transmission, posting, and interactions.

Synthesis requires the learner to bring together ideas to form new ones. Collaboration is recommended to enable students to see multiple perspectives. The interaction sequence for feedback would then require students—faculty and be supported with interaction tools. If a joint project is actually created, then there would be a need for posting tools as well.

Finally, evaluation can be either an individual or a collaborative task. A judgment is made in this task. Gaining ideas from collaborators can enrich this level of task. Faculty or peers could provide feedback (student—faculty—student or students—peers—faculty). A means for posting and interacting is required to support this task.

THE FRAMEWORK APPLIED

Instructional Systems 448, Internet in the Classroom, offered through Penn State's World Campus (see http://www.worldcampus.psu.edu/), is a highly interactive course with much opportunity for faculty voice. Because of its nature and the philosophy behind its design, it was used to develop the framework and for analysis after. In a second study, Popp (2003) analyzed the consequences of these decisions as defined by tinkering with technology time.

Course Description

This course was created for K–12 teachers, university professors, or a trainer in business and industry context. The course was designed around four cases in which the Internet is used for instructional planning, locating Internet resources to integrate in a lesson, and for producing instructional and learning sites:

- Case 1A: Teacher as Internet Planner
- Case 1B: Teacher as Lesson Planner
- Case 2: Teacher as Integrator
- Case 3: Teacher as Producer

Course Design

By contextualizing the content around the tasks the students already performed, they were provided with relevant exercises that they could use immediately in their teaching practice. While in the class, the students learned
many facets of using the Internet and the World Wide Web; however, the
main focus of the course was to examine and reflect on its pedagogical usefulness to teachers and instructors in the classroom.

The course development team analyzed the various tasks required of
teachers who use the Internet in their classroom. Four goals concerning
using, integrating, publishing, and responding to issues were written.
These goals were broken down further into eight objectives. For each objective, a consistency table as shown in Fig. 8.1 was used to strategically select tasks, supporting skills, interaction, and assessments. Who would be
involved and the LMS tools were included in the table. From this analysis,
11 tasks, their corresponding supporting skills, interactions and assessments were developed.

Fulfilling or Tedious Faculty Voice?

Once the course was developed and offered for several semesters, I, as the
instructor realized how labor intensive it was. There was much opportunity for faculty voice. Perhaps there was too much opportunity, and the
question of tedious time and voice arose. I was not convinced, however, to
change any of the tasks or artifacts that were required because they
seemed essential for course design. This dilemma prompted an effort to
analyze the course requirements through a new lens; thus the interaction
selection framework was created and used to analyze the tasks, then to
identify actual interaction types, interaction sequences, and system tools
required for each of the main tasks (see Appendix A). In the first column,
the objectives are listed along with the task title. The data in the table was
then matched to the recommended interaction types, interaction sequences, and system tools from the framework.

Results

From this analysis, it is evident that interactivity and faculty voice were
highly valued in this course. There were, however, four tasks (the shaded areas—tasks 6, 8, 10, and 11 in the Appendix A) in which comprehension was
the level of activity, yet the interaction was individual. I could see how these
activities would have been better if there had been some collaboration. In
fact, students appeared to have the most trouble and the least interest in
these tasks. Redesigning these tasks to include jointly constructed artifacts

File   Edit   View   Favorites   Tools   Help

Back   Search   Favorites   History

Case 1 – Planner

Objective: Use the web to help plan 3 lessons and develop a strategy for Internet use in your school.

Tasks	Supporting Skills	Interaction	Assessment
1. Find a lesson plan that you can use in your classroom.	• Browse for information on the Internet • Search for information on the Internet using good search strategies.	Send the URL to the class, and to the instructor. With a description of your (non-technical) search strategy, and how the lesson fits in your curriculum. L2L Peer Assessment Tool E-mail	OUTCOME ASSESSED: Found lesson plan WHO ASSESSES: both peers and instructor CRITERIA: 1. Search strategy was straightforward, 2. Lesson plan came from the net, and 3. Lesson plan matches current teaching assignment and is currently usable.
		1. Student uses e-mail to	OUTCOME ASSESSED: Embellished lesson

Start   Micr...   Cas...   Inn...   Dra...   Re: ...   abo...   1:38 PM

Figure 8.1.   Consistency table for selecting tasks, skills, interactions and assessments.

to demonstrate understanding should address the objective more appropriately and improve interest.

The analysis also showed that peer review was also used too much for lower level tasks. Selecting S—S—F would have been more efficient for the comprehension tasks, thus reducing the number of iterations and peer reviews I had to review. These peer reviews should be selected for application, analysis and evaluation.

Finally, the analysis showed that the rest of the decisions were appropriate; therefore, not offering any other suggestions for reducing faculty, and, of course, student load. What remains is to determine if there is a more efficient technology affordance for posting student artifacts or if there are too many course objectives. By changing these other two factors, faculty load may also be reduced.

CONCLUSION

When I designed the Internet in the Classroom online course, I felt very strongly about creating student interactions and having a high level of faculty voice to achieve a high level of presence in the course. When a second instructor took over that course, he felt the effects of many of the decisions I had made with regard to the LMS tools for interactions and postings. When we would get together, we exchanged ideas about how to do administrative tasks more efficiently, and he would ask, "Doesn't it bother you that it takes you six clicks combined with wait time to respond to an e-mail?" I had not thought about it from that perspective before, but did not want to compromise any interactions with students. This goal led me to establish a rationale for including specific types of interactions, and then with his data to select the most efficient means for selecting posting and interaction tools.

The resulting analysis was useful in helping me think through these previous decisions, and I expect in helping me think through task selection, interactions, and tools in my next online course. It also seems studying the means through which Drs. Mathews and Pisupati found their online voices would be a good test of the framework.

REFERENCES

Bloom, B. S. (1956). *Taxonomy of educational objectives. Handbook I: The cognitive domain.* New York: David McKay Co., Inc.

Duffy, T., & Cunningham, D. (1996). Constructivism: Implications for the design and delivery of instruction. In D. H. Jonassen (Ed.), *Handbook for research on educational communications and technology* (pp. 170–198). New York: Macmillan Library Reference.

Grabowski, B. (2003). Generative learning contributions to instructional design. In D. H. Jonassen (Ed.), *Handbook for research on educational communications and technology* (2nd ed., pp. 719–743). Mahwah, NJ: Lawrence Erlbaum Associates.

Grabowski, B., & Curtis R. (1991). Information, instruction and learning: A hypermedia perspective. *Performance Improvement Quarterly, 4*(3), 3–12.

Grabowski, B., Koszalka, T., & McCarthy, M. (1999). *Web-enhanced learning environment strategies handbook*. State College, PA: Penn State University.

Hannafin, M., Hill, J., & Land, S. (1997). Student-centered learning and interactive multimedia: Status, issues and implications. *Contemporary Education, 68*(2), 94–99.

Hill, J., Hannafin, M., & Domizi, D. (2005). Resource-based learning and informal learning environments: Prospects and challenges. In L. T. Hin & R. Subramaniam (Eds.), *E-learning and virtual science centers* (pp. 110–125). Singapore: Information Science Publications.

Kafai, Y., & Resnick, M. (1996). *Constructivism in practice: Designing thinking and learning in a digital world*. Hillsdale, NJ: Lawrence Erlbaum Associates.

Mathews, J., & Spielvogel, E. (2005, November). *How to [cope] thrive with 400 students: Effective online communication*. Paper presented at meeting the 11th Sloan-C International conference on Asynchronous Learning Networks. Orlando, FL.

Merrill, D. (1994). *Instructional design theory*. Englewood Cliffs, NJ: Educational Technology Publications.

Moore, M., & Kearsley, G. (1995). *Distance education: A systems view*. New York: Wadsworth.

Pisupati, S., DeLuca, M., Gutkowski, M., & Mahan, W. (2005, November). *What should be the enrollment cap of highly interactive online courses?* Paper presented at the 11th Sloan-C International conference on Asynchronous Learning Networks. Orlando, FL.

Popp, D. (2003). *Limitations of the course management system and the impact on faculty productivity in instructional systems 448, a web based offered through Penn State's world campus* [Alfred B. Sloan Foundation Tech. Rep.]. University Park, PA: The Penn State University, World Campus.

Wittrock, M. C. (1974). Learning as a generative process. *Educational Psychologist, 1*(2), 87–95.

APPENDIX A: ANALYSIS OF THE MAIN TASKS USING THE INTERACTION SELECTION FRAMEWORK

INSYS 448 Tasks	Task Level/Product Type	Interaction for Task Engagement or Product Creation	Interaction Sequence for Assessment	System Tools
1. What About an Internet Strategy for My School, Academic or Training Department? You will find, and discuss on-line, relevant information that you will be able to use to create an Internet strategy for your own professional context	Synthesis— bringing together many parts of the issues then Application— writing an internet strategy document	Collaborative Individual	S-S-F S-F-S	Bulletin Board Forums E-mail attachment
2. How can the net help me plan lessons? You will search the Web to locate a lesson plan that you will be able to use in your own professional context	Application	Individual	Ss-P-F	Presentation space with learning community forum feedback, then with e-mail feedback from instructor
3. How can the net help me refresh? You will locate content and background information on the Internet that will help you develop a lesson plan for your own professional context	Application	Individual	Ss-P-F	Presentation space with learning community forum feedback, then with e-mail feedback from instructor

4. How can I collaborate with others on my lesson plans? You will collaborate with another professional over the Internet to help you enhance a lesson plan of your choice	Application	Individual	Ss-P-F	Presentation space with learning community forum feedback, then with e-mail feedback from instructor
5. What's out there? You will work in small groups to create a list of all the types of resources and networking opportunities that are available on the Internet (related to the classroom) and provide an example of each	Synthesis	Collaboration	S-S-F	Collaborative presentation space with learning community forum feedback, then with e-mail feedback from instructor
6. Revisiting (or visiting!) teaching strategies!? You will define, in your own words, six common teaching strategies and describe how each could be applied to a given lesson plan	Comprehension —definitions Application— lesson ideas	Individual	Ss-P-F	Attachment to learning community forum, then e-mail feedback to peer reviewers from instructor
7. Creating (doing?) WELES? You will write two or three (as needed) exemplary Web-enhanced lesson plans based on your own professional context	Application	Individual	Ss-P-F	Presentation space with learning community forum feedback, then with e-mail feedback from instructor

8. How do I classify my websites? You will define the differences between information, instruction, and learning Web sites	Comprehension	Individual	Ss-P-F	Attachment to the learning community forum feedback, then with e-mail feedback from instructor to peer reviewers
9. What's a Template? You will locate a Web template and then use it to post a lesson plan, assessment instrument, classroom information or full lesson to the Web	Application	Individual	S-F-S	Posting to the learning community forum
10. Web-based? Web-enhanced? You will define the differences between the "Web-based" and "Web-enhanced" in your own words	Comprehension	Individual	Ss-P-F	Posting to the learning community forum for feedback
11. How do I produce and post an instructional lesson myself? You will determine, and discuss on-line, which characteristics make up a visually appealing site You will develop an instructional Web page that follows Gagne's nine events of instruction	Comprehension and Application— Gagne's 9 events Evaluation— good web design Application— producing a lesson	Individual Individual and Collaboration Individual	S-F-S student to self S-S-F S-F-S	e-mail attachment Bulletin board forums Student presentation space

APPENDIX B: DEFINITION

Artifacts: Overt products that students create that are subject to self, peer, or faculty review. Required artifacts are selected based on course objectives.

LMS Tools: Affordances of learning management systems that enable transmission of content, posting of student artifacts, interactions between peers and faculty.

Online Interactions: Internal dialogue within an individual or dialogues occurring in collaboration with others such as one's peers or faculty.

Interaction Types: Individual: those dialogues that promote learner construction of new knowledge and artifacts through individual self-to-self, or self-to-content conversation.

Interaction Types: Collaborative—those dialogues with others that promote learner construction of new knowledge and artifacts.

Interaction Sequences: The flow of dialogue for the purpose of providing and offering feedback about artifacts created. This sequence is begun with the student submitting an artifact, then engaging in conversation with either their peers and then faculty or just the faculty.

Task Level: Classifies the type of thinking expected of the learner to accomplish the course objectives. Blooms taxonomy is used to classify the objectives; knowledge, comprehension, application, analysis, synthesis, and evaluation.

Voice: The extension of faculty presence in an online environment.

"Fulfilling" Voice: Faculty engagement with the students about the content they love.

"Tedious" Voice: Faculty engagement with the students, technology in the course, and student about technological frustrations that results in "wait time" and wasted time taken away from fulfilling voice.

Chapter 9

Interaction: The Power and Promise of Active Online Learning

Wilhelmina C. Savenye
Arizona State University

Most educators realize that online instruction is as complex, and involves as many, or more, variables as does face-to-face classroom instruction. This means that to foster student success in online courses, there are no simple answers, easy fixes, or magic bullets. That having been said, research can provide us with tremendous guidance as to ways and means to enhance online instruction to help students learn.

In particular, the communication tools of the Internet, including e-mail, discussion boards, listservs, chat, and teleconferences, allow us to include considerable interaction in online courses. As a consequence, this interaction factor is being used and studied to improve online learning. The power of communication and interaction in online courses is reflected in some of the fundamental definitions of distance education. For instance, Rumble (1997) defined distance learning as "a process of teaching-learning in which the learner is physically separated from the teacher" (p. 3). Moore and Kearsley (2005) then suggested that distance education "is planned learning that normally occurs in a different place from teaching, requiring special course design and instruction techniques, communication through various technologies, and special organizational and administrative arrangements" (p. 2). Communication in online learning is critical. In fact, Tiffin and Rajasingham (1995) argued that education *is* communication, and, further, that computers and the Internet offer significant opportunities for education; at the same time, the role that communications may play in instruction is changing.

Online learning can take many forms. Courses may be offered completely over the Internet; or they may be offered as hybrid courses, in which a proportion of class meetings take place over the Internet; or as blended courses, in which some activities are Internet-based (Savenye, 2004a). The primary focus, though, of this chapter is on fully online courses.

INTERACTION AND ITS FORMS IN ONLINE COURSES

Interaction, not surprisingly, has been defined many ways in online and distance learning. Most distance educators focus on the communication aspects of interaction. McIsaac and Gunawardena (2004), for instance, stated that interaction is "sustained real two-way communication" that is essential to the "teaching and learning transaction" in distance learning (p. 361). Moore (1989) distinguished among three types of interaction, and would characterize interaction among humans in the learning environment as either *learner–instructor* or *learner–learner* interaction, adding that the latter has become more important in online learning. Moore added a third type of interaction—*learner–content* interaction—in which the individual learner derives communicative value from the content in the course. Although this type of interaction may apply to textbooks, it has become a focus of attention in online learning settings as they tend to be rich in terms of mediated resources. The tradition in development of multimedia programs has long been to include frequent and engaging interaction with content, for instance in the form of questions, simulations, and games. This type of learner engagement with content has been called both "interaction" (Allessi & Trollip, 2004, p. 461) and "interactivity" (Allessi & Trollip, 2004, p. 392). A few researchers on interaction as communication have also used the term "interactivity" (Smith & Winking-Diaz, 2004; Tu, 2000).

To these types of interaction have been added several others. Hillman, Willis, and Gunawardena (1994) describe *learner-interface* interaction, which Hanna, Glowacki-Dudka, and Conceicao-Runlee (2000) call *learner-to-technology* interaction. Sutton (2001) described the benefits of vicarious interaction, such as lurking, in which learners in online discussions may learn from reading, even when not necessarily posting messages related to content. Whereas there are students in face-to-face classes who only listen, the issue of what they might be learning has not been problematic because their presence can be directly observed.

In this chapter, we focus generally on these somewhat more standard definitions of interaction as communication among learners, teacher, content, and sometimes interface. However, it is worthwhile to look at recent refinements to these views of interaction in order to further explore how we might add more and better interaction to our online courses.

Roblyer and colleagues presented (Roblyer & Ekhaml, 2000) and validated an extensive rubric (Roblyer & Wiencke, 2004) that was developed to assess and encourage interaction in distance courses. The rubric allows evaluators to rate a distance course, using a carefully described five-point rating scale, on the degree to which the course represents five aspects of interaction; social interaction, instructional interaction, technological interaction, learner engagement, and instructor engagement.

To further show the depth and complexity of interaction, some definitions may be viewed as represented by the uses and benefits of interaction. For instance, Boettcher and Conrad (1999) proposed a continuum of stages of group work that are dependent on learning goals and activities but that ultimately yield a learning community. They suggested that interaction leads to connections among learners, and that these connections become deeper as interaction time, activities, structure, and complexity increase. Interaction thus leads to collaboration, and, depending on the course design, time and tasks, also leads to cooperation.

Similarly, Zirkin and Sumler (1994), based on their study to aid the state of Maryland in its definition of direct instruction, concluded that interaction is really learner engagement or involvement. Others have suggested that these many types of interaction in an online course instead foster the engagement of learners, thus enhancing motivation, retention, and active and meaningful learning. This leads to our discussion of the rationale for including meaningful interaction in our online courses.

BENEFITS OF INTERACTION IN ONLINE COURSES

Interaction is not the "be all and end all" of online learning. It is just one part of the mix for success. However, as Lehmann (2004) said, "communication is what separates true online learning from web-based tutorials" (p. 9).

Some researchers have suggested that interaction does increase student achievement. For instance, Zirkin and Sumler (1994) concluded that K–12 learners in interactive courses achieve as well or better than those in less interactive courses. Brewer (2004) conducted a study with adult re-entry college students working in small asynchronous discussion groups. She found a significant positive relationship between the number of interactions and higher posttest scores. However, caution must be used here, as there are others who have suggested that interaction does not necessarily enhance achievement, especially when measured by test scores (Simonson, Smaldino, Albright, & Zvacek, 2006).

It stands to reason that interaction is likely to be effective for improving learner achievement of goals and outcomes involving learner communication skills and collaboration. For instance, Smith and Winking-Diaz (2004), in an online college psychology course, used various types of interaction strategies to foster deeper engagement. Strategies included a variety of interaction techniques; an instructor–student discussion board, in which students asked the professor questions; simultaneous discussion boards for students about content; having students label their response types; a partnering system to allow students to help each other with discussions; and a method for having students learn about and contribute to a posting board about facts related to course content. These researchers found that students did master the content and also learned through these communication strategies to apply the content in deeper ways and to reflect on course issues as they related to their own lives.

Interaction can also help students learn technology skills. The National Educational Technology Standards (NETS) (ISTE, 2000–2004), many of which can be fostered through interaction, present learning outcomes for secondary and elementary school administrators, teachers, and students. The standards, for example, suggest that students learn to use telecommunications and media tools to publish information and to communicate with their peers, experts, and other audiences. Students also should learn to use technology to collaborate on research with others, and to develop their skills in analyzing and solving problems. Roblyer (2000) has developed a list of activities, many of which rely on interaction, to aid instructors in teaching the NETS technology outcomes.

Considerable research has shown that interaction in distance courses can enhance student satisfaction, motivation, and retention, and these, too, are powerful reasons to increase the levels and types of interaction in online instruction. In an interactive television course, Fulford and Zhang (1993) found, for instance, that students' level of interaction moderately predicted their satisfaction with the course. Interestingly, students' perception of the overall interaction in the course was an even more important predictor of their satisfaction. Chen (2005) found, in her study involving undergraduate college students in a computer-literacy course, that the more interaction in asynchronous online discussion groups, the more positive were students' attitudes about the course. Cottam, Smith, and Savenye (2004) found that increasing specific interactions on the part of college-level Spanish language instructors and their online students increased course retention dramatically.

There are, of course, some constraints and issues related to implementing interaction in online courses. These may include the time it takes to develop the activities (Simonson et al., 2006), the fact that any technology can fail (Lamb & Smith, 2000), accessibility for those who are differently abled, access speed, copyright, and intellectual property issues (Ko & Rossen, 2001; Smaldino, Russell, Heinich, & Molenda, 2005). Students' levels of writing, language, and technology skills, along with issues related to software versions requiring frequent updating, are all issues that can be problematic for instructors implementing interaction in online classes.

INTERACTION AND EFFECTIVE ONLINE COURSE DESIGN

A good online course is an effective blend of content, organization, and interaction. The instructor is responsible for developing accurate, up-to-date content that supports the learning outcomes. Chickering and Gamson (1987) in their principles of good practice for teaching undergraduates, distinguish between what they call the *how* of teaching, from the *what*, that is, the content of teaching. Course planning and interaction form the *how*.

Course planning and organization rely on a teacher's or a developer's skills in instructional design (Dick, Carey, & Carey, 2001; Gagné, Briggs, & Wager, 1992: Smith & Ragan, 2005). Eastmond and Zieghan (1995) provided an excellent overview of how to apply instructional design guidelines to the online classroom. Meyer (2003) suggested that online learning has brought with it a "renewed focus on pedagogy and instructional design" (p. 20). She added that the development of online learning is supported by research in the areas of instructional design, individual differences, and interaction. Moore and Kearsley (2005) concluded that a well-designed distance course relies on an effective balance between presentation and interaction.

STUDENT FACTORS THAT FOSTER SUCCESS

Considerable research has focused on factors that seem to influence students' success in online distance courses, particularly in light of the fact that distance courses often have low retention rates. We know that students with certain characteristics tend to be more successful in distance courses. Individual students vary on many dimensions, yet students who are more successful tend to be more self-regulated, disciplined, motivated, and independent than are students who are less successful. Muirhead (2004) added that successful distance students have a strong work ethic, are good at working in collaborative groups, and are good reflective thinkers. Students who are more experienced with computer skills and online learning also tend to be more successful. Online course technologies currently rely on text, so writing and typing skills are still important.

To support these findings, Roblyer and Marshall (2002–2003) developed and tested an Educational Success Prediction Instrument with students at the Concord Virtual High School (The Concord Consortium, 2005). They found that students who remained enrolled in and passed an online course differed from students who did not succeed in their beliefs with regard to success and self-responsibility and had superior organizational and technology skills. We believe that many, if not most, of these skills that can foster success for students can be learned, and that interaction in online courses can help students learn them.

IMPROVING INTERACTION IN ONLINE COURSES

There are as many different ways to teach as there are instructors. In this section, we aim to provide new and experienced online instructors with some suggestions for using interaction in their courses. Our advice is based on our many years of online teaching, as well as on our research, along with that of our educational technology doctoral students. Along the way, we include hard-won lessons, and issues that continue to be problematic, even long after our online courses are running smoothly and learners are succeeding in them. We include guidelines for improving interaction in an online course before, during, and after the course.

Chickering and Gamson's (1987) "seven principles for good practice" (p. 1) in undergraduate education provide us with a wonderful starting point for improving online courses. Good practice, according to these principles:

1. Encourages contact between students and faculty;
2. Develops reciprocity and cooperation among students;
3. Encourages active learning;
4. Gives prompt feedback;
5. Emphasizes time on task,
6. Communicates high expectations; and,
7. Respects diverse talents and ways of learning.

Chickering and Gamson (1987) specifically included interaction as one of what they consider to be the six most powerful forces in education, which also include activity, expectations, cooperation, diversity, and responsibility. It is clear that almost all of the seven principles—especially encouraging and supporting contact, cooperation, active learning, feedback, and communicating high expectations—may be implemented using various interaction strategies in online learning. Chickering and Ehrman (1996) described how technology can be used as a lever to aid teachers in implementing the principles of good practice. In particular, they describe strategies for using communication technologies, including discussion boards, e-mail, chats, and word processing, and other software communication tools. They also discuss using technology to improve time on task and to support collaborative learning, problem-based learning, asynchronous discussions, real-time conversations, simulations, experiments, group projects, apprenticeships, research, individual and peer-reviewed writing projects, and portfolio development to foster student learning.

ONLINE INTERACTION RESEARCH

Savenye, McIsaac, and their students and colleagues have been studying interaction in online learning for a number of years. The results of these studies provide insight into both sticky issues and success factors in interaction (McIsaac & Gunawardena, 2004; Savenye, 2004a).

Digital Video Cases to Aid Teachers in Learning Technology Integration

One of our studies drove home for us the importance of interaction in online learning materials. In a Department of Education funded project, we developed over 20 video cases for preservice and inservice teachers to use in learning to integrate technology effectively into their classrooms (Savenye, 2005). We initially piloted the first video case, including about 20 minutes of video, interviews with the teacher, and all the teacher's materials, including her lesson plan, in a series of graduate classes that were online. We found that these mostly experienced educators enjoyed the video case and felt they learned a lot from it and the online discussion the case generated. We subsequently used the case with over 200 undergraduate preservice teachers in a primarily face-to-face class that did not include discussion. We found that these less-experienced education students liked the case, but did not have the background knowledge to learn technology integration concepts as well as the more experienced graduate students. It was determined that subsequent use of the video cases would require more scaffolding, more interactive activities, and more discussion to help these beginning educators learn more from these online materials.

Evaluation of a Web-Based Course on Teaching With Technology

In a series of studies on our first fully online graduate courses, we found, happily, that our instructional design and planning paid off, that students generally were satisfied with the courses and learned the outcomes well. Due to the many interactive projects and discussions built into the course, students indicated they felt as much a part of this online course as a campus-based course. The majority also rated the course as being better than many campus courses. They indicated, as lessons learned, that they could use technology well to learn challenging content. However, in line with our discussion of interaction, students suggested even more activities to help them understand the material, more feedback from the instructor, and that they would have preferred even more interaction (Savenye, 2000).

Collaboration and Interaction in Online Group Learning

Chen (2005) developed an online group learning activity within what were over 20 sections of a traditionally face-to-face undergraduate computer literacy course. After some preliminary training in Blackboard and online searching, students were divided into groups of about six students, who all came from different sections of the course. Each group was given the task of learning how to set up an ergonomic computer station. They were supported through structured activities and discussion forums, which included either of two different types of threading; directions that either included, or did not include, structured question starters. Students worked in their groups to conduct online searches to answer ergonomics questions and to develop a short report describing an ergonomic computer setup. The group reports were graded, and each student's learning and attitudes were also measured individually using a quiz and an attitude survey. One result of the study was that the students were not much influenced by the structured versus unstructured threading conditions, as they found both to be well organized.

Chen's study illuminates several issues in using interaction in online group learning. The first is that students said they wanted to know the students in their groups; they did not like having to work with students they did not know and could not get to know well during the brief 2-week activity. This issue is particularly critical for students in semester-long online courses; we build activities into the initial weeks of our online courses that require students to get to know each other in natural task-related ways. We use discussion forums every week, so that students learn each other's views and interests related to topics both in and outside the course. We also include a few optional forums in our courses, at least one related to the course in general, but also an online café that allows students to get to know one another more socially. That interaction in group learning is critical was supported by Chen's finding of a significant positive relationship between the number of interactions a group made, and their attitudes; the more interactive the group, the more positive students were in their attitudes toward the course.

Another issue that was important to the students in Chen's study was communicating socially, at least for students in one condition. Students in both the more and the less structured threaded forums mastered the objectives about equally well and made about the same number of task-related postings. However, those in the less-structured forums posted almost double the number of socially related postings than did those in the more structured forums. These findings support the research of Saba and Shearer (1994), who found that the less structure in online communications, the more off-task dialogue. However, we find it interesting that only the social dialogue increased. This is not necessarily detrimental, because students learned the content about equally well, and they had indicated that it was important to them to know one another.

Finally, an issue common to group learning in many environments is that Chen's students were frustrated if students in their groups did not pull their weight. We return to this issue, as supporting group work is often critical in online courses that rely on interaction.

Communication Platforms, Peer Interaction, and Dialogue

Castro (2005) conducted a qualitative study in which she investigated student perceptions and patterns of dialogue in an online graduate seminar course that used both discussion forums and chat as platforms for interaction. Castro found that students tended to prefer discussion boards for discussing course content, especially when graded on their postings. Students' reasons included that they have more time to reflect on their answers and to write carefully thought-out responses. Although they felt that chats often proceed too quickly, especially with more than five or six participants, they did indicate that chats could be enjoyable and led them to both consider and pose different questions, as a result of being able to quickly see students' many different views.

Castro also found that the chats included a higher percentage of more social postings than did the discussion boards, which may indicate to instructors to use chats to foster students' getting to know one another, as well as to help develop learning community among students and the instructor.

Social Presence to Increase Interaction

Tu's (2000) dissertation study built a foundation for his continuing work on social presence and designs for online collaborative learning communities (2004). In order to develop a theory about social presence in online courses, he investigated the perceptions and communication patterns of graduate students enrolled in a course on the Internet for teachers. Fifty-one students participated in his mixed-methods study. Students were enrolled in either a face-to-face or televised section of the course; computer-mediated communications software was used to develop interactive online activities for both sections.

Tu found that social presence was comprised of three dimensions, including social context, online communication, and interactivity. Familiarity with the other students was a critical factor in increasing interaction, feelings of social presence, and developing a more informal type of learning community. He suggested that instructors build many activities into the early weeks of the course to help students get to know one another.

Tu also recommended that instructors aid students by responding to e-mails in a timely manner, and by helping students learn to communicate more easily with each other, sometimes, for instance, by providing guidance about rules of engagement. Tu's study also raised issues related to language, trust, anxiety, stress, privacy, face-saving, access, timely responding to peers' postings, some confusion in threaded discussions, communication style, the importance of interactivity in online courses, and size of groups, especially when working in chats.

Patterns and Meanings in Online Interactions

Vrasidas (1999) used qualitative research methods, including interviews, observations, and transcript analysis, to study the meanings students attached to their online interactions in a hybrid graduate course. He found students could more easily clear up misunderstandings and confusion in face-to-face compared with computer-mediated interaction. Students liked the freedom to conduct their online interactions at any time or place, however, at times lacked confidence in their technical skills. They raised issues related to chat technology, including being overwhelmed, trouble with turn taking, and overlapping communications. He recommended training students and providing time for them to learn how to use the communication technologies early in the course.

Vrasidas concluded that class structure and size influence interaction, as do instructor feedback and student experience with online computer-mediated communication technologies. His finding with regard to class structure is in accord with our experience and the recommendation of Boettcher and Conrad (1999), and may contrast with the work of Saba and Shearer (1994). In Vrasidas's research, as in ours, more structure in a course balanced with student choice, seems to support more interaction and improved learning.

Voluntary Online Interaction in Online Course Discussions

Blocher (1997) investigated perceptions and strategies related to computer-mediated discussions in a face-to-face course in which these interactions were voluntary. He found that students' reported use of strategies for interacting online, including critical thinking, elaboration, and other metacognitive strategies increased over the span of the course. Interestingly, in contrast to work on group learning, Blocher found a negative correlation between students' reported use of peer collaboration and their engagement in computer-mediated communications in this free-choice situation.

Also in contrast to quite a bit of the research on computer-mediated communication, E. Thompson (personal communication, October 4,

2005) reported that in a cohort-based online business degree program in which discussions are voluntary, many students are participating to a great degree. She is investigating these students' motivations for their high level of participation. Clearly there is more to be studied in terms of online interaction that is voluntary, that is, not necessarily linked to course requirements or activities.

Our discussion of research findings and the benefits of interaction leads us now to consider the practical details of incorporating more and better interaction into online courses.

IMPROVING ONLINE COURSES USING INTERACTION

Planning the Course

An effective online course represents a delicate balance between allowing students control, while supporting them with structure and good course organization. Giving students' choices and self-determination aids them in learning to become more motivated and self-regulated. This is important, because, as we discussed earlier, students who are more independent, disciplined, and motivated tend to be more successful. It is the online instructor's responsibility to build this balance of structure and choice. This is, of course, easier said than done.

Giving learners control, choice, and self-determination comes easily in part in an online course. Students have frequently told me that they value the choices they can make daily and weekly about how, when, and from where they'll participate in the course activities. In many ways, too, especially in a graduate class, students build part of the content of the course through their contributions to discussions, their group work, and sharing their writing and development projects through peer reviews, presentations, group file exchanges, and the discussions.

When possible, we design opportunities for student to have choices. For instance, in one course, among other projects, they are required to write two brief research papers. For these two short papers they are given the choice of building their own topic, or of choosing from nine topics with guided questions and resources. Student moderators, with instructor guidance, if they prefer, also develop their own questions that the rest of the students discuss for the one week and the topic chosen by the moderators. We build additional forums in which students can discuss other course-related and social topics. We also allow students considerable guided choice, in either developing instruction or in writing a research paper for the final project.

At the same time, students working in fully online courses need to be supported with a well-organized course from the beginning. A detailed syllabus and schedule, along with course content, activities, requirements, projects, expectations, and grading should be developed and posted ahead of time, so all is clear to students from the start. An online syllabus is often longer and more detailed than one for a face-to-face course. It may include an overview, course objectives, technology resources and requirements, course projects and assignments, grading criteria, and course and university policies. Sample online syllabi are presented by Ko and Rossen (2001) and Palloff and Pratt (1999).

When planning the course, instructors should consider the tricky issue of depth versus breadth. More content may be covered in a course that consists primarily of information, in the form of readings, PowerPoint® presentations, and even videos, particularly if they are *talking-head* lectures. However, the fact that content is presented does not mean that students learn the desired skills (also true for face-to-face settings). We have found that active learning takes time. Interaction can help students to comprehend, analyze, and evaluate information more deeply, but, again, those activities require students time to accomplish, and must be built into the overall design of an online course.

An online instructor should test and select the components of the online course management system, such as Blackboard, currently used at our university (Blackboard, Inc., 1997–2005). These components can be used to foster interaction and can include surveys to collect needs assessment and other learner data, quizzes, discussion boards, chats, online office hour tools, group work tools, and file exchanges. Other technologies and media can also be developed and incorporated into a highly interactive course. These may include but are not limited to blogs; listservs; instant messaging; systems such as Breeze (Macromedia, Inc., 1995–2005) to incorporate live or archived video and PowerPoint with audio; presentations developed using other software such as Flash for animations; Web-conferencing software for student use and for interaction with experts; and audio conferencing software, such as Elluminate (Elluminate, Inc., 2001–2005).

To enhance the interaction in a course, instructors can now go far beyond lectures and readings. They can include practice exercises for individual or group work, to foster interaction with course content. They can plan discussions, chats, or conferences with experts from anywhere in the world. They can plan asynchronous discussions and synchronous chats about course topics, meaningful learning activities, and projects. They can develop and support, using interactive tools, debates, role plays, simulations, and even apprenticeships.

Students may moderate discussions, do peer reviews, engage in peer tutoring, plan and share projects, and solve realistic problems using problem-based learning techniques. Students may also write, and possibly share, journals. Boettcher and Conrad (1999) also suggested such interaction strategies as note taking, summarizing, and internships, to which could be added reports, presentations, discussions, and reflective logs. They mention, too, field trips, and guest lectures, both of which can effectively be conducted online, using chat, discussion boards, e-mail, and video or audio teleconferencing.

Ko and Rossen (2001) included advice for supporting group learning, including how to divide students into groups, about roles within groups, and how to help students do collaborative learning, which for many is a new experience. They also present ways to have students do cross-cultural exchanges and to interact with experts.

For more ideas for activities to build into a course to promote interaction, The State University of New York's Learning Network site includes a page entitled "50 cool things you can do in your course besides lecture!" (Pickett, 1999). These include, for instance, debate, brainstorming, puzzles, role playing, skits, symposia and many more (for a complete list of activities, see: http://sln.suny.edu/sln/public/original.nsf/0/d66bf6388888dbdf85256c1600 639be7?OpenDocument).

The Week Before the Class Begins

Before the course begins, write students an e-mail describing how to prepare for the course, how to get started, and what they may expect. Cottam and colleagues (2004) developed a *Retention Action Checklist* as a job aid to help instructors support and retain students throughout the semester, but especially in the first crucial weeks, for a foreign language course taught by many instructors. They described what they call a *Successful Start* letter that is a template each instructor adapts and personalizes. The letter welcomes students, directs them to the course web site, and describes the communication tools they will use. It also tells students they are required to read the syllabus and acknowledge they have read it to their instructor by the second week of the course. Instructors are then told to contact students if they do not receive this acknowledgement. All this preparation pays off as the course begins and proceeds.

During the First Few Weeks of the Course

During the first week of the course, if not before, most instructors conduct an orientation, either face-to-face or online, to help students get started. We typically e-mail students quite a bit during the first week. Instructors may choose also to hold chat-based or audio-based online office hours during these weeks and throughout the course. Consider, too, building a discussion board for FAQs, that is, frequently asked questions in the course, and suggesting that before e-mailing you, students check this board. If you have sent a letter or other request for students to acknowledge, as we mentioned, and students do not answer, they may be having technical difficulties; a phone call not only heads off problems early, but students say they appreciate the personal contact.

Based on all we know from interaction and social presence research, the better students know each other, the better they may interact and work together. As in a face-to-face class, instructors during the first few weeks may conduct icebreaker activities that help students learn to use the course telecommunications tools, as well as to become familiar with each other. This will be particularly helpful later as students work in groups.

Again, the more skilled students are with the computer technologies involved in the course the more likely it is they will succeed, be satisfied with, and remain in the course, so the more practice students receive early on with the online course technologies, the better.

Throughout the Course

As difficult as this sometimes is for busy faculty, the instructor is always responsible for what goes on in the course (Hanna et al., 2000). The instructor should be the initial troubleshooter, as students having technical problems, especially in the first weeks of the course, may drop out. It is a good idea to also let students know of technical help offered by the institution.

Lehmann (2004) recommended that instructors interact with students at all times during the course to provide support, motivation, encouragement, and feedback. Muirhead (2001) described the results of a study in which he asked undergraduate students for their ideas of what would improve interactivity. Among their ideas for instructors were helping students stay accountable during weekly discussions; creating more challenging, as well as more open-ended, discussion questions; initiating and maintaining more personalized and active contact with students; using more group projects and chat; and providing more constructive feedback during discussions.

Most online courses use online discussions, chats (with or without whiteboards), e-mail, and sometimes teleconferences, as the technological tools for conducting course activities. Specific suggestions for how to work with each of these technologies are presented in Savenye (in press). In addition to illustrating how to build online courses, Ko and Rossen (2001) described strategies for working with all of these tools. Moore and Kearsley (2005) provided guidelines for conducting teleconferences, as well as using asynchronous discussions and synchronous chat. Hanna, et al. (2000) and Lehmann (2004) focused considerable attention on methods for building and supporting online groups doing cooperative learning. Berge and Collins in their book (1995) and Website (Collins, 2003) provided advice for instructors and their students on how to facilitate and moderate online interaction. Lehmann (2004) also provided tips on how to manage e-mail, as well as on how to use instant messaging, video and audio conferencing.

Evaluate Students and the Course During and at the End of the Course

That students learn is the primary goal of any online course. It is fair and valuable in all courses, but especially those that use many technologies, to use multiple methods to assess what students have learned (Savenye, 2004b). Assessments often include exams and quizzes, which may be administered in person, with proctors at set locations, or more commonly, online. In large classes, instructors often develop computer-scored assessments; however, instructors may also score assessments by hand. Assessments may include written papers, responses to problem-based learning cases and simulations, debates, or projects, completed individually or in groups. Journals and portfolios may also contribute to assessments. Many online instructors use rubrics, or checklists, to evaluate students' performance, and students can use these rubrics ahead of time to determine what is expected of them. We also use these rubrics to guide students as they do peer reviews of each other's initial drafts of papers; we use other rubrics to assess the usefulness of their peer reviews.

Learner interactions may also form part of the assessment of student learning. For instance, we require students to reply to each week's discussion questions by mid-week and to reply to at least one other student's posting by the end of the week. We use rubrics to evaluate to what extent the students have applied what they read about the week's topic in their responses, and how well they have added their own thoughtful contributions to the discussions. Because students are required to serve as moderators for at least one discussion, their work as moderators also is assessed.

Formative evaluation is a critical aspect of developing courses that use new methods and technologies. Evaluation procedures aid instructors in collecting data to use in improving the courses (Savenye, 2004a). The first time we offer a course, we usually administer one or two mid-course evaluation surveys, sometimes accompanied by an anonymous open discussion forum in which students can post comments, questions, or concerns. Measuring student learning and attitudes while the course is going on enables instructors to give students more feedback, and to improve the course on an ongoing basis (Hanna et al., 2000).

At the end of the course, in addition to making final assessments of student learning, we use a survey to collect information about students' attitudes toward the online course. Often in another discussion board, we ask students to describe the main things they learned, and what suggestions they have for improving the course. Cottam and colleagues (2004) also recommended reminding successful students to consider taking the next course in the sequence, or to consider applying for a degree program. Making revisions or at least notes immediately after the evaluation is particularly useful. These notes, too, can be used to improve aspects of technology-based activities in other courses, whether online, hybrid, blended, or face-to-face.

STICKY ISSUES ABOUT INTERACTION IN ONLINE LEARNING

Although we have been successful in our years of online teaching, in thinking about why we teach online, and what we have learned, a few "sticky issues" come to mind. These are issues that are not yet resolved, that continue to arise when we teach online. Some will be solved as our institutions adopt the next new technologies and methods. Some may be ongoing, and we look forward to discussing with our new online learning colleagues these issues.

Time Constraints

We have found that time is always a constraint when teaching online. The first time issue we continually grapple with is the breadth versus depth issue mentioned earlier. We often plan too much into an online course, and have to extend deadlines, for instance, for group activities the first time through. However, at times in a hybrid course, instructors are finding that students learn more in their online activities, in which they interact with the content, peers, and the instructor, than they might if they had been in a lecture-based campus course.

There is no doubt that developing an online course takes considerably more time than developing a campus-based course. Once developed, some instructors say that teaching an online course still doubles their teaching time; others have found methods for streamlining their online teaching tasks. However, we have found that in a truly engaging and interactive course, students need more feedback, more frequently. They typically are working alone to accomplish many of their assignments, and often feel isolated; they send e-mails and post messages that describe this isolation, and often wonder, "Am I doing this right?" When building group activities, instructors will spend considerable time developing the directions, materials, and evaluation guidelines, as well as monitoring groups by e-mail and in the discussion boards.

As many online instructors have found, whereas it takes only a few hours to review papers and then a few minutes to give feedback to campus-based classes or to hand back papers, providing individualized feedback via online discussion boards, file exchanges and e-mail can take more time.

Time is, for course, a constraint for students, too. We have found it effective to give students a clear idea from the beginning of the course and on an ongoing basis, about how much time they should devote to a particular course, and to certain activities. We have revised our expectations, too, based on students' evaluative feedback regarding time constraints.

The Changing Role of the Instructor Who Teaches Online

The changing role of the technology-using instructor has been a recurring theme in educational technology. Not surprisingly, it arises again in online learning; however, we find that the role shift may be becoming more profound.

One issue is that our administrators, colleagues, and sometimes students, think that once a course is online, it is easy to teach, or even teaches itself. Some may say, although the online instructor has the workload record to prove otherwise, that he or she is not teaching, or not lecturing, so the course must take less time. If the course includes video, some may say the instructor need only lecture once and never again, as was the case years ago with televised courses. The real issue, though, is with regard to interaction. We know that interaction is the key to a successful online course, one that can teach more, better, and differently, or certainly as well, as a campus-based course. However, interaction takes work, and that work is not always visible to those outside the course.

In the same vein, although institutions often encourage faculty to teach online, there is not always commensurate support and perceptions of worth. For those who make the effort to build an effective interactive course, the results may or may not be valued by the institution, particularly one that heavily emphasizes research, or one in which faculty decision makers have not taught online themselves.

Another issue in the shifting role of the instructor is related to student control and students' changing roles in online courses. We believe students should have choices; students contribute to the content of the course even if only through their postings in the discussion boards. This can incur problems and discomfort, at times, for instructors. We provide students with guidelines about communicating appropriately, and retain the right to take down highly inappropriate messages. We also monitor students' discussions to make sure we interject to clarify misunderstandings, correct errors, or bring discussions back to the main questions. However, in highly interactive courses, once we have motivated students to be open, honest, thoughtful, and even thought-provoking, when they are all that, grey areas arise that may be uncomfortable for instructors. For instance, when students discussing online learning decide to critique the course they are in, and not all is flattering, instructors have to decide what to do. When students are confused, or irritated, these postings are up for all to see, and respond to. We have found the value of open, but monitored, discussions for students far outweighs any discomfort, but new issues can always arise, and can remind the instructor of his or her, and the students', shifting roles.

Student Self-Discipline

We have found that, as in a campus course, there are always students with motivation issues, or who lack self-discipline, or who have taken on too heavy a course load. It is often easier for these students to fall behind in online courses, and it takes considerable work on an instructor's part to keep them in the course, and help them keep up. We recently were reminded by a student who said that all this feedback each week, and e-mailed reminders to do assignments, had enabled the student to continue to complete the course.

Human Communication Issues

As our earlier review has pointed out, several communication issues are to be grappled with on an ongoing basis in online courses. These include native language, trust when not familiar with each other, supporting group processes, the limitations of text (currently, but technologies are changing) for communicating emotions and meanings, and response times that can sometimes be too slow in discussion boards, contrasted with too fast in chats.

The Double-Edged Sword of New Online Technologies

We eagerly await new developments in online technologies. In particular, audio and video conferencing and presentation tools, such as Elluminate and Breeze, are beginning to help us solve a few of our sticky issues in teaching online. E-portfolio tools also are becoming more supported at our universities, and these, too, enable more interaction, engagement, and deeper learning.

Of course, every new technology and method also requires considerable time to learn. Although these tools are affordances that allow us to help our students learn even better, they often require course redesign. In fact, each time the learning management system or other presentation software is upgraded, components in the course often must be revised as well. In some cases, online instructors spend considerable effort to make new tools and resources available to students in their organization. These efforts may take the form of securing funds for purchasing or licensing new software, or for paying support personnel to develop needed materials such as videos or Flash presentations to aid learners.

CONCLUSION

In conclusion, we hope the reader is not still wondering if it is worthwhile to teach online using rich interaction strategies. We hope that our discussion has convinced instructors that online technologies not only support interactive, engaging activities for learning, but enable our students to learn in ways that are not easy to do, and sometimes not even possible, in a campus-based classroom. An instructor who builds a learning environment that includes active, engaging learning activities that foster critical thinking skills, feedback, motivation, and support for students in learning from each other, will be an effective online instructor (Kearsley & Blomeyer, 2004). Interaction is the foundation. Building that environment supports a learning community of students who are accountable to, and motivated by, each other, as well as the instructor. As Palloff and Pratt (1999) suggest, such learning communities may transform students, and they are also likely to transform instructors and our institutions.

REFERENCES

Alessi, S. M., & Trollip, S. R. (2004). *Multimedia for learning: Methods and Development* (3rd ed.). Boston, MA: Allyn & Bacon.

Blackboard, Inc. (1997–2005). BlackBoard. [Computer software]. Washington, DC: Blackboard, Inc. Retrieved October 3, 2005, from http://www.blackboard.com.

Berge, Z. L., & Collins, M. P. (Eds.). (2003). *Computer-mediated communication and the online classroom*. Cresskill, NJ: Hampton Press.

Blocher, J. M. (1997). *Self-regulation of strategies and motivation to enhance interaction and social presence in computer mediated communication.* Unpublished doctoral dissertation, Arizona State University, AZ.

Boettcher, J. V., & Conrad, R. M. (1999). *Faculty guide for moving teaching and learning to the Web.* Mission Viejo, CA: League for Innovation in the Community College.

Brewer, S. (2004). *Small group learning in an online asynchronous environment.* Unpublished doctoral dissertation, Arizona State University, AZ.

Castro, M. (2005). *Patterns of communication and interaction in online learning using chat and discussion boards.* Unpublished manuscript.

Chen, H. (2005). *The effect of type of threading and level of self-efficacy on achievement and attitudes in online course discussion.* Unpublished doctoral dissertation, Arizona State University, AZ.

Chickering, A. W., & Gamson, Z. F. (1987, March). Seven principles for good practice in undergraduate education. *AAHE Bulletin* [On-line]. Retrieved October 3, 2005, from http://honolulu.hawaii.edu/intranet/committees/FacDevCom/guidebk/teachtip/7princip.htm

Chickering, A. W., & Ehrmann, S. C. (1996, October). Implementing the seven principles: Technology as lever. *AAHE Bulletin*, 3–6 [Online]. Retrieved October 3, 2005, from http://www.tltgroup.org/programs/seven.html

Collins, M. P. (2003). *Resources for moderators and facilitators of online discussion.* [Online]. Retrieved October 3, 2005, from http://www.emoderators.com/moderators.shtml

Cottam, M. E., Smith, V. C., & Savenye, W. C. (2004, October). *Factors that affect distance education student retention in foreign language classes – Interventions that work!* Paper presented at the annual conference of the Association for Educational Communications and Technology, Chicago, IL.

Dick, W., Carey, L., & Carey, J. (2001). *The systematic design of instruction* (5th ed.). New York: Longman.

Eastmond, D., & Zieghan, L. (1995). Instructional design for the online classroom. In Z. L Berge & M. P. Collins (Eds.), *Computer-mediated communication and the online classroom* (pp. 59–80). Cresskill, NJ: Hampton Press.

Elluminate, Inc. (2001–2005). Elluminate Live [Computer software]. Retrieved October 3, 2005, from http://www.elluminate.com

Fulford, C. P., & Zhang, S. (1993). Perceptions of interaction: The critical predictor in distance education. *The American Journal of Distance Education, 7*(3), 8–21.

Gagné, R. M., Briggs, L. J., & Wager, W. W. (1992). *Principles of instructional design* (4th ed.). Fort Worth, TX: Harcourt, Brace.

Hanna, D. E., Glowacki-Dudka, M., & Conceicao-Runlee, S. (2000). *147 practical tips for teaching online groups.* Madison, WI: Atwood.

Hillman, C. A., Willis, D. J., & Gunawardena, C. N. (1994). Learner-interface interaction in distance education: An extension of contemporary models and strategies for practitioners. *The American Journal of Distance Education, 8*(2), 30–42.

International Society for Technology in Education (ISTE). (2000–2004). *National Educational Technology Standards.* [Online]. Retrieved October 3, 2005, from http://cnets.iste.org

Kearsley, G., & Blomeyer, R. (2004). *Preparing K–12 teachers to teach online.* [Online]. Retrieved October 3, 2005, from http://home.sprynet.com/~gkearsley/ TeachingOnline.htm

Ko, S., & Rossen, S. (2001). *Teaching online: A practical guide.* Boston, MA: Houghton Mifflin.

Lamb, A. C., & Smith, W. L. (2000, February). Ten facts of life for distance learning courses. *TechTrends, 44*(1), 12–15.

Lehmann, K. J. (2004). *How to be a great online teacher.* Lanham, MD: ScareCrow Education.

Macromedia, Inc. (1995–2005). Breeze 5 [Computer software]. San Francisco, CA: Macromedia, Inc. Retrieved October 3, 2005, from http://www.macromedia.com.

McIsaac, M. S., & Gunawardena, C. N. (2004). Distance education. In D. H. Jonassen (Ed.), *Handbook of research for educational communications and technology* (2nd ed., pp. 355–395). Mahwah, NJ: Lawrence Erlbaum Associates.

Meyer, K. A. (2003, May). The Web's impact on student learning: A review of recent research reveals three areas that can enlighten current online learning practices. *T.H.E. Journal, 30*(10), 14–24.

Moore, M. G. (1989). Three types of interaction. *The American Journal of Distance Education, 3*(2), 1–6.

Moore, M. G., & Kearsley, G. (2005). *Distance education: A systems view* (2nd ed.). Belmont, CA: Wadsworth.

Muirhead, B. (2001). Enhancing social interaction in computer-mediated distance education. *Education at a Distance, 14*(40). [Online]. Retrieved October 3, 2005, from http://www.usdla.org/html/journal/APR01_Issue/article02.html

Muirhead, B. (2004). Research insights into interactivity. *International Journal of Technology and Distance Learning, 1*(3) [Online]. Retrieved October 3, 2005, from http://www.itdl.org/Journal/Mar_04/article05.htm

Palloff, R. M., & Pratt, K. (1999). *Building learning communities in cyberspace: Effective strategies for the online classroom*. San Francisco, CA: Jossey-Bass.
Pickett, A. M. (1999, June). *SUNY CIT Conference: What works? Instructional design roundtable: 50 cool things you can do in your course besides lecture!* [Online]. Albany, NY: The State University of New York. Retrieved October 3, 2005, from http://sln. suny.edu/sln/public/original.nsf/dd93a8da0b7ccce0852567b00054e2b6/ d66bf6388888dbdf85256c1600639be7?OpenDocument
Roblyer, M. D. (2000). The national educational technology standards (NETS): A review of definitions, implications, and strategies for integrating NETS into K–12 curriculum. *International Journal of Instructional Media, 27*(2), 133–146.
Roblyer, M. D., & Marshall, J. (2002–2003). Predicting success of virtual high school distance learners: preliminary results from an educational success prediction instrument (ESPRI). *Journal of Research on Technology in Education, 35*(2), 241–255.
Roblyer, M. D., & Ekhaml, L. (2000, Spring). How interactive are YOUR distance courses? A rubric for assessing interaction in distance learning. *Online Journal of Distance Learning Administration, 3*(2). Retrieved October 3, 2005, from http:// www.westga.edu/~distance/roblyer32.html
Roblyer, M., & Wiencke, W. R. (2004). Exploring the interaction equation: Validating a rubric to assess and encourage interaction in distance courses. *Journal of Asynchronous Learning Networks, 8*(4). Retrieved October 3 2005, from http:// www.sloan-c.org/publications/jaln/v8n4/v8n4_roblyer.asp
Rumble, G. (1997). *The costs and economics of open and distance learning*. London: Kogan Page.
Saba, F., & Shearer, R. L. (1994). Verifying key theoretical concepts in a dynamic model of distance education. *The American Journal of Distance Education, 8*(1), 36–57.
Savenye, W. C. (2000). Reflections on developing a web-based *Teaching with Technology* course. In J. M. Spector & T. M. Anderson (Eds.), *Integrated and holistic perspectives on learning, instruction, and technology: Understanding complexity* (pp. 191–211). Dordrecht, Netherlands: Kluwer.
Savenye, W. C. (2004a). Evaluating web-based learning systems and software. In. N. Seel & S. Dijkstra (Eds.), *Instructional design: Addressing the challenges of learning through technology and curriculum* (pp. 309–330). Mahwah, NJ: Lawrence Erlbaum Associates.
Savenye, W. C. (2004b). Alternatives for assessing learning in web-based distance learning courses. *Distance Learning, 1*(1), 29–35.
Savenye, W. C. (2005). Learning technology integration from video cases: Development and research issues. In. M. Orey, J. McClendon, & R. M. Branch (Eds.), *Educational media and technology yearbook 2005* (Vol. 30, pp. 110–126). Westport, CT: Libraries Unlimited.
Savenye, W. C. (in press). Improving online courses: What is interaction and why use it? *Distance Learning*.
Simonson, M., Smaldino, S., Albright, M., & Svacek, S. (2006). *Teaching and learning at a distance: Foundations of distance education* (3rd ed.). Upper Saddle River, NJ: Pearson Merrill Prentice Hall.
Smaldino, S. E., Russell, J. D., Heinich, R., & Molenda, M. (2005). *Instructional technology and media for learning* (8th ed.). Upper Saddle River, NJ: Prentice-Hall.
Smith, P. J., & Ragan, T. J. (2005). *Instructional design* (3rd ed.). Hoboken, NJ: Wiley.
Smith, M. C., & Winking-Diaz, A. (2004, Winter). Increasing students' interactivity in an online course. *Journal of Interactive Online Learning, 2*(3). Retrieved October 3, 2005, from http://www.ncolr.org/jiol/issues/PDF/2.3.3.pdf

Sutton, L. A. (2001). The principle of vicarious interaction in computer-mediated communications. *International Journal of Educational Telecommunications, 7*(3), 223–242.

Tiffin, J., & Rajasingham, L. (1995). *In search of the virtual class: Education in an information society.* London: Routledge.

The Concord Consortium. (2005). *The Concord Consortium: Realizing the promise of educational technology* [Online]. Retrieved October 3, 2005, from http://www.concord.org

Tu, C. H. (2000). *An examination of social presence to increase interaction in online classes.* Unpublished doctoral dissertation, Arizona State University, AZ.

Tu, C. H. (2004). *Online collaborative learning communities: Twenty-one designs to building an online collaborative learning community.* Westport, CN: Libraries Unlimited.

Vrasidas, C. (1999). *Meanings of online and face-to-face interactions in a graduate course.* Unpublished doctoral dissertation, Arizona State University, AZ.

Zirkin, B., & Sumler, D. (1994). Interactive or non-interactive? That is the question! An annotated bibliography. *Journal of Distance Education, 10*(1), 95–112. Retrieved October 3, 2005, from http://cade.athabascau.ca/vol10.1/zirkinsumler.html

Using Elaborations of Online Presence to Foster Critical Thinking and Reflection

Roderick C. Sims
Knowledgecraft

Bethany Bovard
New Mexico State University

More learners, especially those in mid-career, are seeking higher education and utilizing the expediency of the "any time—any place" delivery model offered by many providers (Perkinson, 2004). Consequently, the dynamic of the online interaction is becoming increasingly significant in terms of the quality of the teaching and learning experience. Understanding the encounters that result and the different ways that teachers and learners manifest their online presence, especially when they are communicating through asynchronous channels, is critical to the success of the teaching and learning experience. Salmon (2003) spoke of this as e-moderating presence and identified key activities for both the teacher (e.g., course expectations and regular communication) and the learner (e.g., active communication with other participants) as essential to establishing and maintaining an online presence. Nevertheless, our experience also highlights a conflict within online environments, where the expectations of the online learner for regular and frequent support are not necessarily aligned with those of the teachers, who often emphasize self-directed learning and student collaboration in order to support the development of an online community.

One reason cited to explain this potential conflict is that online communication cannot have the richness of a face-to-face environment. For example, Preece (2000) suggested that online interactions typically lack visual signals, logical sequence, and emotive cues, making it difficult for learners to project a social presence. However, given the increase in online learning, we believe it imperative to investigate new levels of communication, rather than basing online interactions on an assumption that face-to-face communication represents the best form of communication and that computer-mediated communication is inherently less effective. Our argument is that we must focus on what is and what will be, rather than on what was and has been the case. The "what is" can be characterized as an emergent social context in which both synchronous and asynchronous communications are the norm—chats, blogs, podcasts, and text messaging are prime examples. Granted, these communications are often made with learners knowing one another through prior physical meeting, but the resulting virtual communication remains "real"(Bennett & Dziekan, 2005). Preece (2000) also indicated that to better understand these online dynamics, we need to borrow from sociology, communications, and social psychology and we argue that to best use online technologies, we need to transcend and develop theories founded in the predigital age. We must go beyond our comfort zone and investigate the characteristics of anticipated future teaching and learning environments to better understand those interactions and dynamics with which we may not feel comfortable but that are likely to be the norm for future generations of learners.

In this chapter, we focus specifically on those online environments that operate in distance mode, with learners geographically dispersed and the primary form of interaction being the discussion forum. This context provides the framework by which to elaborate on existing work relating to the dynamics of the online classroom with respect to social, cognitive, and teacher presence.

Using face-to-face communication as the standard, social presence focuses on the extent to which media can successfully convey a sense of the participants being physically present (Short, Williams, & Christie, 1976). Preece (2000) argued that "social presence, or more practically lack of social presence, can critically influence how people behave online, form impressions of others, and negotiate common ground" (p. 165). Building on that, Rourke, Anderson, Garrison, and Archer (1999) stated that "the ability of learners to project their personal characteristics into the community of inquiry, thereby presenting themselves as real people" (p. 4) was crucial to social presence. However, based on the wider acceptance and use of online learning, we question whether face-to-face should be maintained as the standard of presence. How many learners and teachers now feel present in the online environment even though their interactions are completely virtual? Although these factors of social presence may have been a more significant concern in early online environments, we argue that it is now less of a concern because of our increased familiarity with online communications; we are more adept at projecting our presence through our virtual interactions because we have adapted to the special nature of online communications.

A second online dynamic is cognitive presence, "the extent to which the participants in any particular configuration of a community of inquiry are able to construct meaning through sustained communication" (Garrison et al., 2004, p. 1). This analysis considered discussion interactions in terms of cognitive presence descriptors such as deliberation, conception, perception, and experience and their relationship to facilitating higher order thinking. If we assume that online education is moving toward an educational norm, then we must also assume that effective online environments will consistently manifest this cognitive presence. It is therefore the responsibility of the course designers and developers to create environments and activities that will sustain an appropriate level of reflection and critical thinking.

A third aspect of the online context that links both social and cognitive presence is that of teaching presence, "the design, facilitation, and direction of cognitive and social processes for the purpose of realizing personally meaningful and educational worthwhile learning outcomes" (Anderson, Rourke, Garrison, & Archer, 2000, p.1). Based on our experience, as we come to better understand the dynamics of online teaching and learning (see Palloff & Pratt, 2003) the role of the teacher will no longer be focused on facilitating and integrating social and cognitive presence; rather, that skill will be assumed and the teacher's role will develop to focus more on the outcomes than on the environment. While implementing strategies to enhance social and cognitive presence in our own online teaching activities, one issue we have faced is that learners often do not seek collaborative networks or develop or demand an explicit online social presence. To address this, we implemented a pilot research study to gain better understanding of the online teaching and learning dynamic and how the complex interactions between teachers and an increasingly diverse student population can be better understood, especially with the multiple perspectives those individual learners bring to online courses of study.

These perspectives involve both the educational goals of the learner as well as their level of cognitive development. In terms of goals, the online learners that we have encountered typically fall into three groups; those who are studying online because it is economically attractive, those for whom it is the most convenient (pragmatic), and those for whom the scholarly interactions and collaborations are of prime importance. However, the extent to which these factors impact on a desire for presence remains unclear and is a primary focus of this analysis. To provide a framework for better understanding the cognitive development and interactions of online learners, we have adopted the three levels identified by Perry (1970). The dualistic learner assumes that there is a simple answer to the course topic; the multiplistic learner will recognize that not all answers can be provided whereas the relativistic learner will determine that answers can be derived from many perspectives. These levels also relate to the personal epistemologies of teachers and learners (Hofer, 2004). Learners' personal epistemologies lead them to have beliefs about the nature of knowledge and knowing. Learners who believe that knowledge is certain and simple and that the teacher or textbook is the source of authority for knowledge may not perceive social presence as critical to achieving cognitive presence. They might find less value in social and cognitive presence of other learners because they would not be seen as being able to shed any light on the subject under study. Similarly, they would unlikely to be interested in collaborating to construct knowledge because that would be contrary to their personal epistemology. On the other hand, learners who view knowledge as uncertain and complex with multiple sources of authority and justifications for knowing would be more likely to engage in collaborative knowledge constructions. They would perceive social/cognitive presence of other learners to have as high a value as that of the teacher.

KEY QUESTIONS

Given this background, the research on online presence often assumes a so-called typical adult student and provides guidelines and suggestions on effective presence for that assumed of the typical student. Similarly the discourse on teaching to foster self-directed learning appears to assume that learners are all at the same starting point when, from the authors' own experience as both teachers and learners, this is not the typical case. Consequently we first argued (Sims & Bovard, 2004) that it is essential to discuss the idea of online presence not only from multiple student perspectives but also from a perspective of dynamic design, and posed the following questions for an examination of the online dynamic between teacher and learner:

    1. How can a teacher be present enough (or perceived to be present enough) that learners benefit from their subject matter expertise without being so present that she or he does not inhibit the learners from learning from one another?

    2. Given that learners have different educational goals (e.g., pragmatic, economic, scholarly), and assuming that those goals help form learners' expectations of teacher presence, is it possible (or desirable) for

a teacher to be present (or perceived as present) at different levels for different learners?

3. Given that learners are at different stages of cognitive development (Perry, 1970) and assuming that those stages help form student expectations of teacher presence, is it possible (or desirable) for a teacher to be present (or be perceived as present) at different stages for different learners?

4. What are the implications for instructional design with the maturing of online environments and the varying expectations of learners?

To address these questions, the performance and perceptions of learners within an online course were reviewed from both quantitative and qualitative perspectives in two separate studies; one, a study of learners at Capella University (USA), a for-profit distance university; the other, a study of learners at New Mexico State University (USA), a land grant institution. Through these studies, we position the outcomes in terms of the dimensions of educational goals (pragmatic, economic, scholarly) and cognitive development (dualistic, multiplistic, relativistic).

BEING PRESENT ONLINE

The courses in which the online learners were enrolled were offered by Capella University (USA) and all learners were resident in the United States with the teacher resident in Australia. The learners are typically mid-career, having chosen to upgrade their qualifications to either masters or doctoral level; with professions across the K–12, community college, higher education, health, government, corporate, and defense sectors. By better understanding the perceptions of our learners and how those perceptions are mediated by their goals and personal epistemologies, we believe the online interaction dynamic between teacher and learner can be enhanced.

Presence as a Quantitative Experience

This analysis is based on two sets of data. First, the total number of responses made by both the learners and the teacher to contributions made to weekly discussion topics were recorded in order to develop a profile of weekly presence from a quantitative perspective. Fig. 10.1 represents contributions to an online course over eight weekly units (U1 – U8) and the percentage of the total weekly responses made by the teacher and 2 of the 12 learners. The data indicates that Learner 1 was not as active (quantitatively) in the course as Learner 2, and did not make any contributions during the Unit 2 discussions. On the other hand, Learner 2 was more prolific in responses throughout the course. The teacher's responses represent a high contribution in Units 1 and 2 providing support for new learners, with sig-

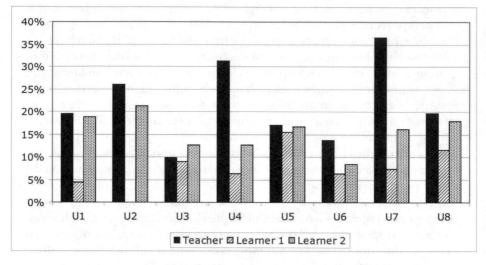

Figure 10.1.   Comparison of teacher and learner contributions.

nificant input in Unit 4 (prior to an assessment piece being required) and Unit 7 (when learners were completing their final projects).

However, although it is possible to imply from this data that the participants (teacher and learner) had comparatively high or low presence within that online learning environment (Anderson et al, 2003; Garrison et al., 2004), this does not give an indication of the substance or perceived value of those contributions by either teacher or learner. More importantly, despite the teacher in this example contributing approximately 20% of all responses, which might be considered a high presence, feedback from learners indicated that this level of visibility did not necessarily provide the desired presence or level of interaction to meet their individual learning needs.

Given this, a basic question emerges: What does it mean to have presence, or to be effectively present, in an online environment? The following analysis provides an assessment of qualitative responses in terms of the factors emerging and the implications for enhancing both learner and teacher presence in an online, asynchronous environment.

Presence as a Qualitative Experience

In order to develop a more substantial view of presence therefore, learners from two courses being conducted by the first author agreed to respond to five questions relating to presence in online teaching and learning. The questions related to what it meant to be present online, to differentiate high and low learner presence as well as high and low teacher presence. Of the 36 learners enrolled, 12 elected to respond to the questions, and not all learners responded to each of the five questions. As a qualitative study, the sample of learners is representative of one instance of online teaching and learning interactions. In analyzing the data and developing conclusions, there is no assumption that these responses can be generalized to all online teaching and learning environments. However, the implications for perceptions of online presence are useful for reflection on a range of online educational interactions. To contextualize the responses in terms of current practice, the impressions of learners from a subsequent offering of the course provide an additional perspective on the data.

The first question asked respondents to indicate their view of online presence, and the classification of their responses are shown in Table 10.1. Of the 11 responses received, the learners focused on indicators such as personal considerations to community and participation to the procedure of completing a course. From a teacher's perspective, although participation and frequency of response are both predictable and observable, it is the personal aspects that a learner can bring to the online environment that can complicate the interaction.

What the different perceptions reinforce is our observation of the complexity of individual differences and learning expectations, the multiple perspectives, that learners do indeed present during online interactions. For example, presence was often related to the flexibility that the environment provides, "it provides me the flexibility in my daily schedule to continue my studies without spending another few nights away from my family. I can study at home or in a quiet place at my choosing." Interestingly, this sense of anytime, anywhere learning appears now to be expected rather than simply a potential feature of the online environment.

TABLE 10.1

Classification of Online Presence

1. *What Does it Mean for You to Be Present in an Asynchronous Online Learning Environment?*

Personal (n = 4)	Participation (n = 3)	Frequency (n = 2)	Community (n = 1)	Procedural (n = 1)
Beliefs	Active	Connected	Being heard	Assessment
Flexibility	Reflective	Rate		
Recognition	Responsive			
	Engaged			

For other learners, the emphasis was on participation and the importance of community to provide the framework for constructive activity—"being present means that I am an active participant in the discussions being held; that I both acknowledge the contributions of my classmates and contribute my own thoughts as well." However, the activity was also linked to the frequency of participation, and the extent to which the learner is part of the dynamic—"when I am able to log-on at minimum every 2 days to participate in the collaborative online discussions and assignments. If I do not keep up this consistent participation, I feel disconnected from the rest of the class." The ability to remain connected is now gaining more research interest as educators begin to question the different ways in which students communicate and socialize (Prensky, 2005).

Alternatively, one learner conceptualized presence as being manifested through their internal state of mind, which aligns with what Reeves (2004) identified as the conative domain. In stating that "presence is a proactive state of mind and activity, where one is in a continual process of defining and refining beliefs and attitudes, with the objective to gain critical insights, through collaborative means, to develop specific competencies," the response highlights that how we participate in an online environment is largely through our construction of personal mental models—not only those in the affective domain but also the conative, which aligns with individual will, determination, and motivation. Given this observation, it is pertinent to ask that, as an online teacher, to what extent can an understanding of a learner's personal beliefs and motivation help balance the way the online teaching process is conducted? From a different perspective, are there presence factors, pertinent to the learner, that extend beyond those described by social and cognitive presence?

Presence for the Learner

There often appears to be a lack of focus of the online learner as an individual bringing multiple perspectives of their presence to the online (in this instance, asynchronous) environment. In analyzing the responses to the second question (summarized in Table 10.2), which focused on the characteristics of learners with a high online presence, two themes emerged; responses related to the characteristics of quality and community aligned with cognitive presence whereas responses related to the characteristic of frequency were more aligned with social presence.

The themes related to the personal theme identified with high course room[1] presence reflected on the dedication of the individual learner,

---

[1]The environment provided by Capella University is known as the course room, and this terminology was used in the questions to elicit responses from the learners.

TABLE 10.2
Classification of High Online Learner Presence

2. What Characterizes Learners Who, in Your Opinion,
Have High Course Room Presence?

Personal (*n* = 3)	**Sample Responses**
Dedication Commitment Energy	It means a dedication in using time management skills to set aside predetermined blocks of time to devote to completing course assignments, posting prepared in depth discussions and responses, and to find this balance between family, work, and studies to be successful.
Quality (*n* = 3)	**Sample Response**
Provoking Proactive Insightful	* Responses that provoke thought are desirable. * Did I learn something or did it make me think or ask further questions, was it insightful.
Frequency (*n* = 4)	**Sample Response**
Quantity Grace Timeliness	Learners who respond to direct questions asked of them within 24 hours of the question or comment being posted. They should not wait until the final day or two of the response period to make all their postings. People who post often/frequently.
Community (*n* = 2)	**Sample Response**
Understanding Dialogue Resources	Feeling, understanding and comprehending the material and having a dialogue with the Facilitator and the other Learners.

which also links to the hypothesis of Reeves (2004) that we must focus on the conative domain (will and determination) to better understand the learner's perception and performance in the online context. One of the valuable outcomes of seeking opinions on the online educational environment is the occasional response that captures the essence of the online dynamic. In this case, one of the respondents offered the following comment, defining presence as:

> people (who) seem to float through classroom discussions, stopping almost gracefully to comment on other learners' thoughts without interrupting their own graceful momentum ... (like) a butterfly stopping briefly here and there while still remaining on course.

What are the characteristics of a learner who might achieve this? How might a teacher perceive this participative activity? What levels of experience and competence might be required to achieve this level of interaction? In the same way that learners perceive positive online presence as relating to a range of characteristics, a similar differentiation arises when low presence is considered. As detailed in Table 10.3, responses highlight issues such as personal events that interrupt and affect the ability to participate as well as contributions being made solely to satisfy course assessment requirements. This latter point highlights the importance of the design strategy that is implemented; for example, in a number of courses in which we have participated, the strategy has focused on analysis of texts and reporting personal analyses of those texts. Aligned with this is an assessment rubric that often requires both posting of individual responses and responding to other learners' contributions.

TABLE 10.3
Classification of low Online Learner Presence

3. What Characterizes Learners Who, in Your Opinion, Have Low Course Room Presence?

Personal (*n* = 5)	Sample Responses
Unbalanced Uninvolved Satisfied	The balance is not there, life all of a sudden starts to get "in the way", and reasons for non attendance become predominantly excuses. Overworked, not committed, possible work/family conflict if the low course room presence spans 3 out of 12 weeks.
Quantity (*n* = 4)	**Sample Response**
Little substance As required Short	One who just interacts because he has to for a grade or just talking to fill the silence or impress the teacher with numbers of postings. Short answers that don't say much, but this can be misleading because even short answers can say something to the person even if it is just that they can relate is important.
Not Applicable (*n* = 1)	**Sample Response**
All have presence	I don't believe there are no learners that have low course room presence in my opinion. Every learner makes an effort to do his or her posts and responses. It may be late or last minute but this may be due to any numerous reasons such as jobs, family or personal problems.
Frequency (*n* = 2)	**Sample Response**
Last Minute	Learners who don't respond to direct questions or comments or wait until the final day of the discussion timetable to respond. They continually post responses late.

This model can result in presence where "one just interacts because he has to for a grade or just talking to fill the silence or impress the teacher with numbers of postings," with the result that neither teacher nor other learners gain from their activity within the online space. Interestingly, one respondent suggested that everyone has a presence, regardless of their contribution or participation. From our observations, it is always apparent when a learner shifts from being an active to a passive participant, but the recognition and acknowledgement of those who could almost be classified as lurkers is less apparent. This initial analysis suggests that learners are aware of the activity of their peers, but there was no reference to learners affecting a class "community" by presenting with a low presence.

The learners who frequent these courses do not appear to exhibit extensive social presence in that context, that is their feedback in this survey did not identify "being themselves" as a factor, and the general implication that they are working more as individuals than as a team also suggests that cognitive presence is more about their own engagement rather than that of a learning community. Consequently, we propose that consideration be made to a fourth manifestation of online presence, that of learner presence, which relates to the continuum of characteristics exhibited by the individual within the context of an online distance education course.

As a follow-up to this study, learners in a subsequent course presented personal perceptions on presence and community building. One of the interesting factors that emerged was the importance of specific activities in the early part of the course to allow learners to express something of their own personality (an element of social presence) that would enhance their ability to work with both their peers and their teacher in the course activities (cognitive presence). Although these may be likened to the *gaining attention* principle espoused by Gagné (1985), there is a difference between an instructional activity and a social activity; and what appears to be happening is that as more and more learners and teachers experience the online dynamic, strategies are being elaborated (from best-practice options such as those proposed by Palloff & Pratt, 2003) that will maximize the opportunities for interaction, critical reflection and community.

Presence for the Teacher

From a different perspective, the learners were also asked to consider the key aspects of online presence for their teachers. As can be seen from Table 10.4, the qualities range from understanding the complexity of the teacher's personal life to expecting a response within 24 hours; some respondents even considered the teacher should respond to every contribution submitted by a learner. However, although the value of carefully considered responses and the provision of additional resources will clearly

TABLE 10.4

Classification of High Online Teacher Presence

4. What Characterizes Teachers Who, in Your Opinion,
Have High Course Room Presence?

Personal (n=5)	Sample Response
Time Management Commitmnet Availability	Setting up time aside to become coaches whilie balancing their own schedules, a teacher in this environment must also be able to respond to student posts during the weekends since many are posted during this time frame.
Quantity (n=1)	**Sample Response**
Over Zealous	Too much comment stifles the courseroom chatter … too much control drives the conversation outside the course room.
Quality (n=3)	**Sample Response**
Reading Responding Resources Visibility Constructive Expectations	This would entail providing unit summary feedback, checking in mid week to respond to Posts, even if it is a brief response with a question or a "how about considering A, B, and C?" This shows that the teacher has actually read the Post. Making an effort to "speak" to all learners in the discussion.
Frequency (n=3)	**Sample Response**
Almost Daily Guidance	These teachers respond to direct questions within 24 hours. They need not respond to every question, but should respond as necessary to steer the discussion or reveal concepts which previously may not have been considered. They should also provide timely feedback on course assignments.

enhance the online experience (Palloff & Pratt, 2003; Salmon, 2003; Sims & Jones, 2003), the variation in expectations of the teacher's presence, and therefore subsequent performance, highlights the difficulty an teacher has in dealing with diverse expectations and learning styles.

With respect to the perspectives on a teacher's low presence, the comments identify factors related to commitment, reliability, and the quality, such as "the teacher that does not provide guidance, such as clarification on assignments or that becomes defensive when assignments are questioned." Additional examples and themes with relation to this are provided in Table 10.5.

In comparing these data, the discrepancies between perceptions of high and low teacher presence and the frequency of responses represent an interesting aspect. Whereas high presence was identified as being active on a daily basis, and providing responses to learners within 24 hours, low presence was seen as visiting the course-room less than weekly. The important

TABLE 10.5

Classification of Low Online Teacher Presence

5. What Characterizes Teachers Who, in Your Opinion,
Have Low Course Room Presence?

Personal (n = 3)	Sample Responses
Disconnected Uncommitted	Those that prefer to stay back but may become disconnected from the group.
Reliability (n = 2)	**Sample Response**
Irregular	Teachers who do not do as those with high course presence or those who state they're going to post or follow-up on something but do not.
Quality (n = 4)	**Sample Response**
Scrutiny Preferential Arrogance Superficial	Teachers who are not truly scrutinizing the quality of the contributions being made by learners and not guiding the discussion to be in line with the direction of the week's unit.
Frequency (n = 2)	**Sample Response**
Not Weekly	Do not visit the course room on a weekly basis allow the learners to facilitate their own discussion for weeks at a time.

issue is not the quantitative frequency of online activity, but that teachers and learners are operating in environments where their expectations of presence will impact on the perceived value of the interactions.

A second consideration of these dimensions of presence relates to the extent to which it is necessary to re-think the way in which online environments are conceptualized. One observation from Sanute (course room communication, November 25, 2005) suggested that as designers it is necessary to view the online course room as a 24x7 environment (whether or not interactions are synchronous or asynchronous) as learners can be present at any time. The implications from this are that design must focus on the "now" of learning compared to learning in a certain time and place ... and therefore we need to reconceptualize the design process (Irlbeck, Kays, Jones, & Sims, in press) to cater for in-delivery modifications and enhancements (Sims & Jones, 2003).

EPISTEMOLOGY AND PRESENCE

In a more recent study, the second author focused on determining the extent to which learners' educational goals and personal epistemologies impacted their perceptions of social, cognitive, and teaching presence in an asynchronous online course that emphasized critical thinking and collaboration. In this master's level course on distance education administration, learners were required to locate relevant resources and discuss them during five 2-week discussions during the semester. The first discussion, facilitated by the teacher, focused on an overview of the course concepts, whereas the remaining four discussions focused on one of four themes related to the administration of distance education programs. These discussions were facilitated by learners, with each team of learners facilitating a 2-week discussion. Every thread in the five discussion topics was meant to help the learners wrestle with a variety of themes and perspectives they would need to understand in order to develop a distance education program. At the same time, the design strategy aimed to enable learners to engage with their personal epistemological framework.

As part of the discussion process, learners were asked to use the critical thinking checklist (Murphy, 2004) to evaluate their posts and include that evaluation at the bottom of at least four substantive posts a week. The teacher used the same checklist to evaluate their posts and to evaluate their accuracy of their self-assessments. The first discussion, Course Concepts Overview, introduced learners to the course and to the critical thinking checklist. During this discussion, the use of the checklist was modeled and the type and quality of posts that were expected was clearly defined. Significant individual feedback was also provided on the learners' own assessments of the quality of their posts. During these 2 weeks, the learners conferred frequently with the teacher as to the nature of the checklist in order to determine if they were interpreting the checklist items correctly.

Over the course of the next four discussions, the teacher participated in discussions to continue to model quality posts; however, individual feedback was restricted to post quality of the discussion facilitators. The facilitators were expected to keep discussions on track and to provide feedback to the other learners on the quality of their posts. During this time, learners asked fewer and fewer questions regarding the checklist—moving from and average of 15 a week in the first weeks down to 3 a week by the end of the third discussion.

Learners' critical thinking levels did improve over the course (Fig. 10.2), with a higher percentage of posts falling into the evaluate and create levels by the end of the course discussions. Student postings were only rated based on the absolute correctness of their assessment, not their relative correctness: A student either over assessed their post, under assessed their post, or correctly assessed their post.

Had the assessments been on a relative scale, giving a higher or lower correctness rating based on how many levels their assessment was off, the learners' overall accuracy would have been seen to improve even more (see Fig. 10.3).

Learners were also asked about their conceptions of, and satisfaction with social, cognitive, and teacher presence. Responses were similar re-

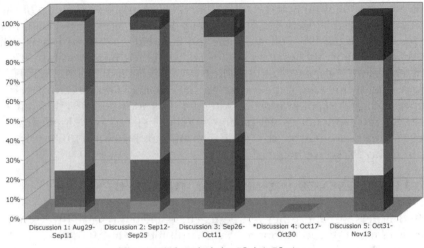

Figure 10.2.   Critical thinking levels of learners.

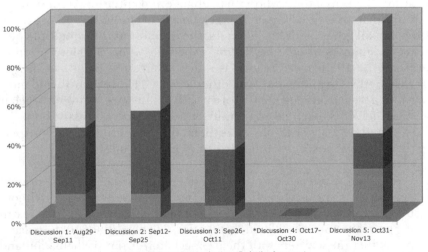

Figure 10.3.   Alternative perspective of critical thinking.

gardless of their goals or cognitive development levels and frequently included timely feedback and some visibility in the course discussions; however, it should be noted that this survey took place at the end of the course Because the teacher had ample time during the course to clarify her expectations regarding collaboration and knowledge construction as well as time to support the learners as they adjusted their own, possibly different, epistemologies, it is likely that the learners came to adopt the beliefs of the teacher by the end of the course. In any event, all learners expressed a generally high level of satisfaction with all forms of presence in the course, even though the majority of learners could be classified as multiplistic and were taking the course for economic reasons (mostly, in order to satisfy requirements to receive financial aid).

ONLINE PRESENCE AND CRITICAL THINKING

The learners we, and other online teachers, encounter are diverse and bring a range of expectations to that environment. In this initial analysis of online learner perceptions, the classification of those perceptions suggests that online presence is complex, diverse, and variable. One explanation for this outcome is the diversity of the learner groups. Although all are looking to further their career through securing a higher degree, some do not have extensive recent educational experience. For some, their work life has a significant impact on their online activity, as their interest is anytime–anyplace learning rather than online collaboration. In contrast, there are others who wish to engage and enter into a community ethos, albeit for a short 12- or 16-week course of study. By seeking input from a small group of online learners, the need to cater for multiple perspectives appears to be a key factor, especially when the perception of presence for the learner relates as much to meeting personal lifestyle needs as it does to interacting with other learners. However, to avoid moving into an environment that is essentially one-to-one between teacher and learner, it is essential to identify strategies that can assist both the teacher and the learner to maximize their online experience. With respect to the questions posed, we offer the following outcomes:

1. How can a teacher be present enough (or perceived to be present enough) that learners benefit from their subject matter expertise without being so present that she or he does not inhibit the learners from learning from one another? It is our contention that in addition to the teacher presenting the learners with their expectations from participation and communication, it is important to model a profile of the learners based

on their expectations for access to the teacher and the communication expected from that teacher. This can involve understanding more about each cohort of learners and adapting course delivery to meet those needs. One way to achieve this would be through an instrument that assesses the presence learners are likely to bring to their studies.

2. Given that learners have different educational goals (pragmatic, economic, scholarly), and assuming that those goals help form learners' expectations of teacher presence, is it possible (or desirable) for a teacher to be present (or perceived as present) at different levels for different learners? Based on the data reported it would appear that it is desirable for a teacher to be present at different levels for different learners. Enabling strategies to achieve this without significant increases in workload would be a key challenge.

3. Given that learners are at different stages of cognitive development (Perry, 1970), and assuming that those stages help form student expectations of teacher presence, is it possible (or desirable) for a teacher to be present (or be perceived as present) at different stages for different learners? Again we would argue that this is certainly desirable, with the possibility that it can occur if the understandings between learner and teacher are better defined at the commencement of their interactions.

4. What are the implications for instructional design with the maturing of online environments and the varying expectations of learners? As we find learners engaging more comfortably in the online context through increasing familiarity with the tools of communication, then we need to create environments where that communication and collaboration can be easily facilitated. The commonly accepted processes of instructional design are not adequate for these conditions and new models and paradigms will be required to realize the potential of dynamic, collaborative online learning environments (Irlbeck et al., in press; Sims & Jones, 2003).

To this end we propose a two-dimensional model (Table 10.6) based on educational goals and cognitive development that provides a guideline on how these interactions might be facilitated. This model is embryonic and is based on our personal experiences and the initial analysis of student perceptions as presented in this paper. However, we also see that this extends existing models of presence (Garrison et al., 2004) to include that of learner presence, which would delineate their specific characteristics that might potentially impact on performance, interaction, and engagement. Although we have used the original levels proposed by Perry (1970), the potential epistemological frameworks used by learners have also been identified (Driscoll, 2005).

TABLE 10.6

Teacher Strategies for Multiple Perspectives of Learners

Cognitive Development		Educational Goals		
		Pragmatic	*Economic*	*Scholarly*
	Dualistic [Objectivist]	* State key criteria * Define outcomes explicitly * Confirm achievement of learning	* Express value of course * Identify key policies	* Establish framework * Assist construction of outcomes * Define theoretical framework
	Multiplistic [Pragmatic]	* Identify relevance of criteria * Enable application of outcomes * Maintain goals	* Assess career continuum * Link expertise of environment	* Examine extended resources * Negotiate contextual outcomes
	Relativistic [Interpretivist]	Negotiate criteria Negotiate outcomes Negotiate support	* Identify outcomes of investment * Note career relevance	* Assume independence * Establish collegial communication * Negotiate alternative outcomes

CONCLUSION

The online teaching and learning environment is becoming more preva-
lent and, with that growth, different forms of interactions and expectations
of both teachers and learners are emerging. In this chapter, we explore the
understandings of learners toward their own online presence and those of
their teachers, and propose that addressing the multiple perspectives that
characterize the groups of online learners is key to a more successful educational experience. Whereas the current models of best practice (Palloff &
Pratt, 2003; Salmon, 2003) provide excellent strategies to manage the me-
chanics of a successful online course, the data considered in this chapter
suggest that the accompanying dynamics of the online experience are
equally complex and require further consideration. One proposed means
to achieve this is to extend current models of presence to integrate that of
the learner and to integrate elements of presence and critical thinking with

new paradigms of instructional design. In making these conclusions, it has to be acknowledged that the data has been provided by learners who are learning independently, at a distance, and within an asynchronous discussion model. As there are many different implementations of online learning, the application of our proposal to other settings will require further investigation. What must be emphasized, however, is the value of developing critical thinking and reflective skills in our online learners, as this brings the online collaborative environment alive.

REFERENCES

Anderson, T., Rourke, L., Archer, W., & Garrison, D. R., (2001). Assessing teaching presence in a computer conferencing transcripts. *Journal of Asynchronous Learning Networks, 5*(2). Retrieved from http://www.aln.org/alnweb/journal/jaln-vol5issue2v2.htm.

Bennett, R., & Dziekan, V. (2005). The omnium project: Establishing online communities to explore collaborative models of creative interaction and education. In H. Goss (Ed.), *Balance, fidelity, mobility: Maintaining the momentum?* Proceedings of the 22nd Annual Conference of the Australasian Society of Computers in Learning in Tertiary Education (pp. 79–88). Brisbane: TALSS, Queensland University of Technology.

Driscoll, M. P. (2005). *Psychology of learning for instruction* (3rd ed.). Boston, MA: Pearson.

Gagné, R. M. (1985). *The conditions of learning* (4th ed.). New York: Holt, Rinehart & Winston.

Garrison, D. R., Anderson, T., & Archer, W. (2004). Critical thinking and computer conferencing: A model and tool to assess cognitive presence. *American Journal of Distance Education, 15*(1), 7–23.

Hofer, B. K. (Ed.). (2004). Personal epistemology: Paradigmatic approaches to understanding students' beliefs about knowledge and knowing. *Educational Psychologist, 39*(1), 1–80.

Irlbeck, S., Kays, E., Jones, D., & Sims, R. (in press). The phoenix rising: Emergent models of instructional design. *Distance Education*.

Murphy, E. (2004). An instrument to support thinking critically about critical thinking in online asynchronous discussions. *Australian Journal of Educational Technology, 20*(3), 295–315. Retrieved on April 22, 2006, from http://www.ascilite.org.au/ajet/ajet20/murphy.html

Palloff, R. M., & Pratt, K. (2003). *The virtual student: A profile and guide to working with online learners.* San Francisco, CA: Jossey-Bass.

Perkinson, R. (2004, August). *An overview of global trends and some perceptions about online delivery by foreign providers.* Keynote presentation to the eAgenda International Roundtable, Surfers Paradise, QLD, Australia.

Perry, W. G., Jr. (1970). *Intellectual and ethical development in the college years.* New York: Holt, Rinehart & Winston.

Preece, J. (2000). *Online communities: Designing usability, supporting sustainability.* Chichester, England: Wiley.

Prensky, M. (2005). What can you learn from a cell phone? Almost anything! Innovate: *Journal of Online Education, 1*(5).

Reeves, T. (2004, August). *The will to fly: Elearning and the challenge of the conative domain.* Presentation to the eAgenda International Roundtable, Surfers Paradise, QLD, Australia.

Rourke, L., Anderson, T. Garrison, D. R., & Archer, W. (1999). Assessing social presence in asynchronous, text-based computer conferencing. *Journal of Distance Education, 14*(3), 51–70.

Salmon, G. (2003). *E-moderating: The key to teaching and learning online* (2nd ed.). London: Taylor & Francis.

Sims, R. C., & Bovard, B. (2004, December). Interacting with online learners: How new elaborations of online presence can foster critical thinking and reflection. In R. Atkinson, C. McBeath, D. Jonas-Dwyer, & R. Phillips (Eds.), *Beyond the comfort zone*. Proceedings of the 21st ASCILITE Conference (pp. 841–850), Perth, WA. Retrieved on April 22, 2006, from http://www.ascilite.org.au/conferences/perth04/procs/sims.html

Sims, R. C., & Jones, D. (2003). Where practice informs theory: Reshaping instructional design for academic communities of practice in online teaching and learning. *Information Technology, Education and Society, 4*(1), 3–20.

Short, J., Williams, E., & Christie, B. (1976). *The social psychology of telecommunications*. London: Wiley.

Chapter 11

A Chorus of Online Voices: Reflections on the Future of Online Instruction

Vanessa P. Dennen
Florida State University

In a mere decade, online learning has firmly rooted itself in the education landscape, a fast-growing vine that connects institutions, instructors, and learners in new ways. What once consisted of a few experimental courses, largely run on homegrown systems, has evolved into entire degree programs on commercially available platforms. Much as the technology and availability have developed, so too have the players and their techniques.

The purpose of this chapter is to meld the voices that appear throughout this book and, while glancing back at what has happened, share thoughts about what may come next. As I reviewed the other chapters, I could not help but nod in agreement and feel comforted by the familiarity of the experiences and principles that were shared by the various authors. Having taught online since 1998, I cannot resist inserting a bit of my own voice and experience, and doing so is consistent with the title and purpose of this volume.

PAST, PRESENT, FUTURE

I recall attending a conference in 1996, a point in time when I had just returned to graduate school after a career that included, among other things, designing and maintaining a corporate Web site. Because I was presenting about the Web myself and was generally interested in new developments, I attended a session about teaching with the Web. The presenter shared with the audience his class, which was being taught entirely online using email and the Web. His Web offerings and pedagogical techniques, then rather unique, would today be considered mundane—just a collection of lecture notes and readings uploaded onto Web pages, with the ability to discuss via a listserv. Few in the audience could readily engage in experience-based discussion. We tried to imagine the class experience. Would the novelty wear off? Would we feel disconnected? Would this be a better way to learn, with less distraction and more convenience? These questions were difficult to answer.

Looking around at my colleagues who teach online now, 10 years after that conference experience, I see a variety of tools and techniques being used. Not only do we use Blackboard, the technology adopted by my university; other tools such as blogs and podcasts have been integrated into our courses. Course activities extend beyond mere reading and discussions; discussion boards may be used to support group work, practice with concept application, presentations, journaling, and peer feedback. We engage in discussions in the hallway and over coffee about what we are doing in our classes and how we are developing our own online voices and styles. This sharing helps us become less isolated instructor voices, and yet it does not make us all the same, just as would be the case for analogous discussions among faculty about face-to-face teaching. Hopefully, within our online degree program, the instructor voices provide a harmonious experience for the learners. Certainly within each class we strive to hear all voices and have them work together toward exploring, understanding, and creating.

I wonder what will we see 10 years from now. It is difficult to project into the future, and past predictions have not always been accurate. Note that teachers have not been replaced by intelligent or adaptive tutoring systems, and in some ways are considered more critical than ever before. Three main areas in which I do think we will see the field maturing and becoming more sophisticated are with regard to (a) tools and technology, (b) increased participants, and (c) professional development. Each of these areas will have an impact on how the instructor's voice is constructed and heard, and each is briefly discussed in this chapter. These three areas seem to be a unifying thread among the other voices presented in this volume. Hopefully, my remarks will build on the many ideas that have been shared so willingly and openly thus far.

FINDING A COMMON KEY

Although each of the preceding authors writes from unique angles, and there are myriad issues on which one might focus when discussing what it means to be an online instructor, there is a common big picture. To use a musical metaphor for these voices, they work in concert like a symphony, each perhaps playing a different part or a variation on a melody or motif, but fitting to-gether in a manner that is coherent and that completes the larger work. Among the many themes found in these chapters are these notions: One's online persona may shift based on the role being played, the discussants, and the tool; the quality of online instruction and interaction need not be mea-sured against a face-to-face example; and instructors should design their courses to capitalize on the potential for human interaction.

Role and Persona

Berge's discussion (in this volume) of instructor roles provides a frame-work for exploring the varied parts of the job. Each role might be consid-ered a persona unto itself, representing a different type of organization and communication that is required of the online instructor. Depending on each instructor's previous online experiences and personal communi-cation style, successful use of each role may vary. For example, the social role can be the element that brings the class together and helps it function as a community. An instructor experienced in large lecture hall classes may not be well prepared to take on the social role in an online setting, where the number of students does not necessarily sway expectations. In-deed, students in an online setting may not immediately be aware of the size of the class if no social interactions are facilitated by the instructor. A full class of 50 could feel like a small and isolated class of five if there are no community development efforts.

Collis and Moonen (in this volume) point out how the managerial role can be quite different online than in a face-to-face setting. Whereas the classroom instructor can briefly describe an assignment and respond in the moment to learner questions about expectations—and those who are absent only have themselves to blame—an online instructor who initially provides insuffi-ciently detailed guidelines may become deluged with questions by e-mail from students who have restrictive work schedules and often desire a reply as immediate as the one they would have in a face-to-face encounter.

Jan Visser's (in this volume) reflections of his life in cyberspace also touch on the notion of persona. From this perspective we can see how one's online identity may differ from a face-to-face one and can be just as fluid and dynamic as a face-to-face one depending on the circumstances. Similarly, Savenye (in this volume) addresses this idea that our online voices convey our presence, stating that it is important to develop a sense of community and know with whom we are interacting online. Issues around social interaction—how one presents and networks oneself on-line—presently are being widely discussed (see, for examples, Downes, 2005; Jones & Peachey, 2005; Kim, 2004; Murphy, 2004; Richardson & Swan, 2003; Shea, Pickett, & Pelz, 2003).

The tools that we use and discussion conventions that have been developed around those tools also shape our online communications. Jan Visser makes this point as he shares the varied computer-mediated interactions he has had with people, some of whom have tragically passed. For example, he found himself and others writing more formally in e-mail than via instant messenger, and using language shortcuts and user profile cues to help shape messaging interactions.

Let us not forget the roles that students play. Learners are seldom passive receptors of knowledge experiencing a course as exactly as the instructor planned with no input of their own. Lya Visser (in this volume), drawing on her own experiences as both distance student and instructor, shares the importance of providing interactions to help diminish potential isolation. Looking beyond just addressing social connections, Collis and Moonen provide a model in which the student can play an integral part in contributing to an online course. Online teaching methods such as the one they and others in this volume describe, which empower the learner to be a co-constructor of knowledge, are founded on some of the tenets of social constructivism. An online class should develop a shared sense of task or mission. This intersubjectivity then encourages the participants to share their perspectives and beliefs (Bober & Dennen, 2001; Master & Oberprieler, 2004). Ultimately a learner's negotiation of knowledge, which includes both external discourse with peers and internal discourse to reconcile course experiences and prior experiences, can result in meaning making (Stahl, 2004) and internalization. Pushing learners into this active role, particular with regards to interacting with peers, often requires guidance and ongoing support.

Quite naturally, learners tend to look to the instructor to set the tone and state expectations. LaPointe (in this volume) reiterates that the learner's role within course interactions needs to be made clear, and the responsibility for this clarity falls on the shoulders of the instructor. Students need to feel a sense of purpose, which can be tied to both audience and role. The rhetorical triangle of *audience*, *persona*, and *purpose* can be used to investigate how a student's contributions fit into the larger discussion of a class and whether or not one's messages provide adequate positioning for actual discourse to occur, as opposed to mere message posting (Dennen & Burner, 2006). The *persona*—the role a student chooses to play—will depend at least in part on who is the perceived *audience* and what the student believes to be the *purpose* of the dialogue.

Moving Away From Comparison

From its inception, online learning has been compared to face-to-face or so-called traditional classroom learning. In terms of learning outcomes, this comparison has been found moot; a meta-analysis of studies has shown no significant differences between the course delivery methods (Russell, 1999). As Sims and Bovard (in this volume) point out and then question, there is an underlying assumption that people sometimes adopt about face-to-face instruction being inherently better than online instruction. This assumption leads to unnecessary comparisons, and in practice has encouraged some online instructors to attempt replication of their classroom-based course (Zemsky & Massy, 2004) rather than the more often appropriate reinvention of those courses for the new medium.

Early experiences in online courses, such as those shared by Lya Visser and LaPointe, indicate that learners are likely to have different types of interactions and experiences within this medium. The medium may liberate some voices that would not be heard in a classroom, and silence others. Students who might not otherwise have the opportunity to take a course often are among the enrolled, a factor that also seems to somewhat nullify comparison. For these students it is not a matter of which medium, but rather if there is a medium that provides them with much-needed flexibility to transcend either location or time.

There still are barriers, in some cases, to successful access for some learners. Naidu and colleagues (in this volume) encountered learners who struggled with access and, once connected, with what to do. Despite the growing familiarity of online learning in some parts of the world and some segments of the population, there still are areas and people for whom it is either not a possibility or not desirable. Clearly this is not a matter of inherently better instructional means and methods, but of selecting the most appropriate means and methods for a given context.

It is likely that comparisons will continue, particularly among those who must choose a medium, who are new to the medium, or who are on the outside of the community of online learners looking in, but I believe that those who have been materially involved as instructional designers, instructors, or learners are less likely to feel the need to measure their online experience against face-to-face ones. Although the initial *hype* about online learning may have been a bit overstated (Zemsky & Massy, 2004), online learning clearly is not a fad; the continuous growth of new programs and enrollment of new students confirms its place and value in the education marketplace.

Designing for Interaction

Interaction, specifically learner–instructor and learner–learner interaction, have become the hallmark of online learning evangelists. Many researchers and instructional designers focus on activities that engage the learner in communication with others, believing that engaging interactions are the key to providing successful and rewarding learning experiences—more important than simply providing content however well designed (DeLacey & Leonard, 2002; Oliver, Herrington, & Reeves, 2006; Palloff & Pratt, 2005; Salmon, 2002).

LOOKING TO THE FUTURE

As we look to the future of online learning, there are two types of considerations to be made. The first type involves changes that are happening around us, such as the aforementioned evolution of technology and tools, increased size of online learner population, and increased professional development opportunities. The second type is indicative of more proactive steps the online instructor may take to address some of these changes. This section discusses where we are now, and were we might be headed.

Evolution of Tools and Technology

Although recent technological changes have seemed in some ways more subtle than the ones that initially brought the field of online learning into being—changes focused on adding new program features more so than new programs, integrating tools for seamless applications, and finding new uses for familiar tools and communications technologies rather than developing significantly new tools and technologies—the pedagogical activities enabled by these developments likely will have a tremendous impact on how online learning is done. In other words, they hopefully will inspire instructors and students to interact in new ways that support learning as well as that allow instructors to fully realize online activities that might have previously been limited by tool capabilities.

   Although I often like to say that I do not allow the tools to limit my teaching, and will find a way to execute a teaching idea, certainly the right tools can make the job easier. Using multiple platforms, which may involve different logins, announcement, and notification, and communication systems can be cumbersome and even burdensome for both learners and instructors. I have found that asking students to blog (see http://www.blogger.com for an example of free blogging software and hosting) and also to use Blackboard within the same class, because each offers its own type of communication support and advantages, requires very clearly delineated guidelines and consistent guidance to avoid confusion over which tool is used when. Initially, having separate URLs, logins, and passwords requires some sorting out. There are many other tools I might like to use that are free and Web-distributed, but I am hesitant to put more of an extraneous cognitive load on students. Thus, integration of tools allowing seamless coordination of activities from the student perspective will be an important development. Not only will integration efforts support more and different types of activities within a given class, it also may relieve some of the instructor's development and management burden, allowing greater focus on the human elements of the course.

One major area in which tool development that might change how online courses are taught is collaboration. A simple communication tool such as a discussion board or chat system may support computer-mediated learner collaboration, but communication between learners is not generic or one-dimensional; educational technology tools are seldom suitable for all potential users and requirements. Specialty tools are being developed to foster specific types of interactions. For example, collaborative writing tools such as whiteboards (http://www.writeboard.com/) may facilitate group work, making it easier for all learners to contribute their voice to a project by keeping the main file in a centralized location and noting who made additions and revisions and when. Such a tool also can help an instructor check to see that all members are participating. It is not that such peer writing practices cannot take place right now, but that they are made easier to initiate, participate in, and manage. Other tools like wikis (see http://www.openwiki.com/ and http://www.openwiking.com for examples), of which WikiPedia (http://www.wikipedia.org) is perhaps the best known, can be used to develop and share a group knowledge base more fluidly than a standard discussion board. Additional collaborative tool functions include annotation, critique (see Flanagan & Egert, 2000), and ranking.

Increased Participants

Over the next 10 years, the number of teachers and students who are experienced with online learning will continue to increase. Online courses are not limited to higher, continuing, and corporate learning environments. For example, in Florida, high school students currently may take online courses via Florida Virtual School (http://www.flvs.net/), and many do. This experience may become increasingly common. With more learners exposed to online courses, or even the possibility of taking online courses, online learning will be considered more of a norm and less of a novelty. I do not mean to suggest that face-to-face learning will be replaced, but rather that online learning will fill the niches for which it is best suited (e.g., professional development, distribution of specialized programs without geographical constraints) and continue to make learning options available to populations who either lack access for any number of reasons.

Recently, I had an experience that vividly demonstrated this idea of increased participants. On a trip home, I found myself sitting in the living room with my laptop engaged in an online discussion with my graduate students. This behavior was not unusual, and my family has come to consider it the norm for me. Seated next to me was my college-aged sister, similarly engrossed in a course offered by a university in another state. On the other couch across from us was a family friend. This woman, who has a professional career in a health-related field, has little computer experience. She, too, was engaged in an online course—her first. She brought her laptop to our house to get help and advice. As we sat there comparing our different versions of Blackboard and the interactions taking place in our classes, my mother entered the room. She commented how she initially thought it weird when I came home with a laptop 5 years ago and claimed to be teaching, but thought it even weirder now to see the three of us tapping away on the keyboards, interacting with our respective classes from the living room. Of course, 5 years ago my sister and our family friend would not have been enrolled in their courses. I think it possible that even my mother, a mediator, might find her way to an online professional development course in the future.

Professional Development and Peer Support

Is there a real need for professional development specific to online instruction? Studies have shown that higher education faculty, who work in an environment where instructors are most often their own instructional designers, are in want of instructional design support for their online courses, at least initially (Bonk, 2001; Kim, Bonk, & Zeng, 2005). Online instructors cannot just look to their organizations to simply provide support. Instead they must make their voices heard outside the classroom and ask for the assistance that they need in order to perform their jobs well and to continue their own professional development.

We typically think of teachers as the leaders or anchors for courses, but they in turn often desire their own opportunities to be participants in a learning community and interact with peers. The first online instructors were largely on their own to figure out pedagogical and technical issues. Assistance may be offered via instructional technology centers on campus, and althoughthese offices excel in helping with technical support and some instructional design issues, they are not a replacement for a community of peers.

In the future, online instructors will likely find an increasing number of local colleagues with whom to share their experiences and ideas as more people join the pool of experienced instructors. First-time instructors may be able to ask the person across the hall for some advice, and in department meetings everyone may nod in agreement when issues related to online learning arise, just as they do now when issues related to the general education courses most people have taken a turn at teaching are mentioned. However, that is not the current situation for most faculty who teach online.

In the traditional higher education environment, faculty members have historically identified themselves by subject matter area. However, online instructors may be a minority in some departments and can feel isolated or unsupported in their efforts if colleagues do not understand what their teaching experience is like and the types of issues they face in the classroom. As some instructors begin to specialize in online instruction, we may see more institutions organized so that faculty also may identify by course delivery method. Locally sponsored groups such as the Blackboard User Group at San Diego State University can help bring together faculty across departments. Of course, online there are various established organizations and outlets for online instructors to share and to learn from each other (e.g., Merlot at http://www.merlot.org and the U.S. Distance Learning Association at http://www.usdla.org) regardless of their location or type of institution.

Some for-profit universities already are structured in ways that acknowledge the differences in teaching environment, with both online and campus faculty bodies. The reasons for doing this are to help facilitate both communication among peers and offering services to meet each group's specific needs. However, care must be taken to not marginalize one group, and online instructors are at a risk here with students located off-campus and classes that take place in cyberspace—a situation that makes parts of their work less visible, but does not necessarily lessen the administrative, instructional, and environmental (e.g., office space) support that they need in order to do their jobs well. Further complicating this situation is that many online instructors in the United States are adjuncts, a group of people whose voice tends to be less heard on the administrative side of academe.

Presently, there are relatively few faculty who teach exclusively online in full-time positions. Most of those who do have these positions are at online universities. As new online programs develop, however, they will have to be staffed with qualified instructors. Most likely one of two things will happen: Either more of the traditional faculty members will begin to teach at least some of their course load online, creating a larger body of instructors who are experienced with online learning or more full-time online positions will be created. Given that an increasing number of graduate students teach online to help support themselves, there should be an adequate workforce of experienced online instructors ready to fill such positions should they materialize.

New Voices Joining the Chorus

Although for many people in a higher and continuing education or training setting, most likely including the audience of this book, online learning is commonplace and perhaps even expected, there will always be new voices joining the online chorus. Will these new voices be prepared to join? And will they be different from the ones we have experienced so far?

Certainly technological expectations have changed, and these expectations in turn impact student voices. In 1999, I had a student enroll in an online class only to find out that she could barely use a computer and did not even have an e-mail account. This student decided that the technological curve was going to be too steep for her to climb during the class period and dropped. The technology served as a barrier to her participation. Other students at that time needed detailed instructions for logging into the courseware and navigating the system. These days I rarely encounter such requests.

Most of the new online students I now encounter at least know someone else who has taken an online course. Their concept of what that means and what may be expected can be quite different from the reality of my class, but they at least begin the course with some ideas of what it might entail. They also know enough to ask some questions up front, demonstrating their own expectations. These students have a greater sense of agency about taking online classes, even when the specific technology, teaching methods, and class expectations may be unfamiliar.

My younger sister, who I mentioned earlier, has years of experience using Instant Messenger and can send complex, albeit lingo-filled, text messages on her telephone faster than she can place a call. Her generation represents many of the new online voices showing up in our classes. These students often are familiar with the technology and comfortable using it in a social setting, but the online voices they have developed may not be well suited to a classroom context. For example, in an undergraduate class I am currently studying, many students compose messages that are exceptionally informal and full of abbreviations such as "LOL" (laughing out loud), "ROTFL" (rolling on the floor laughing), and "l8r" (later). This form of communication has become their norm for online discourse, but it may not match the instructor's expectations. Thus, the students have a fair amount of technological knowledge and comfort as well as already-established online personas. The challenge, then, is to help them develop online voices that are appropriate for course discussion, neither too informal like a chat session with a friend nor too formal like a research paper.

The increased use of Web-based technologies in face-to-face classes may serve as a way to prepare future online learners for the fully online experience. We may expect more and more new online students to not really be new to the medium or its instructional applications, just to the percentage of course time and activities that are exclusively online.

Developing Instructor Personas

Much as online students of the future can be expected to have reasonably well-developed online personas, instructors will as well. These personas will be based on a plethora of earlier online experiences, which will increasingly include online course experiences. Many of the online instructors I know have taken online courses themselves so they can experience another instructor's class and know what it feels like to be an online learner. In the future, however, the pool of online instructors will include more and more people who as learners had experiences in blended and online classes and who observed the online personas of a variety of instructors from the learner perspective. This second wave of online instructors may develop into the online instructors they wish they had, blending the best part of their varied experiences.

Online learning already has pushed many existing instructors to consider or reconsider their orientation toward learning and to change some of their actions in the face-to-face classroom. Often instructors find the ability to hear more student voices in the online class, where the facilitation style, airspace, and sense of thread or topic continuity may be significantly different concepts, refreshing and pedagogically useful. They may, as a result, seek ways to increase their ability to hear student voices in every class, regardless of medium. This is a trend that should continue in the future, extending the impact of online learning to more traditional learning settings.

Pedagogical Tools and Supports

Pedagogical tools to support online instructors still are largely missing from the online learning landscape (Bonk & Dennen, in press). Some tools may lend themselves more readily to certain uses than others. For example, the design of Blackboard (http://www.blackboard.com) can make certain types of activities a bit more difficult to develop than is necessary. The group discussion spaces are set up so that the instructor must start the discussion forums. Although this feature may be desirable during teacher-centered learning activities, when a group space is created to support work teams it is merely a nuisance to both the learners and the instructor that only the instructor can create new forums. Similarly, inflexible controls over who can add content to particular course areas, such as links or glossaries, can require instructor workarounds if learner centeredness is desired.

There is one online learning platform, Moodle (http://www.moodle.org) that claims to be built on principles of social constructivism and constructionism (Moodle, n.d.). Although the product documentation certainly discusses ways of promoting learning communities and learner construction of knowledge, it does not make explicit how Moodle is supposed to support particular pedagogical beliefs. Basically, it is a shell for the instructor and learners to fill in whatever manner meets their needs (Winn, 1992).

Bonk & Dennen (1999) suggested that template-type tools might be developed to support individual instructors with activity design. In particular, activities focused on developing creative, critical thinking, and collaboration skills would be useful. The proliferation of tools has resulted in numerous ways to start a discussion, but few supports for burning questions such as:

- How many learners should be in a discussion group?
- How long should the discussion period be?
- What elements should be included in the discussion prompt?
- Should there be incremental deadlines?

The answers to these questions depend on the type of activity, the level of the learners, and the intended outcomes.

So far, the commercial tool providers have not focused on this area of pedagogical templates and tools, instead developing more sophisticated content development, assessment, and administrative tools. Moodle and Sakai (http://sakaiproject.org) both are examples of open source course management systems that are seeing increasing adoption and, with that, active participation of a user-centered, noncommercial development community. The implications for pedagogical tools are that open source developers might identify this need and fill the gap, both sharing with the open source community and potentially elevating the pressure on the commercial courseware sector to be more responsive to the needs of online instructors.

Qualifying and Quantifying our Interactions

How do we know that our online interactions have been fruitful? Should the measure be satisfaction? Participation? Sense of community? Learning? Both assessment and research are areas in which we attempt to gauge the effectiveness and utility of online interactions. The measurement of online voices is not a simple affair, and traditional methods such as participation counts and content analysis are not sufficient to determine whether learning actually took place and can be attributed to the online interaction (Dennen & Paulus, 2005). For example, a student might post often, but their messages may not be of substance. Another student might post highly accurate mini-essays, but these contributions may be entirely reflective of learning that took place in another setting. Messages that may initially seem irrelevant or insubstantial at first glance, such as a simple question or a brief comment or example, may actually be the catalyst for a series of interactions that foster learning among multiple participants. Thus, figuring out how online learning contributes to the learning or meaning-making process and how to best measure this phenomenon remains a challenge for the future.

CONCLUSIONS

The precise future of online learning may be something that only an oracle can predict, but it seems from the voices heard in this volume that its development will be a thoughtful, interactive process, and likely a student-centered one as well. There are many variables that will influence how the field grows, including technological developments, pedagogical developments, institutional supports, and the influx of a new generation of instructors. Also worth considering is the changing nature of students and their wide variety of prior experiences. The one thing that can be said for sure is that it will be interesting to reflect back in 10 years and see how online learning has grown and how the role and voice of the online instructor has evolved.

REFERENCES

Bober, M. J., & Dennen, V. P. (2001). Intersubjectivity: Facilitating knowledge construction in online environments. *Educational Media International, 38*(4), 241–250.

Bonk, C. J. (2001). *Online teaching in an online world*. Bloomington, IN: CourseShare.com. Retrieved February 18, 2006, from http://mypage.iu.edu/~cjbonk/faculty_survey_report.pdf

Bonk, C. J., & Dennen, V. P. (in press). Pedagogical frameworks for Web-based distance education. In M. G. Moore (Ed.), *Handbook of distance education* (2nd ed.). Mahwah, NJ: Lawrence Erlbaum Associates.

Bonk, C. J., & Dennen, V. P. (1999). Teaching on the Web: With a little help from my pedagogical friends. *Journal of Computing in Higher Education, 11*(1), 3–28.

DeLacey, B., & Leonard, D. (2002). Case study on technology and distance in education at the Harvard Business School. *Educational Technology & Society 5*(2). http://ifets.ieee.org/periodical/vol_2_2002/delacey.html

Dennen, V. P., & Burner, K. (2006, April). *Trilateral talk: Using the rhetorical triangle to promote and analyze learner interactions in threaded discourse*. Presented at the Annual Conference of the American Educational Research Association: San Francisco, CA.

Dennen, V. P., & Paulus, T. M. (2005). Researching "collaborative knowledge building" in formal distance learning environments. In T. Koschmann, T. W. Chen, & D. D. Suthers (Eds.), *Computer supported collaborative learning 2005* (pp. 96–104), Mahwah, NJ: Lawrence Erlbaum Associates.

Downes, S. (2005, October). E-learning 2.0. *E-Learn Magazine*. Retrieved February 19, 2006, from http://elearnmag.org/subpage.cfm?section=articles&article=29–1

Flanagan, M., & Egert, C. (2000). Courseware quality and the collaborative classroom: Implementing IOS courseware to generate seminar-style interactions. *Interactive Multimedia Electronic Journal of Computer-Enhanced Learning, 1*(6). Retrieved June 27, 2001, from http://imej.wfu.edu/articles/2000/1/06/index.asp

Jones, N., & Peachey, P. (2005). The development of socialization in an online learning environment. *The Journal of Interactive Online Learning, 3*(3). Retrieved February 19, 2006, from http://www.ncolr.org/jiol/issues/PDF/3.3.4.pdf

Kim, H. (2004). The relationship between online teacher immediacy behaviors and online instructional effectiveness. In G. Richards (Ed.), *Proceedings of World Conference on E-Learning in Corporate, Government, Healthcare, and Higher Education 2004* (pp. 1954–1959). Chesapeake, VA: AACE.

Kim, K. J., Bonk, C. J., & Zeng, T. (2005, June). Surveying the future of workplace e-learning: The rise of blending, interactivity, and authentic learning. *E-Learn*

Magazine. Retrieved February 19, 2006, from http://www.elearnmag.org/subpage.cfm?section=research&article=5-1

Master, K., & Oberprieler, G. (2004). Encouraging equitable online participation through curriculum articulation. *Computers and Education, 42*, 319–332.

Moodle. (n.d.). Philosophy. Retrieved February 28, 2006 from http://docs.moodle.rog/en/Philosophy

Murphy, E. (2004). Recognizing and promoting collaboration in an online asynchronous discussion. *British Journal of Educational Technology, 35*(4), 421–431.

Oliver, R., Herrington, J., & Reeves, T. C. (2006). Creating authentic learning environments through blended learning approaches. In C. J. Bonk & C. R. Graham (Eds.), *Handbook of blended learning: Global Perspectives, local designs* (pp. 502–515). San Francisco, CA: Pfeiffer.

Palloff, R. M., & Pratt, K. (2005). *Collaborating online: Learning together in community*. San Francisco: Jossey-Bass.

Richardson, J. C., & Swan, K. (2003, February). Examining social presence in online courses in relation to students' perceived learning and satisfaction. *Journal of Asynchronous Learning Environments, 7*(1). Retrieved February 19, 2006, from http://www.sloan-c.org/publications/jaln/v7n1/v7n1_richardson.asp

Russell, T. L. (1999). *The no significant difference phenomenon*. Raleigh, NC: North Carolina State University.

Salmon, G. (2002). *E-tivities: The key to active online learning*. Sterling, VA: Stylus Publishing.

Shea, P. J., Pickett, A. M., & Pelz, W. E. (2003). A follow-up investigation of "teaching presence" in the SUNY learning network. *Journal of Asynchronous Learning Networks, 7*(2). Retrieved February 19, 2006, from http://www.sloan-c.org/publications/jaln/v7n2/v7n2_shea.asp

Stahl, G. (2004). Building collaborative knowing: Elements of a social theory of learning. In J.-W. Strijbos, P. Kirschner, & R. Martens (Eds.), *What we know about CSCL in higher education* (pp. 53–85). Amsterdam: Kluwer.

Winn, W. (1992). The assumptions of constructivism and instructional design. In T. M. Duffy & D. H. Jonassen (Eds.), *Constructivism and the technology of instruction* (pp. 177–182). Hillsdale, NJ: Lawrence Erlbaum Associates.

Zemsky, R., & Massy, W. F. (2004, July). Why the E-learning boom went bust. *The Chronicle of Higher Education, 50*(4). Retrieved February 1, 2006, from http://chronicle.com/weekly/v50/i44/44b00601.htm

Author Index

Subject Index